PENN STATE FOOTBALL

THE COMPLETE ILLUSTRATED HISTORY

Ken Rappoport and Barry Wilner

MVP
BOOKS

DEDICATION

*To my own set of All-Americans:
Helene; Nicole and Dan; Jamie and Eric; Tricia; and Evan.* — BW

Once again, for Bernice. — KR

First published in 2009 by MVP Books, an imprint of MBI Publishing Company and the Quayside Publishing Group, 400 First Avenue N, Suite 300, Minneapolis, MN 55401 USA

Text copyright © 2009 by Ken Rappoport and Barry Wilner

All rights reserved. With the exception of quoting brief passages for the purposes of review, no part of this publication may be reproduced without prior written permission from the Publisher.

The information in this book is true and complete to the best of our knowledge. All recommendations are made without any guarantee on the part of the author or Publisher, who also disclaim any liability incurred in connection with the use of this data or specific details.

This publication has not been prepared, approved, or licensed by Penn State University or the National Collegiate Athletic Association.

We recognize that some words, phrases, model names, and designations mentioned herein may be the property of the trademark holder. We use them for identification purposes only. This is not an official publication.

MVP Books are also available at discounts in bulk quantity for industrial or sales-promotional use. For details write to Special Sales Manager at MBI Publishing Company, 400 First Avenue N, Suite 300, Minneapolis, MN 55401 USA.

Library of Congress Cataloging-in-Publication Data

Rappoport, Ken.
 Penn State football : the complete illustrated history / Ken Rappoport and Barry Wilner.
   p. cm.
 Includes index.
 ISBN 978-0-7603-3510-9 (hb w/ jkt)
1. Penn State Nittany Lions (Football team)—History. 2. Penn State Nittany Lions (Football team)—Pictorial works. 3. Pennsylvania State University—Football—History. 4. Pennsylvania State University—Football—Pictorial works. I. Wilner, Barry. II. Title.
 GV958.P46R36 2009
 796.332'630974853—dc22
                    2009000736

Editor: Josh Leventhal
Designer: Cindy Samargia Laun

Printed in China

On the front cover: (main) Joe Paterno and the Nittany Lions get ready to take the field, 2005 (*Gregory Shamus/WireImage/Getty Images*); (background) Penn State fans cheer on the team at Beaver Stadium, 2008 (*David Bergman/Sports Illustrated/Getty Images*).

On the frontispiece: The Nittany Lion mascot opens the gate for Joe Paterno and the team before a game, 2008 (*Al Tielemans/Sports Illustrated/Getty Images*).

On the title page: Beaver Stadium at dusk, 2008 (*Maxwell Kruger/Penn State University*).

On the back cover: (top, left to right) Derrick Williams is lifted up by teammates after scoring a touchdown at Iowa, 2008 (*Stephen Mally/Icon SMI*); the Nittany Lion mascot runs onto the field prior to a home game against Illinois, 2008 (*Matthew O'Haren/Icon SMI*); Larry Cooney runs the ball against West Virginia, 1948 (*Penn State University Archives*); (middle, left to right) Blair Thomas leaps over the Rutgers defense, circa 1989 (*Collegiate Images/WireImage*); Joe Paterno leads the team onto the field before a game against Iowa, 2007 (*Carolyn Kaster/AP Images*); Daryll Clark celebrates a touchdown against Wisconsin, 2008 (*Andy Manis/AP Images*); (bottom, left to right) Roger Kochman runs the ball behind a blocking Dave Robinson during a win over Air Force, 1962 (*AP Images*); more than 110,000 fans pack Beaver Stadium at the first ever all-stadium "white-out" for a game against Notre Dame, 2007 (*Michael R. Sisak/Icon SMI*); John Cappelletti runs for a touchdown against Maryland, 1972 (*Paul Vathis/AP Images*).

CONTENTS

6	Preface
8	CHAPTER 1 Kicking Off
18	CHAPTER 2 The "M Squad"
24	CHAPTER 3 Buckling Down Under Bezdek
36	CHAPTER 4 The "Hig" Holds On
46	CHAPTER 5 Rip Engle Steps In
62	CHAPTER 6 Off and Running
82	CHAPTER 7 A Heisman Winner in Happy Valley
100	CHAPTER 8 Decade of Champions
114	CHAPTER 9 Blazing New Trails
136	CHAPTER 10 Cooling Off, Collapse, and a Comeback
162	CHAPTER 11 No Ordinary Joe
174	APPENDIX The Penn State Football All-Time Record Book
189	Index

PREFACE

In the fall, State College becomes the third-largest "city" in Pennsylvania. On football weekends, the Penn State campus is exceeded only by Philadelphia and Pittsburgh as the most densely populated area in the state.

The reason? Penn State football. Beaver Stadium, home of the Nittany Lions, seats more than 100,000 and rocks with fans loyal—and loud. It is an experience like no other in the world of sports.

For as long as I can remember, I've loved sports and sports history, and working on this book has been a labor of love. It wasn't too long ago, or so it seems, that I first visited the Penn State campus to research my first book on the Nittany Lions, in the 1970s.

John Morris, then the Penn State sports information director, set up interviews with Joe Paterno and Rip Engle and gave me complete access to his files and photos. My visit included a memorable evening with three old-timers—Dutch Hermann, Joe Bedenk, and Dutch Ricker—who told fascinating stories about their days at Penn State.

I have been back to Penn State on many occasions, and through the years, I have spoken with dozens of Penn State athletes and coaches about the football team.

On Saturdays in the fall, State College becomes the third largest "city" in Pennsylvania, second only to Philadelphia and Pittsburgh, as Beaver Stadium fills with more than 100,000 fans coming from miles around. *Penn State University Archives, Pennsylvania State University Libraries*

Since that first book on Penn State football, I have written many others in the sports field while working for the Associated Press. Because it was my first book, and the first of five about Penn State, the Nittany Lions will always have a special place in my memory bank.

This latest endeavor puts the storied football program in sharp focus with a lavishly illustrated history, covering the 1880s to today. You will see the Nittany Lions as you've never seen them before. Interviews with Penn State coaches and players of the present and the distant past provide deep insight and a rare perspective on more than a century of great college football.

With Joe Paterno's omnipresence at State College, it's hard to imagine anyone else coaching the Nittany Lions. In fact, 13 different men served as the head football coach at Penn State before Paterno. Each of those 13 men made his own special contribution, including Rip Engle, Paterno's mentor. Now in his sixth decade at Penn State, Paterno has been as solidly entrenched as the Nittany Lion statue, one of the most revered objects on campus.

Along with Paterno and Engle, Heisman Trophy–winner John Cappelletti, Hall of Famer Jack Ham, and All-American Kerry Collins are among the many legends who share their thoughts about the Penn State experience.

— *Ken Rappoport*

ACKNOWLEDGMENTS

The authors wish to thank the following people for their help with this book: Genaro Armas, Nancy Armour, Kerry Collins, Paul Karwacki, Bud Meredith, Lydell Mitchell, Dan Perkins, Paul Posluszny, Ralph Russo, Herb Schmidt, Brian Siegrist, and Teresa M. Walker.

In addition to numerous personal interviews, the authors used the following sources in researching this book: the *New York Times*, *Sports Illustrated*, the Associated Press, *USA Today*, the *Sporting News*, the *Penn State Daily Collegian*, the Penn State University Archives, and the Penn State athletic website (gopsusports.cstv.com).

Coach Joe Paterno is immortalized outside Beaver Stadium with a statue depicting him leading the Penn State football team onto the field—something he has done more than 500 times in his career. *Ken Rappoport*

CHAPTER 1
KICKING OFF

Before there was a 100,000-seat Beaver Stadium, it was standing-room only in the early days of Penn State football. *Penn State University Archives, Pennsylvania State University Libraries*

Just before the 1912 football season, a Penn State letterman came back to the campus to help coach Bill Hollenback teach fundamentals to the players.

"What do you think of this year's squad?" Hollenback asked.

"The backfield is good," the old grad said, "but the line is weak."

Hollenback gave the visitor a chance to back up his words.

"He put the ball on the 5-yard line and gave the guy five tries to put it over," recalled Lloyd "Dad" Engle, one of the tackles on that Penn State team.

After the third try, the visitor was back on the 20-yard line and much the worse for wear.

"He decided that he had had enough and admitted that his judgment was a little off," Engle said.

Actually, a lot off. The old grad was facing one of the greatest Penn State football teams of the early days—a juggernaut called the "M Squad," featuring Eugene "Shorty" Miller and Pete Mauthe.

That season, the Lions shut out their first two opponents. After giving up 6 points to Cornell in the third game, they decided enough was enough.

What did they do? They shut out their last five opponents en route to an 8–0 record—the first

full, perfect season in Penn State football history. The Lions outscored their opponents 285–6 for the year.

The old grad, whose identity was lost to history, should have seen it coming. The year before, Hollenback's team had gone 8–0–1.

Any discussion of the first great football team in Penn State history inevitably begins with the 1912 squad.

"Other great teams have represented the Blue and White on the gridiron in past years," noted Penn State's student newspaper, the *Collegian*, "but none accomplished quite as much."

Bill Hollenback grew familiar with turning out unbeaten teams in his brief but highly successful tenure as Penn State's football coach. His 1909 team had gone 5–0–2 before the coach handed the reins to his brother, Jack, for the 1910 season. Bill returned to coach the 1911 team and lasted three more seasons at State College, finishing with a 28–9–4 overall record.

Prior to Hollenback, Tom Fennell was the only football coach to last as long as five years at State College. Fennell, Penn State's first full-time head football coach, posted a 33–17–1 record from 1904 to 1908.

Penn State's first official football team in 1887. Front row, left to right: Watson Levret Barclay, Harvey B. McLean, John S. Weller, Charles Milton Kessler, Charles C. Hildebrand, James Reuben Rose, Harry R. Leyden. Back row: Advisory coach Nelson E. Cleaver, John Price Jackson, John G. Mitchell, James C. Mock, George H. Linsz, John Morris. *Penn State University Archives, Pennsylvania State University Libraries*

THE ORIGINS

Penn State University began playing intercollegiate football in 1887—at least, that's the official word.

Not so the word from I. P. McCreary, who claims to have played on the *original* Penn State football team six years earlier, in 1881. That year, the Penn State squad traveled to Lewisburg to play a contest against Bucknell. The game was played on a muddy field in a drizzling rain that was "a little short of sleet," as McCreary recalled it in letters to his teammates.

Penn State, or State College as it was called then, beat Bucknell 9–0.

News of Penn State's momentous victory took a while to reach the campus at State College. McCreary had made arrangements to send a telegram to the nearby town of Bellefonte following the game. From there, the score could be relayed to State College, which had no wire service at the time.

McCreary's message read: "We have met the enemy, and they are ours; nine to nothing."

In 1892, Beaver Field was fitted for a 500-seat grandstand, complete with roof and flagpoles. It was a sure sign that football was picking up steam at Penn State. *Penn State University Archives, Pennsylvania State University Libraries*

The message was delivered to State College late Saturday afternoon. According to McCreary, the State College postmaster "broadcast the news by writing it big on a sheet of pasteboard and tacking it up over the delivery window of the post office."

George Linsz, a member of the 1887 team, challenged McCreary's claim of the 1881 team as the pioneer of Penn State football. "I am of the opinion that the statement that they played football some time early in the eighties is undoubtedly true," Linsz said. "But I am also of the opinion that this was a rather pick-up aggregation that went into this game, and football was not continuous at Penn State from that date." So, in Linsz's view, 1887 marks the origin of the first *organized* football team and the first year of a continuous program at the school.

Penn State also does not recognize the 1881 team as part of its athletic history. "The nature of the game was considered to be a rugby-style scrimmage," the athletic department noted in its media guide, "thus it is not counted as an intercollegiate football game."

When Linsz stepped off the train at State College for his freshman year in the fall of 1886, he was carrying a battered football with him. Like the credit card of today, he never left home without it. Linsz had played football at the Episcopal Academy of Philadelphia and brought his enthusiasm and knowledge of the game to State College. He loved to kick the ball around on campus with his classmates. Before he knew it, he was in the middle of a movement to bring football to State College. He soon rounded up enough players for a team to represent the university in 1887 and lined up a game with Bucknell.

"There was plenty of enthusiasm at the outset," said James C. Mock, one of the members of the 1887 team. "I recall no opposition among the faculty, and I know that at least two faculty members were helpful."

Among the supportive faculty members was Nelson E. Cleaver, an English professor who had played football at Dickinson and volunteered to help coach the 1887 team.

Along with Linsz (the captain) and Mock, the first official football team at Penn State included Charles C. Hildebrand, Watson Barclay, Harvey McLean, John Weller, Charles Kessler, James Rose, Harry Leyden, John Jackson, John Mitchell, and John Morris.

THE NITTANY LION

They were once known as the "Nittanymen." It's difficult to say exactly when the "Nittanymen" became the "Nittany Lions" as the nickname for Penn State's athletic teams.

According to the Penn State media guide, H. D. "Joe" Mason conducted a one-man campaign in 1907 to choose a school mascot. Mason was on a trip to Princeton with the Penn State baseball team when he saw the Princeton tiger. He decided Penn State should also have a mascot: a lion.

"A student publication sponsored the campaign to select a mascot, and Penn State is believed to be the first college to adopt the lion as a mascot," said the media guide.

Not just a lion—a Nittany Lion. It was named after the mountain lion that roamed Mount Nittany, the stately mountain that overlooks the Penn State campus.

How did Mount Nittany get its name? Well, that's another story.

According to regional folklore, the mountain was formed to honor the spirit of a courageous Indian princess. Her name was Nita-Nee, later changed to Nittany.

The famous Nittany Lion statue on the Penn State University campus. *Ken Rappoport*

The players wore beanies, tight-fitting canvas jackets, knee-length pants, and virtually no padding. Known then as the "Nittanymen," Penn State played its very first game on November 5, 1887. The result was a 54–0 victory over Bucknell.

Bucknell wanted a rematch. Two weeks later, in State College, Penn State scored a 24–0 victory to complete a perfect 2–0 initial season. A good start, but the relatively inexperienced boys from State College still had a lot of knocks to take before turning into a Beast of the East.

In 1889, Penn State was beaten 26–0 by Lafayette and suffered a number of injuries in the game. Four days later, the Lions had to play Lehigh, one of the eastern powers at the time. It didn't matter that Penn State only had nine players to suit up, instead of the normal eleven.

Onto the field at Lehigh went the undermanned Nittanymen. They didn't have a chance and were overwhelmed 106–0. It was the worst defeat in Penn State football history.

Better times were coming.

A GOLDEN TOUCH

First he was a savior, then a turncoat. George W. Hoskins was one of the most intriguing and bizarre figures in the early days of Penn State football.

Hoskins was hired in 1892 to be Penn State's first director of physical training and first instructor of physical education. He is also considered the school's first official football coach. Talk about Penn State getting its money's worth: Hoskins also played center in an era when such double-duty was common practice.

Hoskins had been the athletic trainer at the University of Vermont before his appointment at Penn State. His arrival at State College signaled an upgrade in the football program.

Another sign that football was growing at State College was the decision to expand the stadium. The newly named Beaver Field was getting a facelift—the addition of a 500-seat grandstand with a projecting blue and white roof and three flagpoles.

Still another indication of the increasing relevance of football was that, for the first time, spring practice was held. The number of candidates for the football squad also continued to increase.

Hoskins turned out a succession of winning teams and an overall record of 17–4–4 from 1892 to 1895. His time at Penn State was all positive. But the same couldn't be said after he left the Nittanymen to play for Pitt (then known as Western University of Pittsburgh). Player-coaches switching schools was also common practice in those days.

Facing Penn State for the first time in 1896, Hoskins was now the enemy—an enemy without any sense of fair play. The football game disintegrated into one of the biggest brawls ever seen at Beaver Field, instigated by Hoskins' dirty play, according to the Penn State newspaper, the *Free Lance*.

Penn State's 1892 team won five straight games on shutouts after opening with a loss at Penn. Spring practice made its first appearance at State College that year. *Penn State University Archives, Pennsylvania State University Libraries*

In 1894, this group of footballers led Penn State to its first undefeated season. The squad went 6–0–1 while outscoring the opposition 179–18. *Penn State University Archives, Pennsylvania State University Libraries*

"Not only did trainer and captain Hoskins (center of W.U.P.) make it a disinteresting game," reported the *Free Lance*, "but he gave such an exhibition of the unmanly defiance of all fair rules which degrades the game as to make it a lasting example of the 'antis' who hold up to public opinion."

The brawl, continued the *Free Lance*, "did more injury to the prestige of the game of football than its promoter can repair."

Suddenly, all the good Hoskins had done at Penn State turned sour.

Penn State's football fortunes cooled for a few years before the program was brought back to life by a "Pop" and a "Mother" after the turn of the century.

William Nelson "Pop" Golden compiled a 16–12–1 record as Penn State's football coach from 1900 to 1902 while also serving as trainer. It wasn't his only contribution to athletics at State College. Following the 1902 season, Golden was hired as Penn State's first athletic director. At the same time, he remained on the football staff as an assistant coach until 1909.

During his dozen years at Penn State, Golden presided over unprecedented growth in athletics, most notably in football. He established the first training table, and he helped to raise funds through the alumni and other sources that turned the sport into a profit-maker. On occasion, he also wore the hat of recruiter. Outside of sports, he was a beloved figure among Penn State students, often serving as a guide and mentor.

The 1902 season was Golden's best as coach and featured one of the best individual performances ever by a Penn State back. Andy Smith scored five touchdowns and kicked two extra points in a 55–0 rout of Susquehanna. (Smith then left Penn State to enroll at the University of Pennsylvania.) Penn State shut out six other teams that season en route to a

KICKING OFF 13

"Pop" Golden (left) coached the Penn State football team from 1900 to 1902 and later presided over unprecedented growth in athletics at State College as the school's first athletic director. Dan Reed (right) also coached in the early 1900s at Penn State. *Penn State University Archives, Pennsylvania State University Libraries*

7–3 record. *LaVie*, Penn State's yearbook, called the 1902 season "the most favorable one in the history of the college."

The 1906 season under Tom Fennell was even better: an 8–1–1 record featuring nine shutouts. (Penn State and Gettysburg played to a scoreless tie in the season's fourth game.) Largely responsible for this defensive dominance was William Thomas "Mother" Dunn, Penn State's first All-American.

The 6-foot-3, 200-pound Dunn anchored Penn State's powerful line at center. Teams were so respectful of Dunn that they rarely ran a play through the middle when he was in the game. Realizing this advantage, Dunn became a roving center, moving around wherever the action was. "He delighted in moving around the big men," said Rip Engle, the Penn State coach from 1950 to 1965.

Watching Dunn and the Nittany Lions take on Yale in 1906, Walter Camp, the legendary sportswriter and coach, was impressed—so impressed, in fact, that he put Dunn on his All-America team based on that day's performance. Despite a 10–0 loss to Yale (the only points Penn State gave up all season), Dunn had completely outplayed his opponent.

Dunn was recognized not only by Camp but also by George Trevor of the *New York Sun*. In a 1927 newspaper article, the sportswriter picked an all-time Penn State team. Aside from Dunn, Trevor

PRETTY IN PINK?

Imagine a football team wearing pink as one of its primary colors. That's the way it was at Penn State in the 1880s.

Not the plain-vanilla uniforms of blue and white so familiar to fans today, but actually pink and black. Students chose that combination of school colors in 1887 when football first took flight at Penn State.

"We wanted something bright and attractive," said George Meek, class of 1890, "but we could not use red or orange, as these colors were already in use by other colleges. So we had a very deep pink—really cerise—which, with black, made a very pretty combination."

Soon, according to the Penn State media guide, many students were walking around campus wearing pink and black striped blazers and caps. Penn State's sports teams were very colorful, indeed.

However, there was one little problem: With long exposure to the sun, the pink faded to white. Result: The uniforms were now black and white.

"So the colors were quickly changed to blue and white," Meek said.

Official announcement of the new colors was made on March 18, 1890.

It's been nothing but blue and white ever since.

The Penn State footballers didn't always don the now-classic blue-and-white colors. Back in the early days, it was pink and white—although they weren't wearing helmets back then, either. *Ken Rappoport*

The Penn State football team gets a lift into town by carriage following a victory. Students do the pulling after replacing the horses. *Penn State University Archives, Pennsylvania State University Libraries*

PARKER'S BOAT

After the stagecoach and before the automobile, the train was a popular way to travel in America in the early 1900s. Pennsylvania was no different than the rest of the 48 states.

Visitors from outlying areas came in droves to Penn State games, particularly as the team rose as a football power in the East. One of the most popular ways for fans to get from Bellefonte to Beaver Field in State College was a train nicknamed "Parker's Boat."

Penn State students had two explanations for the unique nickname. According to one version, the conductor, a man named Parker, tried to run his engine through a flooded section of road during a heavy rainstorm. The train stalled, and the passengers were forced to sit in the marooned train for several hours. In the other version, the train was said to rock so much that passengers often became seasick, and thus the reference to a boat.

Such a train was an obvious source of joke material, and one of the countless stories told about "Parker's Boat" involved a disturbed passenger. Suffering through an especially long ride and seemingly no nearer his destination than when he started, the passenger called to Parker:

"Say, conductor, how long have you been on this train?"

"Twenty-seven years," answered Parker.

"You must have come all the way from Bellefonte," another remarked sarcastically.

Three famous Penn State football players from the early days (left to right): Earl E. Hewitt, Andrew Latham Smith, and Leroy Scholl. Scholl is the only Penn State player to win six varsity letters in football (1896–1901). *Penn State University Archives, Pennsylvania State University Libraries*

was especially high on several Penn State players of that era: backs Carl Forkum, "Irish" McIlveen, Bull McLeary, Heff Hirschman, and Ed Yeckley; tackle Andy Moscrip; and kicker Larry Vorhis, who was responsible for many thrilling Penn State moments from 1907 to 1909.

Trevor said Vorhis was Penn State's "most dependable kicker." Vorhis kicked two field goals to trim Cornell in 1907, three to beat Pittsburgh and one to tie Cornell in 1908, one to deadlock Carlisle in 1909, and one to tie Pennsylvania the same year. "That's delivering under pressure," Trevor concluded.

Vorhis' dramatic performances in 1909 were a feature of Bill Hollenback's first team at Penn State. His kicking propelled Penn State to a 5–0–2 record, a sign of things to come.

W. T. "Mother" Dunn was Penn State's first All-American in football, selected by Walter Camp in 1906. The 6-foot-3, 200-pound Dunn anchored Penn State's powerful line at center. *Penn State University Archives, Pennsylvania State University Libraries*

MOTHER'S DAY

At Penn State, he was the "mother" of all centers in his time.

Walter Camp saw William Thomas "Mother" Dunn in action against Yale one day and realized he was watching football greatness. Although Penn State lost the game, Dunn had completely outplayed the Yale center. Camp decided to pencil in Dunn on his 1906 All-America team—the first such honor for a Penn State player.

"Dunn, of Penn State, was the best center of the season," Camp wrote in an article in *Collier's Weekly* in 1906. "He weighs just under 200, is something over six feet in height, active in breaking through, and in diagnosing plays."

Camp described how Dunn "persistently broke through and blocked kicks. Able to run the hundred inside of 11 seconds, he was down under his own side's kicks with the ends."

For many years, Dunn was regarded as the school's all-time greatest lineman. He played four years at Penn State, finishing up in 1906. That season, he led the Nittanymen to an 8–1–1 record. Dunn was the mainstay of a line that held nine opponents scoreless, allowing only 10 points to Yale in Penn State's 10-game schedule.

Dunn's journey from Youngstown, Ohio, to Penn State was not an easy one. When his father died, Dunn started working in the steel mills at a very young age. He also was a chemist for the U.S. Steel Company and a brakeman for the Erie Railroad. When he had saved enough money to go to college, he enrolled at Penn State at the relatively late age of 22.

Dunn was a leader from the moment he arrived on the Penn State campus in 1903, elected to the position of freshman class president. One day, he was leading a group of freshmen across the campus to challenge the sophomores in one of the school "rushes."

"There goes Mother Dunn and all her baby chicks," a sophomore student yelled, and the nickname stuck.

Dunn won the starting center job on the first day of tryout camp and stayed at the position, despite a series of injuries, throughout his career. Not even an injured knee could keep him from dominating a game, as Harvard found out one day.

"The Harvard boys, knowing that Mother had an injury, tried to go for the knee as soon as play started," recalled Rip Engle, who later coached at Penn State. "Instead, the big Harvard center received full treatment from the brace and was taken from the game. The substitute steered clear of Mother's injured knee."

When his football days were over, Dunn became a doctor and moved to Hawaii. Upon his death in 1962, an editorial in the *Maui News* called Dunn "a quiet, friendly man who ministered to the medical needs of the Sunset Side for many years, and acted as friend and counselor for most of the people in the district."

Just like his football days, Mother Dunn still had a large following.

CHAPTER 2: THE "M SQUAD"

Bill Hollenback didn't look much older than his Penn State players. In fact, he wasn't. An All-American at Penn, Hollenback was hired to coach the Nittany Lions when he was just 22 years old.

"The young fellows who had just graduated from college understood the new type of play better than many of the old coaches, and so they were hired," Hollenback later recalled.

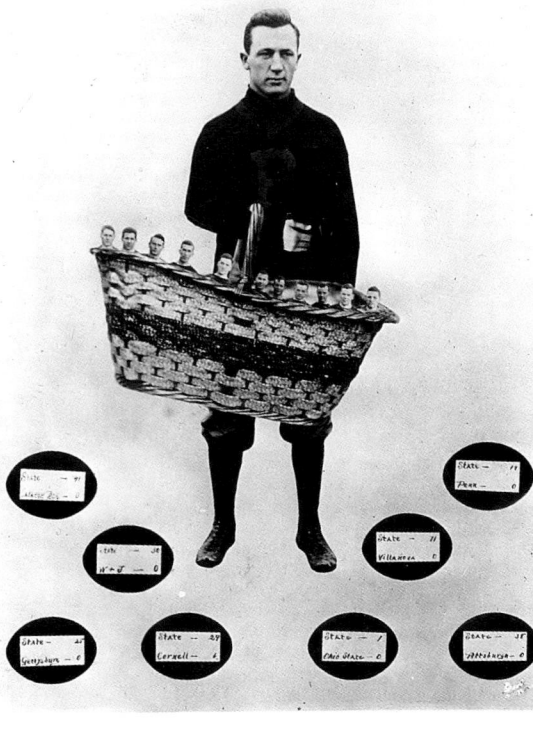

Bill Hollenback carries his great 1912 team, known as the "M Squad," in a basket in this whimsical photo. Known for his fiery locker-room talks, Hollenback led Penn State to a perfect 8–0 record that season. *Penn State University Archives, Pennsylvania State University Libraries*

Football was going through a number of rules changes at the time, including the legalization of the forward pass. Dutch Hermann, who played on the 1909 Penn State team, remembered the beginnings of the pass. It didn't resemble anything like the modern game.

"You didn't have to catch the ball—if it hit you, it belonged to you," said Hermann. "I remember watching a game in 1907 against Pitt. A Penn State guy threw a pass and hit a big Pitt tackle. He didn't know where the ball was; it hit him right in the head. Another Pitt guy grabbed the ball, went in for a touchdown, and they beat us 6–0."

Hermann was thankful he didn't play before the rules changes. Life was tougher for quarterbacks then. "The quarterback would have these large loops on his belt," Hermann recalled, "and a teammate on each side of him would hoist him up and throw him over the line."

Hermann's relationship with Coach Hollenback was solid. "He was a terrific fellow," Hermann said. They had played against each other before Hollenback took the coaching job at Penn State.

"He was a great athlete," Hermann said. "He could run; he could throw."

Hollenback replaced Tom Fennell following a 5–5 season in 1908. Hermann remembered Hollenback as having a fiery locker-room presence. "Back in those days, pep talks were the difference between a winning and a losing football team," Hermann said. "And Hollenback could really inspire a football team."

Action during the Penn State–Penn game on October 28, 1911. The Lions beat Penn 22–6 that day, ending a 17-game winless streak against their intrastate rival. Shorty Miller (far left) scored two touchdowns in the game. *Penn State University Archives, Pennsylvania State University Libraries*

Despite his strong 5-0-2 record in his first year at Penn State, Hollenback suddenly and mysteriously decided to take a similar job at Missouri in 1910. He was replaced by his brother, Jack. No one seemed to object—Jack Hollenback was also a highly respected graduate of Penn, an eastern football power.

"Apparently, he had gone to Missouri on sort of a mutual trial basis," Hermann said of Bill Hollenback. "And for some reason or other, it didn't suit Bill, and it didn't suit Missouri. But since Penn State had designated Bill's brother to take his place temporarily, apparently Bill himself was not so sure when he went out to Missouri that he'd stay."

After brother Jack led the squad to a respectable 5-2-1 campaign in 1910, Bill returned to State College and turned out another unbeaten team in 1911. Then still another in 1912, and that season happened to be perfect. Led by Shorty Miller and Pete Mauthe, the team called the "M Squad" hammered out an 8-0 record.

At 5-foot-5 and 140 pounds, Miller was an unlikely looking football hero. Looks were deceiving: Miller was one of the greatest broken-field runners ever seen at Penn State, according to old-timers.

"He was a little fellow, but he was quick and fast," Hermann said. "Because of his short legs, he could stop and start on a dime without losing speed. I can remember times when he'd get tripped up and would be almost running on his hands before he'd regain his balance. He was a tough man to bring down."

Miller did it all for Penn State—quarterback on offense, deep safety on defense, and punt-return specialist. In an era when teams were still trying to master passing techniques with an awkward oval ball, Miller threw for nine touchdowns in 1912. It was a school record that stood for 50 years, until Pete Liske passed for 12 TDs in 1962.

"He was a left-handed passer, and because of the shape of the ball, he couldn't grip it and had to throw it off his hand," Hermann said of Miller.

Even with his brilliant statistics, Miller didn't think he was the best passer on the team. He insisted that Mauthe had the stronger arm.

"Mauthe would knock down a receiver with a pass," Miller said.

Mauthe was usually recognized more for his powerful running style. The first Penn State player to be inducted into the College Football Hall of Fame, Mauthe rushed for 710 yards in the Nittany Lions' balanced offense in 1912. He was a pressure performer, producing 11 touchdowns, 8 field goals, and 29 extra points.

Dexter "Dex" Very started at right end for Penn State in every game from 1909 to 1912 and was named team captain in 1911. He was inducted into the College Football Hall of Fame in 1976. *College Football Hall of Fame*

Shorty Miller—seen here punting in a game at Beaver Field—was the star quarterback of Penn State's famed "M Squad." His contributions to Penn State football in the early days were sizeable. *Penn State University Archives, Pennsylvania State University Libraries*

Miller and Mauthe shared the glory in the backfield with halfbacks Dan Welty and Robert "Punk" Berryman. The rest of the usual starters were Dexter Very and Al Wilson at ends, Levi Lamb and "Dad" Engle at tackles, Albert Hansen and "Red" Bebout at guards, and John Clark at center.

The 1912 Nittany Lions were as good on defense as they were on offense. They came close to shutting out all their opponents, allowing only 6 points all year—and that one score didn't come against the defense. In the third game of the season, Cornell intercepted a Penn State pass and ran it back for a TD. When Penn State was lining up for Cornell's extra point try, Engle "broke out with the greatest array of cuss words you ever heard," Wilson said.

"I'll be damned if I'll ever stand under another goal post like this," Engle said during the 29–6 win over Cornell.

He never did. The Nittany Lions finished out the 1912 season outscoring the opposition 185–0 over the final five games.

The victory over Cornell was typical of Penn State's performances that season. A *New York Times* story reported, "Penn State's superb physique wore down the Cornell team. . . . The Cornellians at the close of the game were pretty well mauled."

The mauling was so severe, in fact, that Cornell cut off all football relations with Penn State. In the words of the *Cornell Sun*, Cornell's student newspaper, "The visitors were not the sort of aggregation this university cared again to meet on the gridiron. What need to rehearse the deliberate fouls of some of the State College men on Percy Field. Two Cornell players were hamstrung during the contest in a manner the very directness and dexterity of which was evidence of considerable previous schooling in that branch of football."

The newspaper defined "hamstringing" as "the gentle art of deliberately catching a man from behind in the Achilles tendon of the calf in such a way as to effectually incapacitate him for some time to come."

Other tactics used by Penn State, according to the Cornell student newspaper, were ankle twisting and face smashing.

Cornell wasn't the only team to break off football relations with Penn State following the 1912 season. Indeed, the Ohio State Buckeyes didn't even remain on the field for the duration of their game that year.

The Nittany Lions practically scored at will while running up a 37–0 lead over the Buckeyes in Columbus. Throughout the game, Ohio State coach Jack Richards had been complaining to officials about what he considered Penn State's unnecessary roughness. Finally, it came to a boil late in the fourth quarter, when Ohio State sent a play through tackle and guard. The Buckeyes' runner was tackled too hard for Richards' taste, and he pulled his players off the field with about five minutes left in the game.

"The Ohio State players started off the field," Engle recalled. "We had no idea they were leaving but thought they were going to try some sort of spread or trick formation. So we started following them."

That was the signal for the crowd to come out of the stands. Fights broke out on the field. Finally, the Penn State players escaped to their locker room.

The Nittany Lions got out of town safely, but the game left a bad taste and ruptured relations between the schools. It would be another 44 years before the football powerhouses of Penn State and Ohio State met again on a football field.

Above: Shorty Miller was usually out in front of the field when chasing the football. He quarterbacked the great 1912 Penn State team, including this 14–0 win over Penn at Franklin Field. *Penn State University Archives, Pennsylvania State University Libraries*

Left: Pete Mauthe, one of the stars of the 1912 unbeaten Nittany Lions, was a fullback who could tear a line to shreds with his powerful bursts. *Penn State University Archives, Pennsylvania State University Libraries*

HOLLENBACK BOWS OUT, HARLOW STEPS IN

Hollenback remained two more years as the Penn State coach, never coming close to the success of the 1912 team. Following a 5–3–1 season in 1914, he left Penn State and was replaced by the popular Dick Harlow, an assistant coach.

"He had a knack of rallying the entire student body and staff behind the team," noted Rip Engle, who played for Harlow at Western Maryland years before Engle launched his own coaching career at Penn State. "I remember that it snowed the whole week before the last game of my senior year—that was December 12th [1929] against Maryland. Harlow had the campus so much behind the team that each day the students and even some faculty members showed up with shovels and brooms and cleared off the practice field."

Stories of Harlow's heroism as a player at Penn State would fill a book. Playing tackle in 1910 and 1911, Harlow's toughness was legendary. Once, before a game with Pitt, he broke a bone in his ankle. In those circumstances, a player usually goes to the hospital. Harlow went back to the football field.

"We made an issue of it," Harlow said. "Either I played, or we'd all be mad. Pete Mauthe, the captain, demanded that I have my rights, and Hollenback gave in. They made a plaster cast for my leg."

Harlow came to the field on game day on crutches.

"I got rid of them in the field house," he said. "Then I went out and played the whole 60 minutes. After the game, I went back on crutches for six weeks."

As a player, Harlow was renowned for his ability to break through lines and block punts. In his senior year at Penn State, he made 17 such blocks in five games.

When he turned to coaching, blocking punts were an important part of his football philosophy.

"It generally changes the whole course of a game when it happens," Harlow said. "When you block a punt on a team, they never have the same confidence again."

Engle remembered Harlow as a highly superstitious man during their time at Western Maryland.

"Western Maryland played its home games in Baltimore Stadium," Engle said, "and whichever seat we took in the bus for the drive from Westminster to Baltimore for the first game of the season was the seat we had to sit in on each succeeding trip.

Dick Harlow demonstrates the art of dropkicking to some of his players on the 1915 team. Harlow made an impact at Penn State as both a player (1910 and 1911) and a coach (1915–1917). *Penn State University Archives, Pennsylvania State University Libraries*

"I remember that we had to pass through Druid Hill Park in suburban Baltimore en route to the stadium, and although there were some 20 roads through there, old superstitious Dick made the driver take the same route every time."

Away from the field, Harlow was a soft-spoken scholar who collected flowers, birds' eggs, stamps, and Chippendale chairs. On the field, he could be a tough guy, challenging his players in physical ways.

"They say Dick was a holy terror when he played at Penn State, and I can believe it," Engle said. "I've seen him walk up to a big lineman who had been loafing, grab him by the nape of the neck, and give him a boot in the seat."

Harlow usually got even better results from players with his oratory.

"He was an effective psychologist, locker-room orator," Engle said. "In many games, his dressing-room talks were the difference between victory and defeat."

At Penn State, Harlow took over a talented team featuring the great Bob Higgins. Higgins would later become an accomplished Penn State coach in his own right. As a player, he was the stuff of legend as a receiver who caught countless memorable passes.

In November 1915, Penn State and Lehigh were in a scoreless tie at Beaver Field. With time running out, Higgins scored a touchdown on a pass from Stan Ewing that covered 15 yards.

Hold on. The Nittany Lions were penalized for having too many men on the field.

Back in the huddle and a few yards farther back, the quarterback called the same play. He passed to Higgins in the same general area. Higgins gathered in the ball and scored a virtual replica of the first TD to carry the Nittany Lions to a 7–0 victory.

Higgins was equally brilliant on defense, and he was a top kicker as well. After college, he played pro ball for the famed Canton Bulldogs alongside the legendary Jim Thorpe.

The story is often told about the time Thorpe failed to show for a game, and Higgins was called on to impersonate the great runner. He went onto the field wearing Thorpe's jersey number, and he was heavily taped underneath to fill out the bigger uniform. He had people fooled—for a while, anyway.

Before he became a beloved football coach, Bob Higgins was a top-flight end for Penn State, winning All-American honors in 1915 and 1919. *Penn State University Archives, Pennsylvania State University Libraries*

Higgins, one of only five players in Penn State football history to letter in five seasons, was the star of a high-powered offense. The Lions peaked under Coach Harlow in 1916, when they outscored opponents 348–62 en route to an 8–2 record. The Nittany Lions' offense in this era simply overwhelmed many opponents, as emphasized by a 99–0 victory over St. Bonaventure and an 80–0 win over Gettysburg in 1917.

Harlow's teams went 20–8 in the three years he was head coach (1915–1917). He joined America's war effort in 1918, leaving the Lions in the hands of Hugo Bezdek.

BUCKLING DOWN UNDER BEZDEK

CHAPTER 3

Head coach Hugo Bezdek poses with his assistants (left to right): Dutch Herman, Bezdek, Dick Harlow, and Bill Martin. The beloved Harlow left for Colgate and took many of Penn State's top players with him before the 1922 season. *Penn State University Archives, Pennsylvania State University Libraries*

Tough guy. That was Hugo Bezdek's reputation when he took over as the Penn State football coach in 1918.

One story that illustrates his toughness comes from the time Bezdek worked as a baseball scout for the Pittsburgh Pirates and traveled with the team. On one train ride from Pittsburgh to New York, Bezdek got into a heated dispute with one of the Pirates' pitchers, Burleigh Grimes, a future Hall of Famer. They came to blows, fighting all the way from one city to the next. When they got off the train, Bezdek and Grimes shook hands.

"He was tough," said "Lighthorse" Harry Wilson, a Penn State All-American running back in the 1920s.

"But he put out and demanded that others put out, too. He taught good football, and he insured that you were in condition to play 60 minutes. He would be the first to tell you that he was not running a popularity contest."

Indeed not.

For your consideration: "Bloody Tuesday."

"On Monday, we'd have a long practice and warmup, and the second and third team would scrimmage," recalled Joe Bedenk, an All-American lineman in that era. "Then on Tuesday, the first team scrimmaged against every defense in the world, until everybody was dead on their feet."

Bezdek was one coach who would not baby players. Bedenk recalled that he once broke a collarbone while tackling dummies in practice. Despite the seriousness of the injury, Bedenk was back on the field three days later.

Bezdek ordered Bedenk to take 21 laps around the field. After all, Bezdek reasoned, there was nothing wrong with Bedenk's legs even though his collarbone was broken.

"I ran 21 laps around that damn track," Bedenk recalled years later.

Bezdek's favorite remark when a player suffered a leg injury was, "Cut it off."

Once, it so happened that Bezdek himself suffered a leg injury while he was in a foot race with one of his players. As he was being escorted off the field, one of the spirited Penn State players, protected by darkness, shouted, "Cut it off."

Feared but fair. That's the way many of Bezdek's players described him.

Said Dutch Ricker, a Penn State tackle in the 1920s, "If you worked hard and played fair and square with Bez, you got along with him. But if you were a chiseler, he'd make life miserable for you."

As for Bezdek's work ethic, few coaches in America drove their players harder. His general philosophy was that the players who worked the hardest during the week would have the most success on Saturday.

"We were so well conditioned and so much tougher than the teams we played," Bedenk said.

That would account for Penn State's 30-game unbeaten streak in the early 1920s, the second longest in school history. During that time, the Nittany Lions made their first bowl appearance in the 1923 Rose Bowl.

ALL-AMERICAN JOE

The offensive line has been called the engine room of a football team, the engine that makes everything else go. Without Joe Bedenk, the Nittany Lions would have had a hard time getting started in the 1920s.

Bedenk, an All-American guard, was a big factor in Penn State's 30-game unbeaten streak and appearance in the 1923 Rose Bowl.

"We were running guards in those days," Bedenk once recalled. "I used to open holes for Killinger and Wilson," speaking of Glenn Killinger and "Lighthorse" Harry Wilson, two of Penn State's greatest running backs in the 1920s.

Of course, players went both ways in those days. But Bedenk was renowned for his work on the offensive line, clearing paths for the Penn State runners.

"They said I had two personalities, a sort of Jekyll and Hyde," Bedenk said. "I was a nice person off the field, I'm told, but a son of a gun when I played football."

A native of Williamsport, Pennsylvania, Bedenk was initially drawn to Penn State for baseball. The coach at the time was Hugo Bezdek, the former Pittsburgh Pirates manager. Bezdek also was the football coach. He immediately noticed Bedenk's rugged 192-pound build and invited him to join the football team. Bedenk accepted, but was almost immediately sorry he did. He recalled practices called "Bloody Tuesdays" when players scrimmaged "until we were almost dead."

"Those scrimmages were brutal," Bedenk said.

But they usually translated into Penn State victories and personal glories for Bedenk. In 1923, Bedenk was picked for Walter Camp's All-America team on the basis of performances such as in the 21–3 victory over Navy, during which Bedenk cleared the way for three touchdowns by Wilson that day.

After his playing days, Bedenk went into coaching. Most notable was his association at Rice with John Heisman, whose name is on college football's most coveted individual trophy.

Bedenk later returned to State College to serve as an assistant under coach Bob Higgins. Bedenk himself coached the 1949 team in a transitional period before the arrival of Rip Engle. He also took over the Penn State baseball program for many years before his retirement in 1962.

Joe Bedenk was one of Penn State's greatest linemen in the 1920s, leading interference for a strong running attack. Later, he was a Nittany Lions coach in both baseball and football. *Penn State University Archives, Pennsylvania State University Libraries*

Above: Penn State went undefeated in 1920, including this 13–0 victory over Gettysburg in the season's second game. It was the Lions' first of four shutouts that year. *Penn State University Archives, Pennsylvania State University Libraries*

Below: For much of its football history, Penn State's greatest rival was the University of Pittsburgh. The Lions held the early advantage, with 13 wins in the first 22 meetings, but a 16-game winless streak against the Panthers followed. The teams are shown here facing off in a sea of mud at Pittsburgh's Forbes Field in the early 1920s. *Penn State University Archives, Pennsylvania State University Libraries*

Observers walking into a Penn State practice might have thought they were in the wrong place. The players were dancing—yes, dancing! It was Bezdek's idea to improve his players' footwork. The players, big and small, all were doing the Charleston, the craze of the nation. It wasn't quiet, either. Imagine the noise when those beefy football players started dancing in cleats on a tanbark pavilion.

Bezdek, who had coached under the legendary Amos Alonzo Stagg at the University of Chicago and coached Oregon to a Rose Bowl triumph in 1917, was full of innovations, which caught the attention of the eastern football establishment. According to coaching giant Glenn "Pop" Warner, the spinner play was one of the most effective of Bezdek's innovations.

"So successful were these plays that for several years after Hugo Bezdek originated the play, Penn State raised havoc with nearly every team it met," Warner recalled in a newspaper article in the 1930s. "As early as 1921, Glenn Killinger made All-American halfback largely on the long runs that developed from this play. Later, Harry Wilson ran wild for Penn State on the same play."

Bezdek's version of the spinner involved some elaborate ball-handling trickery by the quarterback, who handed off to one of his backs after spinning around. The rest of the Penn State runners plunged into the line, each making opponents believe that he had the ball.

Bezdek also was credited with having a hand in the development of the screen pass, the staggered ends on defense, and the roving center, which allowed a defensive lineman to move around freely in an early incarnation of the linebacker position. He also perfected the quick kick and the onside kick to such an extent that rules had to be rewritten.

In the early part of Bezdek's coaching career at Penn State, he had the help of Dick Harlow. The former coach had returned from World War I and served as an assistant to Bezdek.

"That was a great combination, Dick and Hugo," Bedenk recalled. "Hugo was the iron man just kicking you all over the place, and Dick was the fellow who would come back and soothe you."

Harlow left for Colgate before the 1922 season, and things would not be the same for a while. Many of Harlow's best players followed him, leaving a void of talent at Penn State.

"Harlow left, and seven of our good football players went with him—just the nucleus that made it a good football team," Bedenk said.

Nevertheless, Bezdek continued to coach winning football, with only one losing season over the next eight years. To say that Penn State waltzed away from many of its opponents wouldn't be far from the truth.

Opposing teams soon learned to expect the unexpected when facing Bezdek's Nittany Lions. In a game against Pop Warner's Pitt team on Thanksgiving Day 1919, Penn State was in a kicking situation, backed up on the 7-yard line. The Panthers fully expected the Lions to punt. But upon taking the snap from center, Bill Hess threw a short screen pass to Bob Higgins, who raced 90 yards for a touchdown.

The Panthers were flabbergasted by the play. It started the Lions on their way to a rare win over their intrastate rivals—by a convincing 20–0.

"Taking liberties with Glenn Warner is done about as often as . . . a landlord reduces the rent," quipped one writer, alluding to the famous Pitt coach.

Higgins, an All-American and captain of the 1919 Penn State team, was one of the stars on Bezdek's post–World War I powerhouse, along with Glenn Killinger, Joe Bedenk, Charley Way, Hinkey Haines, Duke Osborne, Mike Palm, and Dick Rauch.

Bezdek was hired not only to coach football at Penn State, but also to head the department of physical education. Shrugging off a limited four-game schedule in 1918 (1–2–1) because of World War I, the Nittany Lions came to life with a strong showing in 1919.

In Bezdek's first full season as head football coach, the Nittany Lions sustained only a 6-point loss to Dartmouth en route to a 7–1 season. The Lions followed that with a 7–0–2 record in 1920 and 8–0–2 in 1921.

The 1920 season featured a victory over Dartmouth in a classic game. But it came at a cost.

"We were really beat up in the Dartmouth game," Killinger said. "We won, but what a bunch of cripples turned out Monday."

No one had given Penn State a chance against Dartmouth. The score was 7–7 late in the game, when Killinger intercepted a pass at midfield and carried the ball to the Dartmouth 7-yard line. Joe Lightner then hammered in for the winning TD.

The game also had historical significance: It was Penn State's first official Alumni Homecoming Day, which brought 1,500 former students back to State

Action during Penn State's Homecoming game on October 9, 1920. The Nittany Lions beat Dartmouth 14–7 in the early stages of what would be a 30-game unbeaten streak, extending from October 25, 1919, to November 3, 1922. *Penn State University Archives, Pennsylvania State University Libraries*

THE ORIGINAL SCATBACK

"I loved to go off-tackle, inside. I see an opening, and I'm gone! I was one of those quick boys, you know."

Charley Way had to be—he was only 5-foot-9 and weighed merely 125 pounds when he started playing football for Penn State in 1917. Way's college career was interrupted by World War I. He was ready to resume his football play in 1920 after putting on a few pounds. That year, he earned All-American honors on the Walter Camp team, as Penn State roared through an undefeated season.

The All-American recognition classified Way as one of the top running backs in the early years of Penn State football. He has another distinction: one of the first successful walk-ons in school history.

"I went out for the team, but I wasn't a scholarship boy," Way said in an interview in the 1970s. "It was the scholarship boys who got the preference. I only weighed about 125 pounds at the time, and my right hand was split open from playing baseball. I wasn't ready for football."

Way's father was a carpenter and only worked in the summer. Way classified his family as "poor."

It didn't stop him from going to Penn State.

"You could go up there without much money in those days."

Way had been a four-sport letterman at Downington (Pennsylvania) High School. It wasn't until his sophomore year in college that he was given a chance to make the Penn State football team.

He didn't start out as a halfback but a quarterback, and second string at that. But when the first-stringer was injured, Way took over for good.

Despite his running style as a halfback, Way managed to avoid any serious injury.

"I never liked to run the ends, because it was too long a way around," he said. "I just liked to run inside. It was more direct that way."

He made Nebraska pay one Saturday in 1920, when he "reeled off a couple of long runs," as Way recalled. "The first time I had the ball, I ran for 53 yards. The next time I got my hands on the ball, I scored a touchdown."

And Penn State whipped Nebraska 20–0. It was one of the games that put Way over the top in contention for the All-America team.

After college, Way played professional football with the Canton Bulldogs and also did some coaching on the high school and college levels. He later worked for the Internal Revenue Service before retiring as a gentleman farmer outside of Philadelphia.

Program cover from the Penn State–Nebraska game at Beaver Field on November 6, 1920. It was the first meeting on the gridiron between these two future football powerhouses. The Nittany Lions won, 20–0. *Penn State University Archives, Pennsylvania State University Libraries*

College. Following the game, celebrations took place all over the Penn State campus. "After these," wrote alumni secretary Edward Sullivan, "the alumni came up to the Armory to enjoy the cider, pretzels, and smokes."

Penn State was developing a reputation as a tough place for visiting football teams—hard to get to and a difficult place in which to play. The Nittany Lions were forced to schedule many of their big games away from home, earning them the nickname, "The Nittany Nomads."

In 1921, the Lions logged 8,200 miles, including a memorable trip to Cambridge, Massachusetts, to face a rugged Harvard team in a battle of eastern powers.

The Nittany Lions, though banged up considerably with injuries to top players, had won the first four games of the season. The injury count included fullback George Snell, who was left in State College with a throat infection. Injuries continued to plague Penn State once the game against Harvard started. Running backs Pete Redinger and Frank Hess were knocked out, leaving reserves to fill the gaps.

The first half belonged to Harvard. The Crimson scored two quick touchdowns and led 14–7 at intermission. The complexion of the game started to change in the third quarter, thanks to Penn State's "Lighthorse" Harry Wilson, who had not seen any action in the first half.

"We were sitting in open bleachers," Wilson remembered of his spot on the bench with the reserves. "Bezdek turned to me and said, 'Wilson, warm up!' I got a little nervous. I got up and ran around and around until I got pooped. I was so tired that I had to sit down and rest."

Wilson was not down long before he heard his coach growl, "Where's Wilson?"

Up popped Wilson again, this time racing onto the field. On the next play, Wilson took a handoff and, as the *New York Times* described it, "found a break in the Harvard left wing and drove through cleanly. He kept his feet beautifully and broke into a clear field almost immediately." The report continued:

> The only Harvard player between Wilson and the Harvard goal line was Charley Buell, who stood far down the gridiron and waited. Wilson drove straight toward the Harvard quarterback [playing defense], watched him set to make a tackle and then swerved to the left again. [Roscoe] Fitts drove across the field also and both he and Buell threw themselves at the runner. Buell caught Wilson and threw him on the eight-yard line, but the players rolled over and then Wilson was held by Buell, with the goal line only four yards away.

Penn State captain and quarterback Glenn Killinger (right) shakes hands with Georgia Tech captain Judy Harlan prior to their meeting at New York's Polo Grounds on October 29, 1921. The Lions were triumphant, 28–7. *Penn State University Archives, Pennsylvania State University Libraries*

"LIGHTHORSE" HARRY WILSON

In the 1920s, the Navy football team saw a lot of "Lighthorse" Harry Wilson. Too much, in fact.

The highly visible halfback was usually showing his back to the Middies while running for touchdowns. And it didn't matter if he was playing for Penn State or Army.

As an All-American at Penn State, Wilson scored three times against the Midshipmen in 1923, including one touchdown on a 95-yard kickoff return. That was all the Nittany Lions needed in a 21–3 victory.

Later, as a star halfback at Army, Wilson scored a touchdown and kicked extra points as the Cadets played the Middies to a magnificent 21–21 tie in the 1926 game, considered the greatest of all Army-Navy tilts. Navy coach Bill Ingram characterized Wilson's play as the "greatest halfback performance" he had ever witnessed.

Under the loose eligibility rules of the day, West Point allowed college athletes to play for Army despite graduating from another school. Thus, Wilson played for both Penn State and Army—seven years in all! (Wilson also spent a year playing football and basketball on the freshmen teams at Penn State).

"I think West Point was the only school where I could do that," Wilson once said of his two-college career. "I know that Navy wouldn't let you do that."

Wilson, presumably nicknamed "Lighthorse" by a Philadelphia sports reporter because of his graceful running style, was a native Pennsylvanian. He attended two prep schools and graduated from Sharon High in 1920.

He could have played football almost anywhere, but decided on Penn State because his brother, Lloyd, was an alumnus.

Wilson caught the attention of coach Hugo Bezdek when he broke off a long run in a 21–21 tie with Harvard in 1921. Wilson's college football career was off and running.

Wilson maintained that it took courage to play football in the 1920s, considering the lightweight uniforms the players wore. "There wasn't much protection," he recalled.

No less courage than Wilson needed to go on bombing raids in the Pacific during World War II. He made 48 of them and earned the Distinguished Flying Cross before retiring as a U.S. Air Force colonel.

"Lighthorse" Harry Wilson is shown here in a pass-throwing pose, but he left his mark in the Penn State football annals primarily for his running exploits, including a memorable 56-yard dash against Harvard in 1921. *College Football Hall of Fame*

Incredibly, Wilson had pulled off a 56-yard run from scrimmage the very first time he touched the ball all day. From the 4-yard line, it took three plays for Penn State to score. Lightner carried the ball over, and after Penn State kicked the extra point, the teams were tied at 14.

"Up to that point, it was the longest run ever at Harvard Stadium," Wilson said of his long dash from scrimmage. "I guess that run helped me make first team."

It also inspired Penn State to another score. Killinger led the Lions to the Harvard 19 as the third quarter ended. Early in the fourth, Lightner scored his third TD of the day to give Penn State a 21–14 advantage.

Back came Harvard to tie the game, as Buell threw a 15-yard touchdown pass and kicked the extra point.

Darkness was now descending on Harvard Stadium. It was an eerie setting, the lights of cigarettes "looking like fireflies," according to Bedenk.

Reported the *Penn State Alumni News*: "The match, with its fifteen-minute quarters, carried the contest into darkness. It was darkness and time the Penn State eleven was fighting against in the last few minutes of play."

The Nittany Lions drove the ball deep into Harvard territory, only to run out of time.

A 21–21 tie. No, a *magnificent* 21–21 tie.

"Starting at three o'clock and battling with tremendous fierceness until it was so dark that the players could not be distinguished one from another, from the stands in which more than 30,000 spectators were straining their eyes, the teams fought each other to a standstill," reported the *Times*.

NITTANY LIONS MAKE THEIR FIRST BOWL

Rose Bowl day, January 1, 1923. Where was the Penn State football team? The Southern Cal coach wanted to know. The Southern Cal team wanted to know. The 53,000 fans wanted to know.

Where were they? The Lions were stuck in the Rose Bowl parade traffic.

"Some of the Rose Bowl people took us down to see the Parade of Roses on the day of the game," recalled Harry Wilson. "It was so jammed that we had a hard time getting out when we had to leave. We had to drive our cars on the sidewalks."

The 1922 Penn State team—sitting pretty on the Nittany Lion, thanks to some trick photography—started off the season 5–0 but stumbled to finish 6–4–1. *Penn State University Archives, Pennsylvania State University Libraries*

As a result, the Nittany Lions were late for the first bowl game in their history. Elmer "Gloomy Gus" Henderson, the Southern Cal coach, was gloomier than ever when the Nittany Lions finally showed up to inaugurate the new stadium in Pasadena, California. The Lions' late arrival held up the game for 35 minutes, according to the *New York Times*.

Adding to the day's steamy temperatures, Henderson and Bezdek nearly came to blows at midfield. The furious Southern Cal coach accused the Penn State coach of purposely holding up the game so that the temperatures could cool off for his players. The two were separated, but not before Bezdek no doubt got in a few choice remarks.

In the days leading up to the Rose Bowl game, things were far more pleasant for the Nittany Lions. They made the rounds of the movie studios and met Douglas Fairbanks Sr. and Mary Pickford, two of the top stars of their day.

"[Fairbanks] was a nut for keeping in shape," Wilson recalled. "He showed us his parallel bars and rings where he'd condition himself."

The Nittany Lions knew all about getting into shape. They had practiced in a foot of snow in the East before taking a train to California for the bowl game.

Although the team left a week early in order to get acclimated to the weather, it didn't seem to do much good.

"It was awfully warm out there," Wilson said, "and we weren't used to it. After practicing in that California heat for a while, I found that I couldn't stand up. All of us were pretty pooped."

Wilson, along with Bedenk, was one of the few players left from the powerful 1920 and 1921 Penn State teams, which had gone undefeated.

The 1922 team clearly wasn't as good as its predecessors. In November, the Nittany Lions had their historic 30-game unbeaten streak halted by Navy. By the time they got to the Rose Bowl on January 1, they had lost three of their last four games. The Rose Bowl invitation to Penn State had gone out before those games, but there was little regret by the Rose Bowl committee of its choice.

"The selection of Penn State comes as a direct tribute to the great record compiled in the past four years under the coaching of Hugo Bezdek," noted the *Penn State Alumni News*, "and is made regardless of victory or defeat during the present season."

Following a season-ending loss to Pitt, the Nittany Lions took a short rest. Then Bezdek took a squad of 30 on a four-day train ride to Pasadena. According

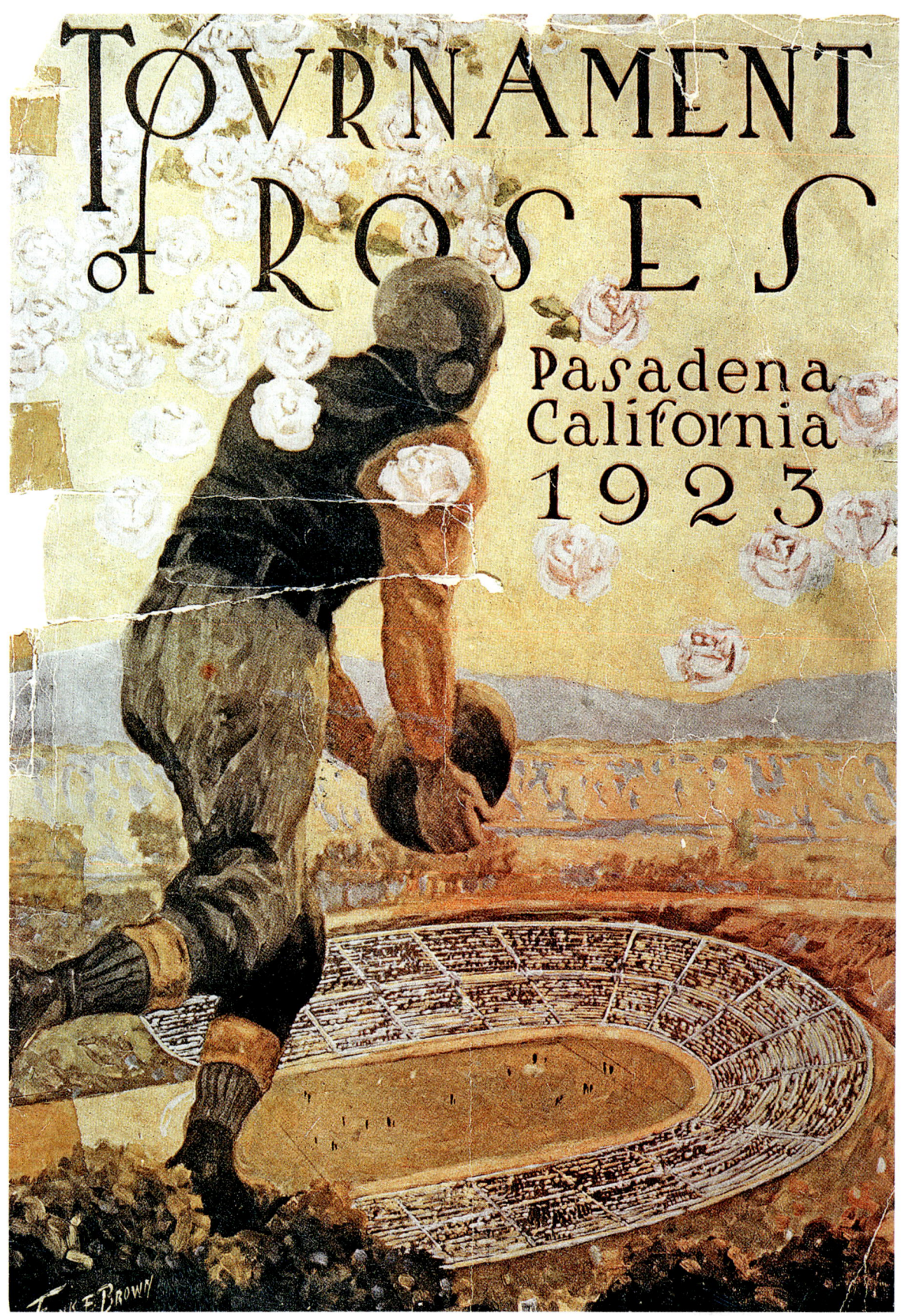

The Tournament of Roses program from the 1923 Rose Bowl, a real keepsake for Nittany Lions fans. It was Penn State's first bowl game. *Penn State University Archives, Pennsylvania State University Libraries*

Hugo Bezdek's Nittany Lions were not as good in 1922 as they had been in two previous undefeated seasons, but Penn State garnered its first invitation to a postseason bowl game nevertheless. Alas, the Lions lost to Southern Cal, 14–3, in the Rose Bowl. *Penn State University Archives, Pennsylvania State University Libraries*

to one Pennsylvania newspaper, the football players were "standing the long trip to the coast in fine fashion." The players did some sightseeing along the way, including a stop at the Grand Canyon.

After arriving in Pasadena, the Nittany Lions went through a strenuous workout under the blazing California sun. Unfortunately, it cost them another top player, when Bedenk suffered broken ribs.

Southern Cal was favored to win the Rose Bowl, but it meant nothing to Henderson. To the Trojans' coach, the glass was always half empty, and he was constantly offering dire predictions for his teams. Fortunately for Southern Cal, Henderson was usually wrong.

But at the 1923 Rose Bowl, the Trojans struggled through the first quarter without scoring a point. Penn State posted 3 on a 20-yard field goal by quarterback Mike Palm.

Late in the second quarter, momentum swung Southern Cal's way. A long gain by halfback "Ironsides" Baker featured a Trojans drive that ended when fullback Don Campbell plunged a yard over center into the end zone. The Trojans took a 7–3 halftime lead into the dressing room as "blaring bands, full-throated cheers from the rooting sections and waving banners" filled the stadium, according to a Pasadena newspaper.

After Penn State failed to make a first down on the first series of the third period, Southern Cal took over, as Baker and Campbell supplied the running punch. Baker scored from the 1-yard line to put the Trojans up 14–3.

Although, according to the *Times* report, "both teams were visibly exhausted in the final period," the Trojans appeared to be less exhausted than the Lions. They dominated the fourth quarter, and only a magnificent effort by the Penn State defense kept Southern Cal from scoring more touchdowns.

Final: Southern Cal 14, Penn State 3.

Some observers said that the climate had been a factor in Penn State's loss, but Coach Bezdek refused to hide behind any excuses. "I don't think [the weather] had anything to do with the outcome of the game," he said. "Southern Cal was too fast for us."

A BULLETIN AND A BREAKING POINT

The Rose Bowl wasn't the only significant event for Penn State in the 1922 season. It was also the year that the Nittany Lions started their longstanding and colorful rivalry with Syracuse.

The Lions and Orangemen played to a scoreless tie in their first meeting in October 1922. It wasn't until 1927 that a Penn State team was able to beat Syracuse. In another heady, defensive struggle that typified their encounters, the Nittany Lions fell behind 6–0 in the first period before staging a fourth-quarter rally in one of the rivalry's most exciting games. Penn State won on a late field goal by captain Johnny Roepke.

"The State followers, who passed a miserable first three quarters, saw a rejuvenated eleven leap at the Orange in the final period," the *New York Times* reported.

Unable to pierce the Syracuse line on the ground, the Nittany Lions had gone to the air and "resorted to deadly passes for gains." Penn State quarterback Cy Lungren finally swept around left end for a touchdown that tied the game 6–6.

The "Beaver Field Pictorial" was a nice souvenir from the Navy-Penn State game in October 1923. The Lions defeated the Midshipmen 21–3 in the Homecoming game. *Penn State University Archives, Pennsylvania State University Libraries*

It wasn't long before the Nittany Lions were driving for another score. This time, Lungren called for a placement kick, and Roepke knocked the ball through the uprights for a 9–6 lead.

Syracuse wasn't finished, however. In the closing minutes, the Orangemen drove from their goal line to the Nittany Lions' 10-yard line. That was as far as they got.

"The 90-yard march was ended when the whistle blew for the end of the game," reported the *Times*.

Roepke was one of Penn State's biggest stars during this period, a scoring machine known as the "Masked Marvel" because he wore headgear with a leather face guard. In 1927, the "Marvel" exploded for a 28-point performance against Gettysburg and 27 against Lafayette—an amazing total of 55 points in two games.

Roepke could do it all for Penn State—everything but save Bezdek's coaching job. By now, the football program was in decline, and Bezdek's best years were behind him. Following a 3–5–1 season in 1928, the Penn State campus was sharply divided between the anti-Bezdek and pro-Bezdek camps.

Matters didn't get any better for the beleaguered coach when the Carnegie Report was released in 1929. The report, simply called "Bulletin 23," was four years in the making and harshly condemned the subsidization of college athletes. It focused on what investigators called "the deepest shadows that darken American colleges"—athletic scholarships.

Penn State was among a minority group that endorsed the report and urged a cleanup in college athletics. With no scholarships to hand out, Bezdek was at a distinct disadvantage against other schools. Given the circumstances, it was remarkable he could lead the Lions to a 6–3 season in 1929. But he couldn't beat Pitt, which was a sore point during his Penn State career. In 12 games against their fierce intrastate rivals, Bezdek's Lions were a lackluster 1–9–2.

For that reason alone, many at Penn State thought Bezdek should be fired. He was fired—as coach. As it was announced, Bezdek "volunteered" to leave the sidelines to take command of the complete athletic program.

Bezdek was allowed to choose his coaching successor. He chose Bob Higgins, one of the most popular players in Penn State football history.

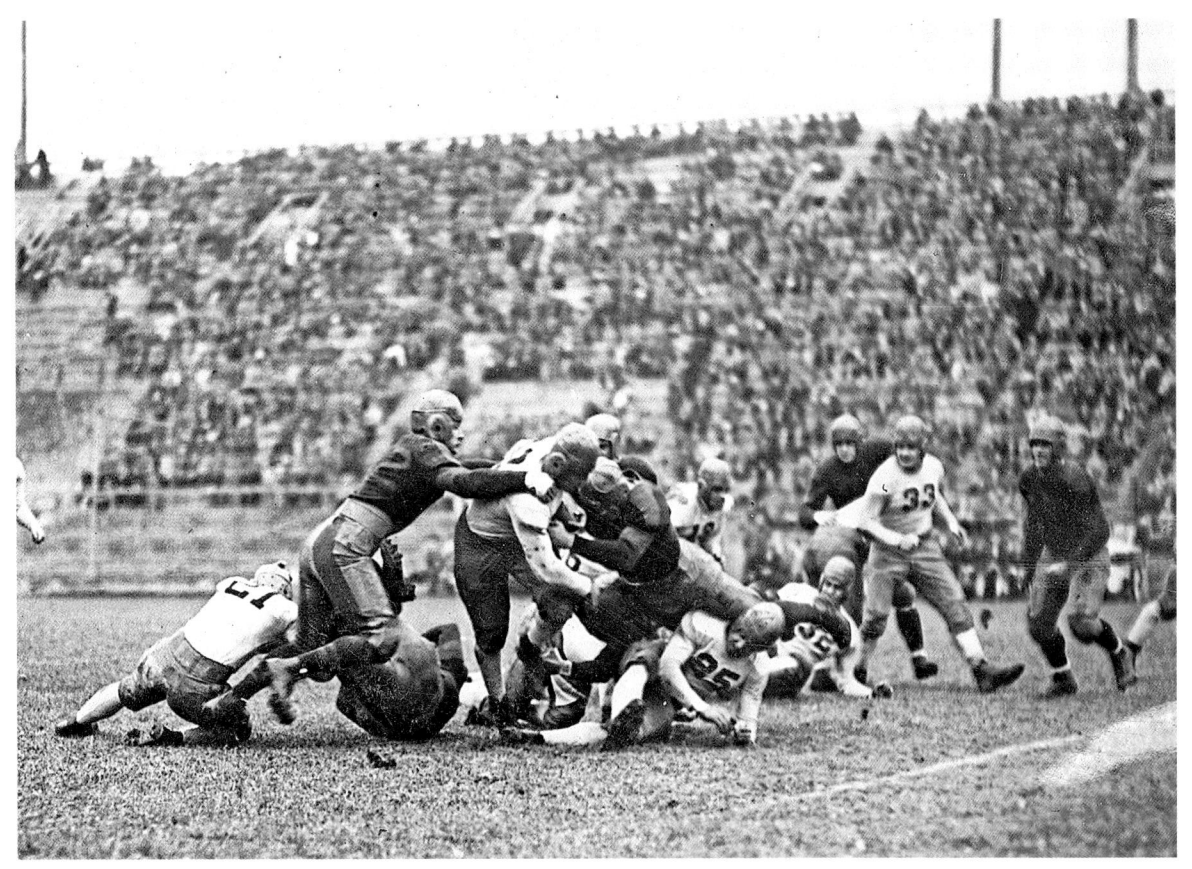

Penn State–Syracuse games were often rough-and-tumble affairs. The long-standing rivalry began in 1922, and the Orange usually ended up on top during the early years, with the Lions winning only 2 of the first 14 meetings. *Penn State University Archives, Pennsylvania State University Libraries*

It's Alumni Day at Penn State on October 25, 1924, and Beaver Field is packed. Nittany Lions fans went home unhappy following a 10–6 loss to Syracuse, one of the school's emerging football rivals. *Penn State University Archives, Pennsylvania State University Libraries*

THE "HIG" HOLDS ON

The Great Depression hit America following the stock market crash of 1929. Penn State football was also on the decline.

"Our football team was really low," said Joe Bedenk, an assistant under new coach Bob Higgins. "We couldn't beat a good high school team. I could tell you about some of the boys who played for us; oh, boy! We had guards weighing 148 pounds. Our blocking back was only 138."

Penn State was among a group of schools that had banned athletic scholarships as part of a nationwide purity campaign to clean up "professionalism" from amateur sports.

"We couldn't even buy meals for our players," Bedenk said.

As a result, the Nittany Lions had a tough time recruiting elite players. And Higgins, who had taken over on the sidelines for Hugo Bezdek in 1930, was faced with an enormous, almost impossible task.

It was no surprise that Penn State had one losing season after another under its new coach. Worst of all, Higgins couldn't beat Pitt.

Coach Bob Higgins brought respectability to Penn State football, but not before his teams struggled through seven straight non-winning seasons. Pictured with Higgins are (left to right) Woody Petchel, Bill Luther, Bill LaFleur, and Fran Rogel. *Penn State University Archives, Pennsylvania State University Libraries*

Higgins, known for having a good sense of humor, liked to tell this story about his early struggles as the Penn State football coach:

One day, after another loss to Pitt, Higgins approached a Penn State rooter. "I asked him for a nickel to call a friend," Higgins recalled. "He gave me a disgusted look, tossed me a dime, and muttered, 'Here, call both your friends.'"

Apocryphal or not, the story makes the point: A onetime football hero at Penn State, Higgins was not always the most popular man on campus in the 1930s as the football coach.

Higgins struggled through his first seven seasons as head coach, posting a combined record of 21–33–3 from 1930 to 1936. The low point came with a 2–8 showing in 1931. Ticket prices for Penn State's home games were $1.10 at the time. Fans complained that the Nittany Lions had nerve charging that much for games.

"When you get licked as often as I did in those terrible 1930s," Higgins once remarked, "you get over being a tough guy."

In 1937, Higgins finally produced a winning season at 5–3. But even then, Penn State sustained a sixth straight loss to Pitt.

It wasn't until 1939, during Penn State's second winning season in 10 years under Higgins, that the Nittany Lions finally beat Pitt. The score was 10–0, in a typical defensive struggle.

The win was an emotional one not only for Higgins, but for his wife, Virginia, as well. Virginia Higgins had been upset when her husband was taken to task by the editor of the student newspaper, the *Daily Collegian*, following a 47–0 thrashing by Cornell.

As the story goes, following the win over Pitt, Virginia Higgins took her revenge. Walking up to the student editor, she lifted a heel and deftly placed a kick on his rear end. With a smug smile, she walked away, satisfied that her foot was right on target.

By the end of the 1930s, Penn State was winning more games, thanks in large part to the alumni. The school couldn't officially sanction it, of course, but many of Penn State's well-to-do graduates began offering summer jobs as an enticement to promising players.

"We had no organization with the alumni at that time to even collect any money," Bedenk said, "but things began to pick up along about 1938 and 1939."

Indeed, things started to turn around for Bedenk and Penn State. Although the Lions had a losing record in 1938 (3–4–1), they posted some impressive victories: 33–0 over Maryland, 59–6 over Lehigh, and 33–6 over Syracuse. Running back Chuck Peters scored two touchdowns in the game against Syracuse, including an 80-yard run off tackle. The 1939 team improved to 5–1–2, including the 10–0 victory over Pitt and a 10–0 shutout of Pennsylvania, another of Penn State's familiar tormentors.

One of the alumni who helped Higgins build stronger teams was Casey Jones, a former teammate and longtime friend of the coach. Jones served as an unofficial scout for "Hig," supplying several good players, such as John "Shag" Wolosky and Negley Norton. Higgins' adherence to the single-wing offense and a powerful defense did the rest. "A coach can do just as much with a single wing as he can with the T-formation," Higgins insisted.

It was the defense, though, that everyone was talking about. Penn State set several national pass-defense records during the 1938 season.

Head coach Bob Higgins poses with co-captains John Economos and Sam Donato in 1937. The team went 5–3 that year to give the Lions their first winning season under Higgins. *Penn State University Archives, Pennsylvania State University Libraries*

Things started to turn around for Penn State in the early 1940s behind a tough defense. Posing with Bob Higgins in 1942 are John Kerns (No. 77), John Jaffurs (No. 63), and Aldo Cenci (in uniform). *Penn State University Archives, Pennsylvania State University Libraries*

Despite missing three years to military service, All-American lineman Steve Suhey was a key contributor for the Nittany Lions in the pre– and post–World War II era. He also contributed three sons who played for Penn State in the 1970s. *College Football Hall of Fame*

Leon Gajecki, a center who was named an All-American in 1940, described those teams as strictly defensive minded. "We had a hard-nosed team. It wasn't a team of offensive power; but then again, not too many clubs had a lot of offense in those days."

Like many of the Penn State players of that day, Gajecki came out of a small western Pennsylvania coal-mining town. The Colver native, once a 96-pounder, worked hard to get his weight up so he could play college football. Although he had bulked up to 180 pounds by the time he arrived in State College, he was the smallest man on the team.

As a senior in 1940, the 6-foot Gajecki had built up to 225 pounds, and he was recognized as one of the top centers in the nation.

Gajecki was a star player on a team that included the great passing combination of Bill Smaltz to Len Krouse, plus outstanding runners in "Pepper" Petrella and Chuck Peters. Smaltz and Krouse returned in

1941 to help Penn State win seven of nine games, including the second victory in three years over Pitt, this one a convincing 31–7 triumph.

Like many other schools, Penn State's football program was affected by World War II. Many of the Nittany Lions' top upperclassmen joined the battle, leaving mostly freshman to play varsity ball.

"We talked to these kids," Bedenk said of the departing players, "and told them to please come back after the war. We knew if they did, we'd have some pretty good teams at Penn State."

Good teams, indeed. But no one, not even Bedenk, could imagine how good the 1947 team would be.

BOB HIGGINS' GREATEST TEAM

The war ended in 1945, and prosperity began.

On college campuses across America, veterans returned under the GI Bill to finish their education—some to play football as well.

The depleted Penn State squad had posted four straight winning seasons during the war years (1942–1945), but things looked even better when the players returned from military service. "After the boys came back from the war, we had a good ball club in 1946, but we couldn't get completely together," said end Sam Tamburo. "Then things fell into place in 1947."

The Nittany Lions opened the 1947 season with a 27–6 victory over Washington State. They followed with a 54–0 whipping of Bucknell and a 75–0 beating of Fordham.

"This was a strange game," center John "Shag" Wolosky said of the Fordham contest. "We were winning by 30–0 or 35–0 in the first quarter, and we were punting on first down [so as not to run up the score]. They would try to score; we'd intercept and go for a touchdown. At halftime, it was 55–0, and they were still doing the same thing. The whole second half was that way."

Penn State's big scores and tough defense started to attract attention from the national media.

"The sportswriters started coming up when it became apparent to some of them that maybe Penn State was going to have a good team that year," said Negley Norton, a tackle on the 1947 team. "And they spent more time watching the line practice than they did the backs. We had just a smothering defense. Everybody just flew in there."

The defense absolutely was the featured part of the team, particularly the line.

The Nittany Lions had their way with Fordham on October 11, 1947, romping past the Rams 75–0. Here, the Lions pull off their standard reverse play, called "33 on 3." Quarterback Chuck Drazenovich handles the ball, with Bob Williams (No. 42) and Wally Triplett (No. 12) also in on the action. *Penn State University Archives, Pennsylvania State University Libraries*

Penn State halfback Elwood "Woody" Petchel (No. 41) picks up yardage against Syracuse at new Beaver Field in 1947. The Lions won handily, 40–0, on their way to an undefeated season. *Penn State University Archives, Pennsylvania State University Libraries*

"Your job wasn't as much to score or run as it was also to defend," said Wally Triplett, who did double-duty as a running back and defensive back. "You took great pride in that. And those western Pennsylvania boys were good at that. If they weren't going to Penn State, they would have been in the coal mines. That was the type of people we had."

Doing the major share on the defensive line were John Wolosky at center, Steve Suhey and Joe Drazenovich at guard, Negley Norton and John Nolan at tackle, and Sam Tamburo and John Potsklan at the end positions.

Higgins' team also featured a solid single-wing running game led by Jeff Durkota, Penn State's top scorer in 1947 with 10 TDs, and Fran Rogel, who led in rushing yardage with 554.

Rogel was a great inside runner with powerful legs and a good sense of balance. He was nicknamed "Punchy" because he seemed oblivious to everything on the football field, except the signals.

When he did hear the referee's whistle blowing a play dead, Rogel usually thought it was too fast. "Hey, mister, don't blow that thing so fast—I'm never down," he would admonish the referee.

Then there was Elwood Petchel, another character and a player whom Higgins called "the best back of his weight in the country." At 145 pounds, Petchel looked more like the ball boy than a ball carrier. The undersized halfback was also the source of many funny stories.

In one game against Navy, Petchel tried to tackle a Middies runner but wound up as a piggyback rider. As he passed the Penn State bench on the back of the runner, Petchel shouted, "Hi, ho, Silver!" mimicking the cry of the Lone Ranger, popular then on radio.

Ed Czekaj was the kicking specialist and played a key role in the Lions' 6–2 season in 1946. He was back in 1947 to lend his kicking skills to the Penn State offense, which received less recognition than the defense but was, in fact, ranked among the top five teams in the country.

After Penn State whitewashed Syracuse 40–0, the Lions had their first real test in West Virginia. They managed to hold off the Mountaineers 21–14 in a close call—or maybe not so close.

"We beat them only 21–14, but we had two, three hundred yards to their minus yardage," Wolosky said. "A lot of those teams had minus yardage."

The Lions scored their winning points on a long pass play from Petchel to Triplett in the third quarter, snapping a 14–14 tie.

The Nittany Lions' wrecking crew rolled on: 46–0 over Colgate, 7–0 over Temple, 20–7 over Navy, and 29–0 over Pitt.

It didn't pay to get the Nittany Lions angry. Early in the Navy game, Potsklan complimented a Middie for one particular block.

"Sure, it was a good block," the Navy player replied, "you're playing in the big league today."

When Potsklan went back to the huddle, he reported what the Navy player had said. It inspired a bigger effort by the Lions as they swept by Navy, with Durkota scoring two touchdowns.

"We were loose and just tried to go out and have a good time," Tamburo said. "We weren't shooting for an undefeated season; we weren't worried about breaking records, just playing football to our best capabilities."

JEFF DURKOTA

Like many players of his era, Jeff Durkota's college football career was divided into two parts: prewar and postwar.

Durkota liked the second part better. He led the Nittany Lions with 10 touchdowns during a tremendous unbeaten season in 1947.

"We didn't pass too much; we just bolted our way through," recalled Durkota, who scored four of his touchdowns in a 75–0 laugher over Fordham.

A native of western Pennsylvania, Durkota played end as a freshman at Penn State in 1941 because that had been his position in high school. In his sophomore year, he was converted to a wingback because he was one of the fastest men on the team.

He was soon racing on snowy mountain slopes rather than football fields. Following his sophomore season, Durkota was part of the U.S. Army ski troops that fought in the Italian Alps during World War II. Durkota was in the 10th Mountain Division, a famed American fighting force.

Following the war, Durkota reinserted himself into the football scene at Penn State. He was one of many veterans asked to come back by the coaching staff.

"We were bigger and smarter," Durkota recalled of the legendary 1947 Lions. "That's why we had such a good team."

Shutouts were a common element of the season. The Nittany Lions held six of their nine opponents without a point while outscoring all opponents 319–27 overall. Penn State set remarkable defensive records en route to the school's first appearance in the Cotton Bowl.

After college, Durkota played in the All-American Football Conference with Cleveland, Buffalo, and Los Angeles.

Durkota went into private business following his retirement from pro football, eventually owning a car dealership in Pennsylvania.

Jeff Durkota (No. 14) led the undefeated 1947 Nittany Lions with 10 touchdowns. He is shown here with his backfield mates Bobby Williams, Chuck Drazenovich, and Joe Colone. *Penn State University Archives, Pennsylvania State University Libraries*

Above: Guards Robert Ross (No. 63) and John Simon (No. 61) block for Bill Luther against West Virginia on October 25, 1947. The Lions held on to beat the previously undefeated Mountaineers 21–14 in a memorable game. *Penn State University Archives, Pennsylvania State University Libraries*

Right: Penn State fans bring the goalposts down following a 29–0 victory over Pitt that completed a perfect regular season in 1947. It was the team's sixth shutout of the year. *Penn State University Archives, Pennsylvania State University Libraries*

Nevertheless, records were broken. Along the way to a 9–0 record—the first perfect regular season at Penn State since 1912—the Nittany Lions outscored the opposition 319–27 and set defensive standards hard to match:

- Fewest yards allowed in a game (minus 47 against Syracuse).
- Fewest average yards allowed rushing per game (17.0).
- Lowest average allowed per rush (0.64).

Next stop for Penn State: a bowl game. But first, the Nittany Lions had to clear up a problem involving the racial makeup of the squad.

PENN STATE'S FIRST COTTON BOWL

After the 1947 season, the Nittany Lions were invited to play in the Cotton Bowl against Southern Methodist University (SMU), the unbeaten Southwest Conference champion. But there was a problem.

Segregation was still in force in Texas, as it was in many places below the Mason-Dixon Line. Like many other schools, SMU had a color barrier, making it school policy not to play against teams with African-American players. Penn State had two African Americans: Wally Triplett and Dennie Hoggard.

"Some of the guys did want to go, but the majority said, 'Look, we all go or none. We're stuck with that,'" Triplett recalled. "So when Southern Methodist heard that, they said they would break their color barrier and play us."

It was a big decision for SMU. The clash would be historic, the first time that an African American would play in the Cotton Bowl.

Higgins was bringing 40 players with him, plus his staff, and another question had to be answered: Where would they stay in Dallas, a segregated town?

"The school arranged for us to stay at the navy base outside of Dallas," Triplett said. "That's where they could house us and feed us, and we had room to practice."

The base, located 14 miles outside of Dallas, wasn't exactly what the team had in mind. The players were looking forward to more luxurious accommodations.

"We were 26, 27, 28 years old, four years in the service," Czekaj recalled. "We were there for the bowl game, but we were sleeping in double-decker bunks—navy barracks, navy chow, you know. Like our World War II days."

"And," added Wolosky, "we were not allowed off base. So we didn't like it very well."

After several days of fierce practices, Higgins finally turned his players loose. Reported the *New York Times*: "Some of the players attended movies, a few were guests at the SMU-Wyoming basketball game, and others just went sightseeing."

There had been a more festive atmosphere when the Penn State squad first arrived in Dallas. Members of the Penn State Club greeted the team in a Dallas suburb, where the local sheriff "arrested" the Penn State coaches on warrants, charging them with "crossing a

WALLY TRIPLETT

Wally Triplett never considered himself a trailblazer. But somehow the role kept finding him, whether he was playing football at Penn State, returning punts for the Detroit Lions, or working in the Michigan racing industry.

Along with Dennie Hoggard, Triplett was the first African American to play in the Cotton Bowl. He was also the first black player to be drafted by a National Football League team and the first African-American racing clerk in Michigan.

Triplett said that he didn't set out to be the first black racing clerk in Michigan, "but I stayed with it and that was part of my resume for 35 years."

Another part of his resume: After 60 years, he was still ranked second in punt return average at Penn State (16.5 yards per carry over three years). He once returned a punt 85 yards against West Virginia.

Besides his race, Triplett's background was different in another way from the other players on the Penn State team, most of whom had come from the coal mines of western Pennsylvania and from meager conditions. Triplett came out of one of the elite suburban schools in Philadelphia on a senatorial, not a football, scholarship. It wasn't long before Triplett proved his worth as a football player.

Following service in the Korean War, Triplett was drafted by both the Detroit Lions of the NFL and the Brooklyn Dodgers of the old All-American Football Conference (AAFC).

"The All-American Conference sought out a lot of the black kids from schools and started to try to compete with the NFL," Triplett said. "The NFL held mostly to their policy of discrimination and did not seek to draft [black players] until the year I came along in 1950."

Triplett signed with the Lions, purely for monetary reasons. Detroit offered him a contract worth $700 more than the Dodgers' offer.

Triplett was unaware at the time of the significance of his decision. Although African Americans had played in the NFL before, they had all been selected by coaches outside of the drafting system. George Taliaferro, an African-American halfback out of Indiana, had been drafted six rounds earlier than Triplett—making him the first black player drafted—but Taliaferro opted to sign with a team from the AAFC. Thus, Triplett became the first drafted African American to play in the NFL.

Triplett didn't wait long to make an impact in Detroit. In a 1950 game against the Los Angeles Rams, the 5-foot-10, 173-pound Triplett returned four kickoffs for a team record 294 yards. He scored three times, including once on a 97-yarder.

Following his football career, Triplett was still rushing ahead and breaking down doors.

Wally Triplett runs the ball against SMU during the 1948 Cotton Bowl. The game was a breakthrough moment, with African Americans Triplett and Dennie Hoggard in the lineup for the Nittany Lions. *Penn State University Archives, Pennsylvania State University Libraries*

Woody Petchel tosses a touchdown pass to Wally Triplett in the third quarter of the 1948 Cotton Bowl. The score tied the game at 13–13, but Ed Czekaj missed the extra point. *Penn State University Archives, Pennsylvania State University Libraries*

state line without a southern accent." Higgins played along with the gag and allowed himself to be handcuffed for the rest of the journey into Dallas.

Upon their arrival at the main station, Penn State players were greeted by hundreds of people, including a high school band. In true western style, each of the players received a 10-gallon hat.

The game shaped up as a classic matchup between SMU's strong aerial attack and Penn State's powerful single-wing ground game. The Nittany Lions' mission was clear, according to Higgins: "Stop Doak Walker, and break up Southern Methodist's passing."

Walker was a nationally renowned player, the biggest star of the SMU team. He did it all: passing, running, and kicking extra points. Walker was a heroic-looking figure, the exact opposite of Penn State's Petchel, the Nittany Lions' 145-pound wonder.

"He will be the smallest man on the field and that, no doubt, includes the water boys," said Chester L. Smith, sports editor of the *Pittsburgh Press*.

But looks were deceiving.

"With that 145 on the hoof," Smith continued, "Elwood can do about all there is to be done with a football. He is one of the most remarkable little men I have ever seen in football, and he could, possibly, steal the show."

While Penn State was making history by fielding two African-American players, history was also being made in the stands. Part of the state delegation from Pennsylvania included Dennie Hoggard's mother, whose husband happened to be a state senator.

"They had her sitting on the 50-yard line with everybody else," Triplett said. "That was a big thing. It gave us an opportunity to break down barriers in the segregation of the fans."

The Pennsylvania delegation, along with the rest of the 47,000 fans, witnessed a fast start by SMU. As usual, the All-American Walker was in the middle of things.

First, he threw a 53-yard touchdown pass to Paul Page and kicked the extra point for a 7–0 SMU lead in the opening quarter. Then, he capped a 63-yard drive with a 3-yard plunge over right tackle in the second period. This time, Walker missed the extra point, leaving the Mustangs with a 13–0 lead.

Credit Shag Wolosky with Walker's miss on the extra point.

"I moved myself over the center," Wolosky recalled. "And I jumped center just as he snapped, so I was standing there when Doak Walker went to kick the ball. He just kicked it on the side."

Late in the first half, Petchel got the Lions going after Larry Cooney returned the kickoff 22 yards to the Penn State 35. Petchel completed a 17-yard pass, then tore off 16 more yards on the ground.

The Penn State attack was slowed by a penalty and two incomplete passes. But Petchel fired a 36-yard scoring pass to Cooney, and Czekaj followed with the extra-point kick to cut SMU's lead to 13–7 at the half.

"At halftime, we realized they were tough, but they weren't that tough," Joe Drazenovich said. "None of us at halftime thought we were going to lose."

With Petchel leading the attack in the third quarter, the Nittany Lions moved the ball 44 yards to SMU's 1-inch line. But the Mustangs stopped Penn State with a great goal-line stand. The Texas team then punted out of danger.

Back came the Lions behind Petchel, who fired a running pass to Triplett in the end zone. This time, Czekaj missed the extra-point kick, leaving the score tied at 13–13. That's the way the game ended.

Czekaj had to live with that missed extra point for some time.

"My only claim to fame is I missed the extra point in the Cotton Bowl," recalled Czekaj, who later became Penn State's athletic director. "I got it wherever I traveled: 'You're the guy that missed the extra point that lost the Cotton Bowl.' No matter where I went, they always remembered that. Doak Walker missed one, too, and they've forgotten about that."

The 1948 season featured a 7–1–1 record, including a 14–14 tie against a strong Michigan State team memorable for more than just a fiercely fought game. At the time, Beaver Field seated only 17,700. Somehow, they managed to squeeze 23,000 into the stadium, matching the biggest previous football crowd at State College.

"Twenty-three thousand fans poured into the little stands, edged up to the sidelines, climbed trees, sat on top of cars, and even brought stepladders," said one writer. "There was hardly room on the benches for the players and coaches."

Obviously, Beaver Field was ill equipped to handle such an overflow. The place looked like a "dump heap," according to one observer. "You never saw so much debris in your life as the crowd left."

Penn State officials decided to expand the stadium to nearly twice its size to accommodate the increasing demand for football tickets. Penn State athletic director Ernie McCoy was making an effort to line up more intersectional games.

That was not the only change taking place at State College. Because of failing health, Higgins was forced to retire after the 1948 season, at the age of 54.

Bedenk won a power struggle for the head coaching job in 1949, but his tenure only lasted one year.

Welcome to the Rip Engle era.

For 50 cents you could buy a program to the Cotton Bowl on January 1, 1948. Memories of the classic 13–13 tie between Penn State and SMU are priceless. *Penn State University Archives, Pennsylvania State University Libraries*

Halfback Larry Cooney runs the ball during Penn State's 37–7 win over West Virginia in 1948. The Lions posted a 7–1–1 record that season, Bob Higgins' last as head coach. *Penn State University Archives, Pennsylvania State University Libraries*

RIP ENGLE STEPS IN

Rip Engle (front row, second from left) led Penn State to an overall record of 104–48–4 during his 16 seasons as the head football coach. Note young assistant coach Joe Paterno behind Engle. *Penn State University Archives, Pennsylvania State University Libraries*

When Rip Engle was offered the job of head football coach at Penn State in 1950, he had a problem. He was the new guy in town. Incoming coaches usually bring along their own staff, but not at Penn State.

Engle was forced to retain Bob Higgins' entire coaching staff. That included Joe Bedenk, who had coached Penn State to a 5–4 record after taking over for Higgins for a one-year stint in 1949. Engle could only bring along one assistant. That assistant was

Halfback Lenny Moore, seen here breaking around the defense during a game at Beaver Field, led the Lions in rushing every year from 1953 to 1955 and graduated as the school's all-time rushing leader with 2,380 yards. *Collegiate Images/WireImage/Getty Images*

Joseph Vincent Paterno, who had played quarterback for Engle at Brown from 1946 to 1949.

Engle admittedly had misgivings about taking the Penn State job.

"I had never met these coaches," he said. "They were all single-wing coaches. The whole staff had been there long before me. And then Joe Paterno had never coached, although I knew he had great possibilities. It was a pretty precarious situation. I just wondered how smart I was, really."

Engle was a popular choice among the students. The same couldn't be said of the Penn State football staff.

The new coach had a talk with his staff, telling them that he didn't know or care where their loyalties were. But if they were going to win, he told them, he needed their complete loyalty.

He would soon have it.

Engle had built a reputation in eastern football. One of the pioneers of the wing-T offense, he had helped the Brown football program gain respectability. Facing quality Ivy League opponents, as well as other good football teams in the East, Engle's squads had compiled a 28–20–4 record from 1944 to 1949. Before that, he had worked on the Brown staff as an assistant, and prior to that, Engle coached championship teams on the high school level in Waynesboro, Pennsylvania.

His style was usually low-key and curse-free.

"He never swore," remembered Bob Mitinger, a top receiver who played for Engle in the late 1950s and early 1960s. "He would say, 'God love you, son, surely you can give a little better effort than that.' 'Dammit' and 'hell' were the worst words Rip Engle ever said."

One might say that Engle was destined to coach Penn State football. After all, at Western Maryland College, Engle had played for Dick Harlow, the former Penn State player and coach, and it was Harlow who got Engle into coaching in the first place. Harlow later lent his support to Engle when he was up for the Penn State job.

"I never expected to be a coach," Engle said. "I got out of school right after the Depression, and that was the only kind of job I could get. Coach Harlow had two jobs for me coaching, and I couldn't find another job to save me. Otherwise, I would have never been a coach."

Engle's story began in Elk Lick, Pennsylvania, where he worked in the mines as a teenager.

JOE PATERNO'S FIRST RECRUIT

Jim Garrity is the answer to a Penn State football trivia question: Who was the first player recruited by Joe Paterno?

OK, so no official records are kept of such things, but Garrity and Paterno are forever linked in Nittany Lions football lore, at least in their own minds.

"He has said on many occasions that I was first," Garrity said.

At the time that Garrity was exploring his options for playing college football, Paterno was an assistant to head coach Rip Engle. Fresh out of college and eager to make an impression, Paterno was also a strong recruiter for Engle. In Garrity's case, Paterno worked extra hard to steal him away from Kentucky.

Garrity, a top-flight receiver from Pittsburgh, was all set to play for Bear Bryant at the southern school. It didn't stop Paterno, who continued to show up with another assistant, Earl Bruce, to see Garrity play. Paterno talked to Garrity at a high school all-star game. He visited his parents, extolling the virtues of Penn State football. It was an indication of the kind of aggressiveness Paterno would later show as a head coach.

Just three weeks before Garrity was supposed to leave for Kentucky, he changed his mind. He was going to Penn State.

Garrity decided it was best to stay closer to home so that his parents could see him play. Plus, he believed that because of Paterno's age, the young coach could relate to college kids.

Paterno, who guided the offense then, had made a big catch in this sure-handed receiver.

In 1953, Garrity led the Nittany Lions in receptions. In 1954, when he was a co-captain, Garrity tied Jack Sherry for the team lead in receptions.

The Nittany Lions forged a solid 20–7–1 record during Garrity's time there (1952–1954), but they failed to earn a bowl bid in an era when far fewer postseason opportunities existed.

A generation later, Garrity's son, Gregg, would make up for that. He played on four bowl-winning teams at Penn State, including the 1982 team that won the school's first national championship.

"I started work when I was 14, every summer," Engle recalled in a 1970s interview. "You had to be 16 to work in the coal mine. The inspectors would come. They used to check. I was big then, and I grew fast."

Engle moved up the ladder to the position of mine inspector at age 19, but he was desperate to break the shackles of mine work and go on to higher education.

He attended Blue Ridge College in Maryland, where he played in the first football game he ever saw. He then went on to Western Maryland, where he developed into one of the top receivers in the state.

When he went into coaching in the 1930s, Engle applied the lessons he had learned from Harlow. He also brought to coaching the lessons learned from one particular mule he worked with in the mines.

"That mule taught me how to work," Engle said. "He was always happy working. He was only a small mule, but he could outwork all the rest of the mules together."

When the mule died, Engle wanted to stuff it but didn't have enough money. "We skinned it, and we had that skin for 20 years."

One of Engle's biggest thrills at Brown was beating Colgate in one of the big upsets of 1944.

"We had a group of 17-year-olds and wartime rejects," Engle remembered, "and it was a lean year for victories."

Engle would find a richer pool of talent when he took the Penn State job. He also got plenty of support from Higgins, who still carried a lot of weight at the school, even in retirement.

"He never second-guessed me," Engle said of Higgins. "He never came in, never bothered me. He'd say either, 'I don't know,' or he'd be on your side."

A new policy came along with a new football coach: scholarships.

As at most colleges, the Penn State football team had benefited from the GI Bill, which paid education costs for players returning from World War II. That was about the only time it could be said that football players got a free ride during the Higgins era. Since the early 1930s, Penn State had committed to a no-scholarship policy for athletes.

Engle's arrival signaled a new era at State College. In his very first season, Engle was given the luxury of 45 scholarships. It was enough to get him going in the right direction. Under the new coach, Penn State was hoping to become more than just an eastern power.

First, the Nittany Lions had to learn how to beat Pitt.

Although the Lions had put together a three-game winning streak over the Panthers in the early 1940s, their overall record against their longtime intrastate rivals had been a sore point at Penn State. Since 1913, Penn State had managed to beat Pitt just six times in 34 games.

After Penn State went 11 straight years without a victory over Pitt, the series was suspended for three years, from 1932 to 1934. It resumed in 1935 with—naturally—another loss by Penn State.

When Engle took over as head coach in 1950, the Nittany Lions had lost five of their previous six games with Pitt. Suffer no longer, Penn State fans! Engle's first year not only produced a winning season (5–3–1), but a victory over the hated Panthers in the season's final game. In fact, the Nittany Lions won four of their first five games against Pitt during the Engle regime.

The game that got Penn State "moving," according to Engle, occurred at Pitt in 1952. Pitt had one of its strongest teams in years and had posted notable wins over Ohio State, Notre Dame, and Army. A win over the Nittany Lions would send Pitt to the Orange Bowl. The Panthers and their fans had already packed to go to Florida.

But Pitt didn't figure on Jack Sherry, who had come from Philadelphia to State College on a football scholarship and wound up playing basketball as well.

As time was running out in the first quarter of the game on November 22, 1952, Sherry intercepted a pass by Rudy Mattioli at midfield and returned the ball to the Pitt 29.

When the second period got underway, quarterback Tony Rados moved the Nittany Lions through the air. Buddy Rowell finished the drive with a 3-yard blast through the guard hole.

In the fourth quarter, Sherry picked off another pass by Mattioli at Pitt's 36 and returned it 25 yards. A roughing foul put the ball on the 1-yard line, and Rados took it in on a quarterback sneak. Bill Leonard, who had kicked both extra points, also had a field goal. Penn State shocked Pitt 17–0 to wreck the Panthers' Orange Bowl plans.

At the end of the game, the Pitt students started throwing oranges at their own bench from the stands.

"I thought maybe they were going to throw them at us," Engle said. "It was too bad. I felt sorry for the Panthers from that standpoint. But it was a great victory for Penn State."

While Penn State's schedule was heavily accented with eastern teams, Engle's Lions did not shy away from playing national powers. In the opening game of the 1954 season, they traveled to Illinois to face the nation's No. 1 team. The Illini featured J. C. Caroline, Mickey Bates, and Abe Woodson, billed as the "nation's fastest backfield."

"Nobody gave us a chance," Engle said.

The Illini, 14-point favorites, scored first to take a 6–0 lead, rousing a boisterous crowd of 54,000.

Back came the Nittany Lions behind Jesse Arnelle, a 6-foot-8, 228-pound junior end who also starred in basketball at Penn State. Arnelle recovered a fumble by Bates on the Illini 28-yard line and then caught a 24-yard scoring pass from Don Bailey to put Penn State in front 7–6.

In the second quarter, Bailey ripped off a 50-yard run. He then broke loose for 6 yards and, as he was about to be tackled, tossed a lateral to Lenny Moore. The Lions' halfback went the final 12 yards for the TD to give Penn State a 14–6 lead, enough to hold off a late charge by Illinois. The final score was Penn State 14, Illinois 12.

"Penn State displayed midseason form and was so strong down the middle that the Illinois fullback, Bates, seldom took a shot at it," reported the Associated Press.

Rather it was Moore, the Penn State halfback, who was making people sit up and take notice. He had scored a touchdown and was the featured runner in Penn State's "tornado-like attack," as described by the AP. That attack produced 279 yards on the ground, almost twice the total produced by Illinois' famous backfield.

Roosevelt Grier was a tough lineman for Penn State in the early 1950s before going on to play 11 seasons in the NFL for the Giants and Rams. *Penn State University Archives, Pennsylvania State University Libraries*

"He seemed to be able to change directions in mid-air," Engle said of Moore during a 1972 interview reflecting on his years at Penn State. "No one ever got a clear shot at him."

Engle knew he had a gem in Moore from the first time he saw the halfback score a touchdown in the 1953 opener against Wisconsin. Moore, just starting his sophomore year, dashed around end and raced 65 yards for a touchdown. Although the TD was called back because of a penalty and Penn State lost the game 20–0, Engle knew he had found the breakaway runner he so desperately needed.

"He had great mental toughness," Engle said of Moore, who would go on to star in the National Football League (NFL) with the Baltimore Colts and be inducted into the Pro Football Hall of Fame. "You could get an idea of his ability if you could have seen him walk over to the broad jump pit one evening, after a hard practice, and with his uniform on, broad jump 22 feet."

Moore was just as good in the defensive backfield, according to Engle. But it was his running ability that brought him notice. Game after game, Moore continued to build a reputation as one of the best running backs in America. West Virginia coach Art Lewis said, "Moore scared you every time he got the ball."

The performance against Illinois in 1954 started Moore on a 1,000-yard season, an accomplishment that was more meaningful then because teams only played 9 games (or 10 if they wound up in a bowl). Moore rushed for a career-high 1,082 yards as the Lions went 7–2.

Graduation losses the following season cost Penn State, and the Lions slumped to a 5–4 record.

"We weren't really a good team," Engle said. "We did have Moore and Milt Plum in the backfield, but our line was one of the lightest in major college football."

As a result, Moore's production dropped off in 1955, although he was still one of the most dangerous backs in the college game.

When Penn State faced Syracuse that season, the Nittany Lions had the difficult task of drawing up a game plan to stop the great Jim Brown. So far, no one had done so.

"He was running over and around most everyone," Engle said.

Brown, later to go on to a legendary Hall-of-Fame career with the Cleveland Browns, was the featured runner in the Syracuse attack. A human battering ram, Brown was a heavy-duty runner who ran over people and usually hurt them. Moore's style, in contrast, was more speed and deception than brute force.

Penn State finished the 1955 season by getting snowed in by Pitt at Beaver Stadium, 20–0. The Lions ended the season with a disappointing 5–4 record after going 7–2 the year before. *Penn State University Archives, Pennsylvania State University Libraries*

JACK SHERRY

Jack Sherry claims a distinction that no one else can in Penn State sports history: He's the only athlete to play football and captain a Final Four basketball team.

"I'm sure that's never happened before or since," said Sherry, who played both sports at Penn State in the 1950s.

Basketball seemed to be his best sport at West Catholic High School in Philadelphia, although it was a football scholarship that got him to Penn State. He was recommended by his high school coach, Mike Kearns, and handed the scholarship sight unseen. Kearns had played football at Penn State with Sever Toretti and Jim O'Hora, longtime line coaches.

There was a small problem at first. When Sherry went out for spring football, he had a rough time.

"They didn't even invite me back the following fall," Sherry recalled. "That's how bad I was. I was overwhelmed with the toughness. I wasn't tough defensively in blocking and tackling."

In the meantime, Sherry played some basketball with his dorm team. Recognized as a prime basketball talent, he was invited to try out for the Nittany Lions' freshman squad.

"I started that week," Sherry said. "And I was the high scorer the rest of the year. That's how bad Penn State basketball was."

Before long, he was starring on the varsity and helping the Lions go to the NCAA tournament in 1952. Although the Lions were knocked out in the first round by Kentucky, Sherry won approval from the football coaches for his leaping ability and soft hands. They decided to give him a second chance in football, this time placing him at safety and receiver.

"I could catch the ball," Sherry said. "I had good hands. Most basketball players had good hands."

During the 1952 season, Sherry stood out with eight interceptions, tying him with Don Eyer for team high. The highlights of his football career were the two interceptions he pulled down against Pitt to set up touchdowns as Penn State upset the Panthers 17–0 and wrecked their chances for the Orange Bowl.

In 1954, Sherry captained one of Penn State's greatest basketball teams. The Lions advanced to the Final Four, where they lost to a great LaSalle team featuring Tom Gola. Penn State then knocked off Southern Cal for third place in the NCAA tournament.

Jack Sherry made his mark in two sports at Penn State. He was the only athlete in school history to letter in football and lead the basketball team to a berth in the Final Four. *Penn State University Archives, Pennsylvania State University Libraries*

Later that year, Sherry played end on the 1954 football team and tied Jim Garrity for the receptions lead with 11 in a ground-oriented offense. Although Sherry averaged 14.5 yards a catch, he never considered himself a football star.

"I was basically a basketball player playing football," he said.

The matchup of two of the country's best college runners was made for hyperbole. And the game lived up to all of it.

Syracuse was hoping to break a no-victory jinx at Beaver Stadium that was then going on two decades. For a while, it looked like the Orangemen would.

Brown blasted over for a touchdown from 2 yards out to give Syracuse a 7–0 lead in the first quarter. Then Brown scored on a pass reception in the second quarter to cap a 68-yard drive. Brown, who had kicked the extra point after the first TD, missed his try for the second, leaving the score at 13–0.

Then Joe Sabol, Penn State's third-string fullback, who also played in the backfield on defense, intercepted a pass by Syracuse's Ed Albright and eluded three tacklers before he was brought down on the Orangemen's 10-yard line. Plum passed to Billy Kane, who jumped into the end zone to cut the Syracuse lead to 13–7.

When Brown scampered 52 yards on a kickoff return in the third quarter and later scored a TD from 6 yards out, then kicked the extra point, Penn State found itself trailing 20–7.

It didn't look good for the Lions. But suddenly they "caught fire," as Engle recalled. "Moore made some great runs, Plum's passing started to click, and the whole team was inspired."

In the third period, Penn State drove 59 yards for a touchdown. Moore took the ball the final 2 yards for the score to trim the lead to 20–14.

In the fourth quarter, Syracuse was driving for a touchdown and advanced as far as the Penn State 9. Plum, playing safety on defense, made an interception in the end zone to stop the threat. The quarterback then led Penn State on a drive of its own from the 20.

The AP report described the drive: "Moore took a pitchout and rambled 22 yards. Plum passed to Bobby Allen for 16 more. Moore went 13 off tackle and Bill Straub ran 14 to the Syracuse 12. From there, the Lions did it the hard way in four plays."

Moore carried on two of the next three plays before Plum scored from the 1-yard line. Then the quarterback kicked the placement that won the game for Penn State, 21–20.

The final tally in the individual battle of the backs: Brown gained 159 yards on 20 carries, scored three touchdowns, and kicked two extra points. Moore gained 146 yards on 22 carries, scored a touchdown, set up another during Penn State's winning 80-yard drive in the fourth quarter, and "tackled savagely" while playing defense, the AP reported.

In quarterbacking the victory, Plum also placed himself in the pantheon of Penn State's greatest individual football performances.

It wouldn't be the last time that Plum would star in an important game for the Nittany Lions.

A BIG WIN AT OHIO STATE

The 1950s marked a renaissance in college football. Gone were the World War II veterans that had filled rosters, leaving younger players to take their spots. The kids were replacing the men all over the nation.

And Penn State, armed with scholarships, continued to recruit as aggressively as any college in the country. Among the newcomers to Penn State during this time were Moore, Plum, Roosevelt Grier, Arnelle, and Sam Valentine.

The credit for bringing such players to State College went to Engle's assistants, who worked tirelessly year-round at their recruiting jobs. As the offensive coach, Joe Paterno discovered some gems in quarterbacks and receivers, many of them from Pennsylvania.

Bob Mitinger, one of the top receivers at Penn State in the 1950s, recalled how he was snared by Paterno: "I went up to Penn State one time as a junior and [coach] Earl Bruce introduced me to Joe. Joe turned around and said, 'You're number 59 from Greensburg High, aren't you?' I was impressed by his remembering me, and we discussed plays and everything."

The best measuring stick for how good the Nittany Lions were during the mid-1950s is how they fared against some of the nation's ranked teams outside the East.

When the Nittany Lions knocked off top-ranked Illinois in 1954, it turned some heads.

In 1956, the Lions seemingly had to prove themselves all over again when they traveled to Ohio State for a game against the unbeaten Buckeyes. It was the first time the schools had met on a football field since the controversial 1912 game that ended in a massive brawl.

Dick Hoak shared quarterback duties on the Nittany Lions and went on to star in the pros as a running back for the Pittsburgh Steelers. His peak performance at Penn State came in the 1960 Liberty Bowl, when he directed five touchdown drives in a 41–12 victory over Oregon, earning him the MVP award. *Penn State University Archives, Pennsylvania State University Libraries*

"They had Jim Parker, one of the best running guards in football," Engle recalled. "He was quoted in the papers as saying that Ohio State really would show the 'invader from the east' just how good Big Ten football really was."

Plum remembered how angry he got watching Woody Hayes on his TV program discuss the weekend's game. He felt that the Ohio State coach didn't give Penn State much respect.

"He spoke about Penn State for about three minutes, and then got on to the following week's game with Texas Christian," Plum said. "So I think it got a few guys mad. And then the next morning, we had our pregame meal, and I was one of the last out of the restaurant to board the bus. And the woman there, the hostess, said, 'Well, boys, give it the best you can.' We weren't supposed to win. An eastern team just doesn't beat a Big Ten team. That was written in stone then."

The Buckeyes had won 20 of their previous 22 games and had captured back-to-back Big Ten titles in 1954 and 1955 to go along with a national championship in 1954. The Nittany Lions, already with a loss in their first three games against eastern competition, had the double disadvantage of playing before a hostile crowd at Ohio Stadium numbering 82,584.

Penn State players give coach Rip Engle a ride following their stunning 7–6 victory over Ohio State in Columbus on October 20, 1956. The Buckeyes were three-touchdown favorites and had won 20 of their previous 22 games. *Penn State University Archives, Pennsylvania State University Libraries*

Penn State's airborne Andy Stynchula blocks a punt by Syracuse in this 1959 game between the longtime rivals. The Orangemen came out on top, 20–18, in one of the greatest ever played at Beaver Field. *Penn State University Archives, Pennsylvania State University Libraries*

Under Rip Engle, the Lions made four visits to bowls, including twice to the Gator Bowl. In 1961, they beat Georgia Tech; in 1962, they lost to Florida. *Penn State University Archives, Pennsylvania State University Libraries*

None of this seemed to affect the Penn State players, who came into the game as three-touchdown underdogs. The teams battled to a scoreless tie after one quarter, and then two. The second quarter featured a 55-yard punt by Plum that settled on Ohio State's 1-yard line, but the Nittany Lions failed to take advantage. Closest thing to a score in the second quarter was a field goal attempt by Ohio State from the 18 that missed the mark.

In the third quarter, Penn State drove 60 yards to the Ohio State 14 before losing the ball on a fumble. The Buckeyes then put on a drive of their own, going 83 yards before they were stopped by Bruce Gilmore's interception in the end zone.

The mighty defensive struggle continued through the third quarter and then deep into the fourth.

Three-touchdown underdogs? Penn State looked every bit the equal of the Buckeyes.

Plum, a do-everything quarterback, then made the punt of his career with a 73-yarder that died on Ohio State's 3-yard line. Unable to move out of the coffin corner, the Buckeyes punted to their 45.

There were less than five minutes left in the game.

"We knew that this was our last chance," Engle said. "The drive that followed—well, I've never seen one so free of mechanical or mental errors."

Plum moved the Lions downfield, and 13 plays later, Gilmore banged over from the 1-foot line. Plum converted the extra point for a 7–0 Penn State lead.

Back came Ohio State. Leo Brown caught two long passes to highlight a drive that carried the Buckeyes to the Penn State 3.

Don Clark plunged into the end zone for 6 points, but Frank Kremblas, who had missed the 18-yard field goal attempt in the second quarter, missed the extra point.

The Nittany Lions escaped with a 7–6 win, one of the biggest in their history.

"It was the one perfect football game I've ever been connected with," said Engle, who coached 16 seasons at Penn State following his six years at Brown. "Both offense and defense were just perfectly planned and perfectly executed, and we just happened to guess right."

Penn State senior and team captain Sam Valentine played the game of his life at linebacker. Valentine had wanted to play for Ohio State out of high school but was rejected for being too small. Now, four years later, he got his revenge.

"Sam and his teammates put 83,000 people in Buckeye Stadium into a state of shock that day," Engle recalled. "Ten minutes after the game, they were still sitting frozen in their seats."

The Nittany Lions paid the price with an unusual number of injuries in the all-out physical game.

"We took the train back," Plum said, "and I'll tell you, we were banged up. It looked like one of those old Civil War movies . . . everybody lying around with legs propped up and bandages."

BOWL VISITS BECOME A HABIT

The Penn State football schedule in the 1950s featured the usual suspects: Pitt, Syracuse, West Virginia, Rutgers, and Army, among others. There were also a number of first-time opponents.

In 1957, the Nittany Lions played Vanderbilt and Marquette for the first time in their history. In 1958, Furman University joined the opposition. And in 1959, it was Missouri and VMI for the initial time on Penn State's ever-evolving schedule.

The Lions continued to travel extensively for games, but as the 1959 season approached, one item was still missing from Rip Engle's itinerary: a trip to a bowl game.

Penn State had only played in two postseason games in its entire 72-year history—the 1923 Rose Bowl and 1948 Cotton Bowl—and came away without a victory in either game.

MILT PLUM

Talk about a player doing it all for his team, and then some.

As was the style of the day, Milt Plum played on both sides of the ball—quarterback on offense and safety on defense—for Penn State in the 1950s. Plum also took on the assignment of the team's punter.

"I didn't leave the field too often," Plum said. "Somebody told me I had the most time played in nine games one season."

As a defensive back, Plum intercepted seven passes one season. He could have had two more but knocked them down because they were on fourth down.

Plum had his best year statistically as a quarterback in 1956, when he led the team with 675 yards passing and six touchdown passes. But it was one of his punts that gained him a lasting place in Penn State football lore.

In a game against Ohio State, Plum launched a 72-yard coffin-corner punt that pinned the Buckeyes deep in their territory. After the Buckeyes were unable to move the ball and were forced to kick, Penn State was in great field position. The Lions went in to score and pulled off a huge upset over the heavily favored Buckeyes.

During his pro football career from 1957 to 1969, mostly spent with the Cleveland Browns and Detroit Lions, Plum became an All-Pro quarterback. For many years after his retirement, he held the NFL record for career pass completion percentage.

His backfield partner at Cleveland was none other than Jim Brown, one of the greatest runners in pro football history. Like the Nittany Lions, the Browns were a run-oriented team, and Plum was a superb ball-handler who was perfect for the style.

The link between Plum and Jim Brown went back to their college days, when Brown played for Syracuse. In the 1955 Penn State–Syracuse game, Plum made one of the most memorable tackles in Penn State history when he cut down Brown in the open field.

"He was off to the races," Plum said. "I had an angle on him and was able to get him."

Plum starred in both football and baseball at Woodbury (New Jersey) High School. He hoped to do the same at Penn State, but had to concentrate on football because of the demands and competitive nature of the quarterback position.

"There were always three quarterbacks fighting it out," said Plum, a good-sized QB for the day at 6-foot-2 and 185 pounds.

Plum's versatility eventually won over the coaching staff.

"In those days, you did everything," Plum said.

And few did everything as well as Milt Plum.

Milt Plum was a do-everything quarterback in the days of two-way football, rarely leaving the field. He helped Penn State upset mighty Ohio State in 1956. *Penn State University Archives, Pennsylvania State University Libraries*

Gutsy "Riverboat" Richie Lucas was a three-year starter for the Lions (1957–1959). In his senior season, he earned All-American honors by leading the team in rushing and passing yardage on the offensive side of the ball while leading in interceptions on defense. *College Football Hall of Fame*

In 1959, Engle had one of his best teams at Penn State. Despite a limited number of bowls at the time—there were only eight bowl games in 1959—the Nittany Lions seemed to have a legitimate chance to finally land a postseason berth that season.

One of the main reasons was Richie Lucas.

Just call him "Riverboat Richie," a nickname he earned for his daring quarterback play from 1957 to 1959. He brought excitement to Beaver Field.

"We knew we had a gambler on our hands, a real good one," Engle said of Lucas, one of Penn State's all-time great quarterbacks. "He had so many qualifications for gambling: the nerve, the timing, the finesse."

Finding Lucas was a happy accident for Engle. Actually, at the time, the Penn State coach had been looking at another kid from Pennsylvania, Bethel High School quarterback Jerry Eisaman. While watching films of Eisaman, Engle couldn't help but notice a ubiquitous Glassport High defensive back making most of the tackles and intercepting most of the passes. It was Lucas. Engle immediately gave up on Eisaman and induced Lucas to come to Penn State.

Lucas looked like a choirboy but had mischief in his heart and usually a trick or two up his sleeves on a football field. He gained his reputation during his sophomore year in a 1957 game against West Virginia.

Throughout the game, the big West Virginia linemen had been putting pressure on Penn State's punters. Late in the first half, on fourth down with 5 yards to go, Engle ordered Lucas to punt.

Everyone in the stadium expected Lucas to punt. Everyone but Lucas, that is. He decided to run instead. The move caught West Virginia flatfooted; Engle was just as surprised. Lucas dashed 25 yards for a first down, and the play sparked the Nittany Lions to a 27–6 victory.

When Lucas was asked why he disregarded Engle's order to punt, he responded typically: "When he sends in a play, I treat it as a suggestion."

All-American honors eventually came Lucas' way. He set a Penn State single-season record for total offense with 1,238 yards in 1959. That same year, Lucas finished runner-up in the Heisman Trophy race to Billy Cannon, the highest finish for a Penn State player before John Cappelletti won the honor in 1973.

With Lucas leading the charge to an 8–2 season in 1959, the Nittany Lions gained their first bowl bid under Engle. They were invited to the Liberty Bowl in Philadelphia.

"The Liberty Bowl was trying to get established," said Sam Stellatella, a rugged lineman who was one of the primary kickers on the 1959 squad. "They wanted to establish a major bowl game in the northeast."

Penn State's opposition was Alabama. It would be the first time the Nittany Lions faced the Crimson Tide and their iconic coach, Bear Bryant.

Until that point, postseason bowls were played in warm-weather spots such as Miami, New Orleans, Dallas, and Pasadena, California. These games could usually be played comfortably outdoors. The Liberty Bowl would be the first bowl game played in a cold-weather site. And the weather would be a factor.

"It was extremely cold," Mitinger said of the game in Municipal Stadium.

And windy.

Coach Rip Engle and quarterback Richie Lucas try to warm up during a practice at Beaver Field in late 1959. The Nittany Lions were getting ready to face Alabama in the Liberty Bowl game in Philadelphia—Penn State's first bowl game under Engle. *Penn State University Archives, Pennsylvania State University Libraries*

Penn State halfback Roger Kochman (No. 46) lunges into the end zone for a touchdown against Alabama in the 1959 Liberty Bowl. It was all the Lions would need in their 7–0 victory over Bear Bryant's Crimson Tide. *AP Images*

At one point near the end of the first half, Alabama was forced to punt.

"They're deep in their own territory, about on their own 20-yard line," Stellatella remembered, "and they're kicking into a gale wind. And the wind just took that ball and pushed it back. So we recovered the ball with a couple of minutes to go in the half around their 20-yard line."

Toward the end of the regular season, Engle liked to put in a trick play "to keep the guys interested," according to Stellatella. "So we put in the fake field goal."

Galen Hall, who had replaced an injured Lucas in the first half, knelt to take the snap while Stellatella moved into position to kick the ball. Stellatella faked the field goal, and Hall took the ball and rolled right.

Roger Kochman, Penn State's star halfback, flared out to the left. Hall threw the ball across the field, and Kochman caught it in the vicinity of the 5-yard line. He breezed into the end zone, and Stellatella added the extra point for a historic 7–0 Penn State victory.

The win not only marked the first bowl victory for Penn State, but also the only time that the Nittany Lions would beat a Bear Bryant team.

"We just got a good ol' thrashing," Bryant said. "We were fortunate not to be beaten by four or five touchdowns. They outhit, outblocked, outsmarted, and outcoached us."

The same could have been said by Oregon after the 1960 Liberty Bowl. Penn State returned to Philadelphia and administered a 41–12 beating to the Ducks behind a magnificent performance by Dick Hoak, who shared the quarterback duties with Hall on two distinct teams: the "Regulars" and the "Reddies."

"I guess that was about as good a day as I've ever had," said Hoak, who won the Most Valuable Player award after directing five of Penn State's six touchdowns. He scored twice himself on rollouts and completed a 33-yard TD pass to Dick Pae.

Hoak, who would go on to success in the NFL, was one of the reasons Penn State made bowl visits a habit in the early 1960s. Among the other key players of the period were Mitinger and Dave Robinson, two of the best ends on any team in the nation, along with linemen Glenn Ressler and Chuck Sieminski, and Kochman at halfback. Mitinger, Robinson, Kochman, and Ressler all were named to the All-America team.

"It means everything, All-America," said Ressler, a fierce competitor who later became an All-Pro guard with the Baltimore Colts. "That's what you're there for, when you're rewarded. That's the pinnacle."

Penn State's newfound bowl successes came in the midst of other historic happenings at the school and for the football program.

Old Beaver Field, named for James A. Beaver, a former Pennsylvania governor and school trustee, had been relocated to more spacious surroundings across campus before the 1960 season. The Penn State administrators hoped the new site would be just as lucky for them as Old Beaver Field, where the Nittany Lions had fashioned a 184–34–11 record.

The new stadium was 50 percent larger than the original, seating 46,284. It was one of the most beautiful settings for a football game in America, affording fans a good view of the scenic mountain ranges that surround the campus.

On the field, Penn State continued to roll. The Lions notched yet another bowl victory in 1961 with a 30–15 decision over Georgia Tech in the Gator Bowl. Dave Robinson played one of his greatest games for Penn

Coach Rip Engle is surrounded by three of his top players of the early 1960s (left to right): end Dave Robinson, tackle Chuck Sieminski, and halfback Roger Kochman. *Penn State University Archives, Pennsylvania State University Libraries*

State and took home the Most Valuable Player award. The events in the days leading up to the Gator Bowl made it an even more satisfying moment for Robinson.

The only African American on the Penn State team, Robinson had to deal with a number of race-related problems in Florida. One such incident came when the team went to a movie theater in St. Augustine after practice.

When the players walked in to take their seats, an usher told Robinson that he had to sit in the balcony, a space reserved for blacks. In a great show of unanimity, the entire team went upstairs to sit with Robinson and watched the movie from there.

Robinson then took his frustration out against Georgia Tech.

Dave Robinson confronted many challenges on and off the football field. He encountered racial prejudice in Jacksonville, Florida, during Penn State's trip to the 1961 Gator Bowl, yet he persevered and earned MVP honors in the Lions' 30–15 win over Georgia Tech. *Penn State University Archives, Pennsylvania State University Libraries*

"He was just a demon," said Penn State tackle Jerry Farkas.

Robinson made a long-remembered play in that game when he leaped over two blockers and forced Georgia Tech quarterback Stan Gann to fumble. Robinson recovered, leading to a Penn State touchdown.

"It was just a very athletic play," Farkas said. "But I did play next to him and you could just sense all the frustration was coming out in that game, and to his advantage, he channeled it well."

That season, the Nittany Lions won the Lambert Trophy as the best team in the East, an honor they would repeat in 1962.

Despite an upset loss to Florida in the 1962 Gator Bowl, the Nittany Lions completed a flashy four-year run that included three victories in postseason competition and an overall record of 34–10.

"I look back on my career at Penn State and remember that we were all well schooled in fundamentals," Kochman said. "That was one of the reasons that we had a certain degree of success."

Still, eastern football was not as highly regarded as other regions of the country. Penn State hoped to change that type of thinking by playing a more intense national schedule.

During the 1960s, teams such as California, Oregon, Air Force, Rice, Missouri, Miami, Illinois, UCLA, and Ohio State lined up against the Nittany Lions.

"We were trying to stretch a little bit and get some national recognition for the program, and probably even more so for eastern football at that time," said quarterback Pete Liske, who played from 1961 to 1963. "It wasn't just for Penn State. The schools in the East really weren't getting much respect from the rest of the country."

In the early days of college football, beginning with the Princeton-Rutgers game in 1869, the East was long considered the seat of power in the sport. The Ivy League had virtually written the book on college football with various innovations, rules changes, and star players.

The emergence of the major conferences in the 1920s and 1930s, particularly the Big Ten, changed the power structure of college football in America. It was far more popular than professional football,

Dave Robinson (No. 89) leads the way for ball carrier Roger Kochman (No. 46) during a 20–6 win over Air Force in 1962. Both players were named first-team All-Americans that season. *AP Images*

and fans eagerly followed the heroic exploits of such players as Red Grange at Illinois, Ernie Nevers at Stanford, Bronko Nagurski at Minnesota, Sammy Baugh at TCU, Don Hudson at Alabama, and the legendary "Four Horsemen" of Notre Dame.

By the 1950s and 1960s, major conferences such as the Big Ten, Southeastern, Southwest, Big Eight, and Pac-8 ruled college football. Eastern football, made up mostly of independents, was generally not considered to be in the same class as those power conferences. Without the lure of a conference title or guarantees of playing in high-profile rivalries, eastern teams had a more difficult time recruiting elite athletes. National championships, once considered a birthright of the Ivy League and other eastern schools, were now a rarity in that region of the country.

Other changes were on the way for the football team in Happy Valley, most notably at the head coaching position. After a 5–5 season in 1965, Engle walked into the school president's office and announced he was quitting.

"I felt that football began to lose its charm, began to lose its fun," Engle said. "I went to the president, and he said, 'Well, you can still be our coach five more years.'

"And I said, 'Well, that's when I want to get out—when I can still be your coach.'"

Rip's replacement was no surprise: Joe Paterno. And a new era was born in Penn State football.

Like the mailman, halfback Roger Kochman delivered for Penn State in all types of weather. Here he gets a block from Al Gursky (No. 43) while driving through the snow in a game against Maryland at Beaver Stadium in November 1962. *Penn State University Archives, Pennsylvania State University Libraries*

CHAPTER 6

OFF AND RUNNING

So who was Joe Paterno, and how did he get the job as head football coach at one of the most prestigious universities in the land?

Paterno's path to Penn State began in Providence, Rhode Island, where he quarterbacked Brown University under coach Rip Engle. Hardly a world-beater for the Ivy Leaguers, Paterno was, as Engle put it, "the smartest guy on the field. He did things that showed you how much he understood the game."

Paterno figured his days on the gridiron ended when he graduated from Brown. Although he majored in English literature, Paterno assumed that he'd use his Ivy League education to get into law school. How many parents back in his native Brooklyn dreamed of having their children go to a school such as Brown, then on to a career as an attorney?

But Paterno also was intrigued by an offer from Engle, who was leaving Brown for the big time at Penn State University.

"I decided to go along just to broaden my experiences before entering law school," said Paterno, who was placed in charge of converting the Nittany Lions from a single-wing offense to a wing-T.

But it was more than the work that entranced Paterno. It was the place.

Sure, in 1956, Paterno had been the only Lions assistant coach who voted in favor of Engle taking the head coaching job at Southern Cal. (Engle had been a leading candidate for the Trojans' position, and he

Coach Joe Paterno leads his Penn State football team onto the field at Beaver Stadium—a role he would play for 43 seasons ... and counting. *Penn State University Archives, Pennsylvania State University Libraries*

62 CHAPTER 6

Bob Campbell (No. 23) led the stampede of great running backs at Penn State in the 1960s. He was the Lions' top rusher during Paterno's first season as head coach in 1966 and went on to post six 100-yard games in his career. *Penn State University Archives, Pennsylvania State University Libraries*

polled his staff on whether it made sense to switch jobs, and to see who would be interested in heading west with him. Seven coaches voted against the move, with Paterno the lone dissenter.) But Engle, Paterno, and crew stayed put in State College, and not long after, Paterno discovered that he was quite happy in Happy Valley.

Before long, with all pretenses of entering the legal profession (or any other profession) completely gone, Paterno was plotting his future as a head coach—as the Nittany Lions' head coach.

"I grew to love Penn State so much that . . . I dreamed of nothing other than becoming head coach."

Just before Engle retired, Paterno had been offered the head coaching job at Yale. He turned it down following a visit with Engle to the Penn State president's office, which virtually assured him that he would be the next coach at Penn State.

Paterno oversaw some impressive offenses in his years as an assistant, including several teams that averaged well over three touchdowns a game in an era when wide-open attacks were not yet in vogue in the college game. He helped Engle lead the Nittany Lions to four bowl games and three Lambert Trophies. He was Engle's top assistant and confidante. He was the only choice to succeed his mentor.

Fans stormed the Beaver Stadium field following a 13–8 victory over third-ranked North Carolina State in November 1967. It was Joe Paterno's biggest victory in the early years of his head coaching career. *Penn State University Archives, Pennsylvania State University Libraries*

"I knew that Joe would become an outstanding coach," said Engle, who recognized early on Paterno's keen football mind. "His leadership and competitive attitude made him a fine quarterback, and when I came to Penn State in 1950, he was the one person I brought along even though he had just graduated from college. I was aware even then of his potential as a fine coach."

But potential has to be realized, and that can take years. For JoePa, it took one year.

Coming off a mediocre 5–5 record in Engle's final season at State College, the Nittany Lions weren't exactly primed to be world-beaters in their first foray under Paterno. A schedule loaded with powerhouse opponents—the Lions would face three schools ranked in the top five in the nation in 1966—wasn't working in their favor, either.

Paterno was unperturbed. As a 39-year-old rookie head coach, he understood that year one of his regime would be about constructing a foundation for his program. Who knew he was going to build something as lasting as the Colosseum in Rome?

After repeating the 5–5 mark of Engle's final season, Paterno focused those thick-rimmed glasses on a future he was certain would be bright, filled with bowl games and, perhaps, national championships.

He was approaching the school's football future thoughtfully and with care, recruiting some of the best high school talent in the nation, and particularly combing the Northeast; the Lions pretty much already owned Pennsylvania's rich prep-school reservoir of skilled players.

One of Paterno's earliest stars actually was recruited by Engle: Ted Kwalick of McKees Rocks, near Pittsburgh. Engle sold Kwalick as much on Penn State's academic reputation as on its football program, a theme that carried through most of Paterno's reign in State College. Little did Kwalick know that he would wind up playing for Paterno, not Engle.

Kwalick remembered Paterno's uncertainty about which side of the ball to use him on and where to play him on offense or defense. It was an early measure of Paterno's football acumen that he plunked Kwalick at tight end, then watched the youngster develop into an All-American who eventually became an NFL star and a member of the College Football Hall of Fame.

"I feel honored to be Joe's first All-American, but that wasn't really the key," Kwalick recalled. "What we did as a team was so critical. We started out my sophomore year 5–5, and then my junior year 8–2–1. And then my senior year, I think we had the best college defense in the country."

To get to that memorable 1968 campaign, though, the Lions first had to fully adjust to Paterno as the head man.

"Joe's tough," said Charlie Pittman, Paterno's first star running back. "He wants you to put out. He has hard practices and tough discipline on and off the field.

"Some coaches try to get you to love and respect them so you'll do anything for them. Joe's not loved, but he's respected because of the type of person he is. He's really tough and he's intelligent. You're afraid not to respect him."

ALL-AMERICAN BOY

Ted Kwalick had modest goals when he arrived at Penn State.

"I just wanted to get a college education, be a high school football coach, and teach physical education," Kwalick said.

So much for long-range plans. Instead, Kwalick became a collegiate All-American at tight end and went on to have a brilliant career in the pros. He was two players in one: a great blocker and also a threat on short or long passes.

"The tight end position was just coming into fruition at that time," Kwalick remembered. "It was around 1965, '66 when they came out with the tight end, the split end, and the flanker."

Before Kwalick and others redefined the position, the tight end was used to block for running backs. At Penn State, Kwalick added the element of pass catcher. At 6-foot-4, 225 pounds, he was tough to bring down in the open field. NFL scouts said he ran like a halfback once in the open field—a halfback with bullish strength.

Classic Kwalick: In a 1967 game against Syracuse, Kwalick bounced off a number of Syracuse players after making a catch. Then he took off on a 30-yard gain before being dragged down by three tacklers.

During his Penn State career, from 1966 to 1968, Kwalick caught 86 passes for 1,343 yards and 10 touchdowns. He also had the distinction of being Joe Paterno's first All-American, an honor he received in 1967. He repeated in 1968 and thus became only the second Penn State football player twice named All-American. The first to do it was Bob Higgins, also a receiver, in 1915 and 1919.

Kwalick was actually recruited by head coach Rip Engle and Paterno, who was the quarterbacks coach at that time. Paterno and Engle loved everything about Kwalick—everything but his grades. He had academic problems at Montour High School, located outside of Pittsburgh. Engle offered him a scholarship, but only if he improved his grades. He did, and Kwalick became a Nittany Lion.

Kwalick found himself in the middle of a football explosion at Penn State that produced some of Paterno's greatest teams. The era featured two perfect teams and a 31-game unbeaten streak.

Along with Kwalick, those Penn State teams featured several All-Americans: linebackers Dennis Onkotz and Jack Ham, tackle Mike Reid, safety Neal Smith, and running back Charlie Pittman. Kwalick and Onkotz gained All-American status twice.

After college, Kwalick was a first-round draft choice of the San Francisco 49ers and quickly became an offensive force in the NFL. He was an All-Pro in 1972, 1973, and 1974, and he later won a Super Bowl as a member of the Oakland Raiders.

Kwalick returned to the Penn State campus in 1989 when he was inducted into the College Football Hall of Fame.

All-American Ted Kwalick, seen here galloping through the Army defense in 1968, helped to revolutionize the tight end position during his three seasons at Penn State. *Penn State University Archives, Pennsylvania State University Libraries*

Joe Paterno called Dennis Onkotz (No. 35) "one of the greatest linebackers Penn State has ever had." The mobile and athletic defender nabbed 11 interceptions during his college career, including three that he ran back for a touchdown—a school record. *Penn State University Archives, Pennsylvania State University Libraries*

And while the players were adapting to him, Paterno had to adjust to being the head man. To Paterno, that meant be aggressive from the outset—don't back down, on or off the field. Express yourself, whether as an athlete or as a member of society.

"I think you've got to go after things, and you've got to take a chance," he said. "You've got to gamble, and when something appears to be right to you, you've got to take a chance and not be afraid to lose.

"I've always preached to my boys that there's one thing I want you to do and this is don't ever be afraid to lose. If you're afraid to lose, you never have a chance of winning."

That philosophy is something Kwalick and hundreds of other former Nittany Lions players have taken with them after leaving Happy Valley. Paterno also worked to ensure that his players were well-rounded students, largely though his Grand Experiment approach that emphasized the student-athlete.

"I couldn't have been happier with my college experience," Kwalick said. "Joe stressed there's more to life than football. The things I learned from that football experience carried me through a lot of hard times in life."

Paterno also had to learn to carry himself though the hard times. His wife, Sue Paterno, once told *Sports*

Illustrated how despondent he was after finishing 5–5 in his first year as head coach. "He spent the whole summer planning a new defense," she said. "Oh, that was rough, keeping the kids out of his hair and all. He said that if he didn't have a winning season the second year he would quit and go back to assistant coaching. He said it wasn't fair to the kids to be coached by a loser."

Four decades later, this would-be loser was in a race to be the winningest college football coach of all time.

THE SEISMIC SIXTIES AT PENN STATE

One area in which Joe Paterno immediately proved himself was recruiting.

In the mid-1960s, eastern football had its hot spots, particularly Syracuse, Pittsburgh, West Virginia, Maryland, and even Army and Navy. Under Paterno, though, Penn State would begin an era of dominance not just on the field, but in the living rooms of prospects who previously might have had the Nittany Lions on their radar, but not necessarily in the middle of the screen.

From those houses in Haverford and farms in Farmingdale, Paterno and staff would stretch their reach into Ohio, Michigan, and Indiana—Big Ten country—as well as Virginia and the Carolinas—Atlantic Coast Conference territory. Paterno's recruiting tentacles reached into the Deep South to challenge the Southeastern Conference; to the Midwest and Plains states to poach prospects away from the Big Eight; and even to talent-rich California to challenge for players who normally attended Pacific-8 schools.

Perhaps most significantly, Paterno had no qualms about recruiting black players. It simply wasn't part of his makeup to care about someone's skin color, athlete or non-athlete.

When Charlie Pittman came to State College in 1967, the campus was, by his estimation, one percent black. When he left as an All-American (academic and athletic) in 1969, the school had become among the most attractive educational and athletic destinations for minorities in the nation.

It wasn't always a sure thing that Pittman would be a Nittany Lion, however. "I set the Maryland [high school] scoring record in 1966," Pittman recalled, "and then I got recruited by Penn State, Maryland, Syracuse, a lot of Ivy League schools, and Navy. My idol at the time was number 24, Lenny Moore for the Baltimore Colts. In the year that I set the scoring record in Maryland, Lenny set the touchdown record in the National Football League. He had gone to Penn State, and he had played for the Colts. So naturally, that's what I wanted to do."

But Rip Engle was retiring from Penn State, and with Maryland having recently hired Lou Saban as its coach, Pittman verbally committed to the Terrapins.

"I wasn't so sure I wanted to play for some inexperienced coach named Paterno," he recalled.

Charlie Pittman, Joe Paterno's first All-American running back, led the Nittany Lions in rushing for three straight seasons. He opened the door for other great black running backs to follow. Here, he picks up a few of the 161 yards he gained against Navy in the opening game of the 1968 season. *Penn State University Archives, Pennsylvania State University Libraries*

Ted Kwalick (left) and Dennis Onkotz show off the headline announcing their dual selection as All-Americans in 1968. Kwalick was honored in 1967 as well, and Onkotz was a repeat selection in 1969. *Penn State University Archives, Pennsylvania State University Libraries*

But Engle and Paterno were not about to give up on Pittman. They assured him that nothing about the Lions program would change. They finally won Pittman over, but it took a while before he was sure he had made the right move.

"Here I was, this bashful, inner-city kid from Baltimore who had never left his block, and now I was in a new environment," Pittman said. "I questioned to some degree whether I belonged, whether I was good enough to be part of this."

Paterno never doubted it. In those days of racial anxiety, when a new coach at a perennially successful university made the bold step of opening the program's doors to anyone and everyone, it was incumbent upon that coach to fully believe in and support every single recruit. It was Paterno's open-mindedness on such matters that got him inside the front doors of all those homes of black teenagers with skills to match their unlimited dreams.

Paterno was instrumental in encouraging Pittman to believe in his dreams. Pittman recalled how, one day in the locker room, the coach sensed that his new recruit was feeling a little down. "At that point, someone . . . passed us, and Joe stopped him and said, 'Here's the guy who's going to make me a great football coach.'

"Just that statement did so much to boost my confidence that I completely turned it around."

And turn it around he did, to the tune of 2,236 yards rushing and 30 touchdowns for his career. Pittman was named to the All-America team in 1969, making him Paterno's first running back so honored.

With the help of the likes of Pittman and Kwalick on offense and Dennis Onkotz, Jack Ham, Mike Reid, and Neal Smith on defense, the Nittany Lions were about to turn State College, Pennsylvania, into one of the sport's most majestic addresses.

Pittman, whose son Tony would star for the Lions two decades later, knew he played a key role, particularly in attracting top African-American athletes to the school.

"If they don't get me, they don't get Franco [Harris] and Lydell [Mitchell]. Joe and I have this conversation that I'm not the best that ever played there, but I opened the door for a lot of guys behind me. We're living proof that the Grand Experiment works."

For those doubters who considered the hiring of Paterno a "Grand Experiment" in itself, 1967 would be a critical season. The Lions opened with tight losses to Navy and UCLA (a blocked punt being the decisive play) sandwiched around a win over Miami. At 1–2, Paterno made a difficult decision.

The coach benched many of his upperclassmen and went with a slew of sophomores, many at key positions.

"You go with upperclassmen until they prove they can't do it," Onkotz said. "I know I was a lot better than the guy ahead of me. It wasn't even close—a lot of us were. They didn't really have the [senior] players to compete, and we were there. In practice, the first team couldn't run on us, the freshmen. They couldn't block me. The handwriting was on the wall."

That decision brought the Nittany Lions to life. They won their last seven regular-season contests, including victories over rivals Syracuse, West Virginia, and most notably, a 42–6 rout of Pittsburgh. They were just getting started.

Under coach Paterno, Penn State has become synonymous with bowl games. Here, JoePa greets the media before his first postseason appearance, at the 1967 Gator Bowl. The Lions tied Florida State, 17–17. *Penn State University Archives, Pennsylvania State University Libraries*

After tying Florida State 17–17 in the 1967 Gator Bowl, Penn State would win every game during the next two seasons, running its unbeaten string to 31.

Not only did Paterno bring the school back to eastern supremacy, but he lifted it beyond any such geographic borders. Penn State had become a force on the national scene, establishing itself as a title contender for the Alabamas and Nebraskas, Southern Californias and Texases to reckon with.

One major reason was the defense Paterno was putting together. Based on a 4-4-3 alignment, the defensive scheme utilized intelligent, agile, and mobile linebackers. Onkotz was the prototype, and Ham would take the position to a yet-higher level.

Thus was born "Linebacker U."

"Yeah, the 4-4-3," Onkotz recalled almost reverently. "I think if you have athletic linebackers, the linebackers control the game, as long as you have one or two good defensive tackles."

Penn State had those, as well, led by Reid and Steve Smear.

"Those guys could do everything," Onkotz said.

Onkotz also remembered that six Lions on those powerful teams had played quarterback in high school, which meant they were agile and could move.

"Not huge, but very mobile," Onkotz said. "And we were smart."

They were so good that through the first five games of 1968, the Lions had outscored opponents 137–41. After beating Army 28–24—a game in which Kwalick clinched the win by running back an onside kick for a touchdown—the Lions ran off four more easy wins, including a 65–9 humiliation of Pitt.

Becoming the first Penn State squad to win 10 games in a season, the Lions finished the regular season with a perfect 10–0 record. They had moved from the tenth spot in the preseason rankings to third before heading to the Orange Bowl to play No. 6 Kansas.

The Lions' defense in 1968 was practically impenetrable, and the offense was machinelike. The strong offensive line was anchored by the likes of Dave Bradley, Charlie Zapiec, and John Kulka, and later Dave Joyner.

"They made everything go," Pittman said of the offensive line. "Before each game, I sat down and talked with Kulka and Bradley and let them know that I was aware of what they were doing. And that I was thankful."

Kwalick's all-around work at tight end earned him a spot on the All-America team in 1968. Onkotz, perhaps the most single-minded player Paterno ever coached, was also an All-American.

Steve Smear was a star defensive tackle for Penn State, and he teamed with Mike Reid to present a devastating duo during the Lions' unbeaten season in 1968. *Penn State University Archives, Pennsylvania State University Libraries*

LINEBACKER U

OK, roll call!

Jack Ham. Dennis Onkotz. LaVar Arrington. John Skorupan. Ed O'Neil. Greg Buttle. Paul Posluszny. Dan Connor. Brandon Short. Andre Collins. Kurt Allerman. Charlie Zapiec. Brian Gelzheiser. Lance Mehl. Shane Conlan. Dave Robinson.

Quite a list—and that's just a sampling of the stars who helped Penn State earn the well-deserved nickname of "Linebacker U."

It all started with Jerry Sandusky, a former Nittany Lions lineman who joined Paterno's staff as an assistant coach in 1969, became the linebackers coach in 1970, and eventually took over as defensive coordinator in 1977. By the time he retired in 1999, Sandusky had turned out nine first-team All-Americans and many more great ones at the linebacker position.

Posluszny, an All-American in 2005 and 2006, said that what drew him to Penn State was the "whole Linebacker U mystique."

Indeed, pro scouts have been enamored of Nittany Lions linebackers for decades, going back to Robinson in the 1960s. Robinson actually played defensive end for the Nittany Lions before moving on to the NFL, but he was so versatile for Joe Paterno that he was something of a hybrid. In the pros, he was converted to linebacker and helped the Green Bay Packers establish one of football's greatest dynasties.

Robinson encountered many challenges while at State College that were tougher than bringing down opposing ball carriers. He was the only black player on the 1961 squad, and when Penn State was invited to play in the Gator Bowl in Jacksonville, Florida, Robinson was apprehensive. And rightly so.

When the team wanted to eat dinner at the airport restaurant, Robinson was refused service.

"The whole squad walked out," recalled Paterno, then an assistant coach.

It was that kind of support that made top high school players, of all races, covet a chance to play at Penn State. Many of those star recruits were linebackers.

Paterno has fond memories of all of them, from the ultra-aggressive Onkotz and Ham to the athletic Arrington to the versatile Buttle.

"Buttle is as good a linebacker as we've had here," Paterno once said. "He is a complete linebacker. He's a big man, but he plays the pass as well as the run. He's very alert; he's very intelligent. He has great leadership qualities."

Buttle actually expected to play a different position when he arrived in Happy Valley. After being a tight end, defensive end, linebacker, and punter in high school, Buttle told the Penn State coaches he preferred tight end.

"But John Skorupan, who was an All-American linebacker, had just graduated," Buttle said. "So they told me, 'Buttle, you are a linebacker.'"

He went on to earn his own All-American credentials in 1975 before becoming a standout with the New York Jets in the pros.

There was never any question about Jack Ham's best position. He succeeded Onkotz as the leader of the linebackers, and in 1970 he was a consensus All-American and one of the best defensive players in the nation. Ham went on to a legendary pro career, serving as a hammering presence on the dominating Pittsburgh Steelers defense of the 1970s. From there, he was elected to the Pro Football Hall of Fame in 1988 and the College Football Hall of Fame two years later.

Yet, he nearly didn't get to Penn State at all.

Because Ham was only about 185 pounds as a high school senior, he was lightly recruited. His former high school teammate, Steve Smear, was already playing defensive tackle at Penn State, and he vouched for Ham. So Paterno sent assistant coach George Welsh on a recruiting trip to Johnstown, Pennsylvania.

Long story short, Ham received the last scholarship available in the 1966 recruiting season.

Ham would go on to be part of a rugged defensive dynasty at Penn State. The Lions posted 11–0 records in 1968 and 1969. In the 1970 Orange Bowl, the Lions were at their best, forcing nine turnovers, including seven interceptions, against a powerful Missouri offense.

Gelzheiser was a linebacker cut from the same mold as Ham. Smart, instinctive, assertive, and a true leader.

When the Lions went undefeated in 1994, Gelzheiser was the glue. He had been a special-teams stalwart before becoming a defensive regular in 1993, just in time for the school's Big Ten debut.

Joining that conference fit Gelzheiser's style: physical.

"It was just a constant beating," he noted.

And Gelzheiser was handing out a lot of those beatings, even though he played hurt for much of his career.

"Gelzheiser was the guy who was the cornerstone of that defense," said Kerry Collins, the quarterback in that perfect season. "He was a good guy that was a great leader for the time."

Gelzheiser was overshadowed by other Big Ten linebackers who made more tackles and were more spectacular. But, as he noted, "We were unbeaten." His own coaches certainly understood his importance at Linebacker U.

"I don't like to make comparisons," linebackers coach Tom Bradley said during the 1994 season, "but I'm sure Brian stacks up with the rest of them. Any time that we've had great linebackers, the team has been great."

Arrington, Posluszny, and Connor are three, more recent, acclaimed linebackers for the Lions.

In 1999, Arrington won both the Butkus Award as the nation's top linebacker and the Bednarik Award as best defensive player. Posluszny won the Bednarik Award in both 2005 and 2006 and the Butkus in 2005. Connor won the Bednarik in 2007, giving the Nittany Lions an unprecedented three straight in that category. (The Butkus was originated in 1985 and the Bednarik in 1994.)

Arrington, an All-American in 1998 and 1999 and the Big Ten Defensive Player of the Year in 1998, was a dominant performer.

His quickness allowed him to get past blockers and on top of ball carriers and passers before opponents knew what hit them. His agility made him dangerous in pass coverage. His intelligence helped him sniff out plays before they developed.

Arrington was best known for the "LaVar Leap," a maneuver that only a decathlete should be capable of doing. Arrington would leap over an opponent—or several of them, even—to make a tackle, thus assuring himself a longtime presence on highlight reels.

He was almost always spectacular. Against Purdue, Arrington sacked Drew Brees and forced a fumble that he ran in for a touchdown. Against archrival Pittsburgh, Arrington blocked a field goal attempt with four seconds left to preserve the victory.

And in his final collegiate game before turning pro a year early, Arrington sparked a 24–0 romp against Texas A&M in the 1999 Alamo Bowl, accounting for 14 tackles and a sack.

Because he was a bit of a showboat, Arrington never drew lavish praise from Paterno and his staff. But they knew how good he was, and so did the NFL scouts. Arrington was the second overall pick in the 2000 draft, selected by the Washington Redskins, one spot behind fellow Nittany Lion Courtney Brown, who went to Cleveland.

Arrington's enthusiasm and passion also once got him kicked out of a Penn State game—and he wasn't even playing. Arrington was on the sideline rooting a bit too vociferously for his former team against Iowa in 2002 when he was ejected.

Posluszny never had such travails. Not that he wasn't just as fervent about Penn State. His hard play showed it during his brilliant, award-winning college career. His Bednarik and Butkus awards were further evidence that Linebacker U was still in business, in a big way.

"They're both huge honors, but I'd have to say, as a linebacker, that this one [the Butkus Award] means a lot more to me," Posluszny said. "Playing linebacker, to win the Butkus Award means you're the top person at your position, and that's the biggest thing you can do."

Paterno described Posluszny as "everything you want out of a football player—ability, attitude, competitiveness, intelligence."

And the Penn State coaching staff was everything Posluszny could want for his development. Posluszny emphasized the key roles that Paterno and his staff have played in establishing and then maintaining the quality of linebacker play at State College.

Once he got to school and saw that Paterno was "determined to be the coach at Penn State for as long as he could," Posluszny knew he was in the right place.

"It was a great experience to play for Coach," Posluszny said. "Any guy would say that. He has so much valuable knowledge of coaching guys and has seen every situation you can think of. He's dealing with 18- to 22-year-old kids. He knows what we are going through, our problems, what we want to accomplish, and how to handle being on a great football team."

A great football team led by great linebackers.

Joe Paterno poses with two of his star linebackers, Dennis Onkotz (center) and Jack Ham (right), along with the Lambert Trophy, awarded to the best college team in the East. Onkotz and Ham were central to establishing Penn State's reputation as "Linebacker U." *Penn State University Archives, Pennsylvania State University Libraries*

"You play football," Onkotz said of his existence in Happy Valley. "We all went to school, graduated in four years. We didn't get five years like these guys do today. We got a lot of engineers and everything else in that class. I didn't have time. I went from one thing to another. I didn't even have a beer in college."

It seemed as though champagne would be in order when the Lions finished off their first perfect season since 1912 with a gut-wrenching 15–14 win over Kansas in the Orange Bowl.

But just as now, college football had no definitive way of defining a champion. No playoffs. No absolute title game.

In the 1960s and 1970s, the polls decided the national champion. So even after the Lions slowed Kansas' star running back John Riggins and the Jayhawks' prolific attack to finish at 11–0, earning the No. 1 ranking was not to be.

Ohio State got that reward even though the Buckeyes were only 10–0. Coming from the highly regarded Big Ten, while Penn State was an independent that had not faced a ranked opponent before edging Kansas, helped the Buckeyes, as did a 27–16 win over Southern California in the Rose Bowl.

But that did not lessen the Lions' brilliance at the Orange Bowl, particularly in the final minutes.

A long punt return helped set up a Riggins touchdown that gave Kansas a 14–7 lead in the late going. Otherwise, the Penn State defense had performed magnificently.

Kansas had the ball with less than two minutes remaining, but the Lions forced a punt. Penn State coaches ordered "10-Go Charge," an all-out assault to block the punt.

Neal Smith got a piece of the ball, and the Lions took possession on the 50-yard line. Bob Campbell, Pittman's running mate in the backfield, recalled talking with quarterback Charlie Burkhart about the next play. "I told Burkhart to throw downfield for the left goal post, and I would be there."

Tri-captains John Kulka, Mike Reid, and Steve Smear (left to right) enjoy a light moment before the 1969 Orange Bowl. It's unclear if the fresh-squeezed orange juice helped the Lions to squeeze by Kansas, 15–14, on New Year's Day. *Penn State University Archives, Pennsylvania State University Libraries*

Burkhart did, Campbell was, and the Lions had the ball at the Kansas 3-yard line.

Paterno called a timeout to diagram the next three plays. Not that Burkhart was worried.

"Chuck was positively the coolest guy around," recalled Paterno with a chuckle. "He kept telling me, 'We'll win, coach, don't worry.' It was great, but sometimes I wonder if he has quite enough talent to be all that cocky."

Cocky or not, the first two handoffs yielded little. The third play diagramed by the coach called for a handoff to Pittman, but Burkhart thought of a better option and changed the play at the line.

"It was something I'd never done before, never even thought of before," he said.

Faking the handoff to Pittman, the quarterback sped around left end—and scored, making it 14–13 Kansas.

Paterno's reaction to Burkhart's maneuver? None—he was too busy calling for the 2-point conversion.

"Hey, we had won every game during the season," he said. "So if we couldn't win, we'd lose. No ties."

And it looked as if Penn State had earned its first loss since game three of the 1967 schedule when Burkhart's pass to Campbell was knocked down in the end zone. But Kansas had 12 men on the field. (It was one of several times in the frantic final moments that the Jayhawks had too many men on the field.)

Penalized half the distance to the goal line, Kansas then set up with the proper number of players. Paterno had called for a pitch right to Campbell for the 2-point play, but when the crowd noise was so loud that the Lions were allowed by the officials to huddle up again, Paterno changed the play.

Now he called for a sweep to the left, again by Campbell, perhaps figuring the Jayhawks would be concentrating on stopping Pittman.

Campbell surged in to win the game.

"That's what you want," Campbell said. "That's where you want to be if you want to play the game."

But you also want to be atop the football world, and the pollsters denied Penn State such glory.

Ah, sun, sand, and girls. That was the formula for the Nittany Lions as they prepared for the 1969 Orange Bowl with a game of beach football in sunny Florida. *Penn State University Archives, Pennsylvania State University Libraries*

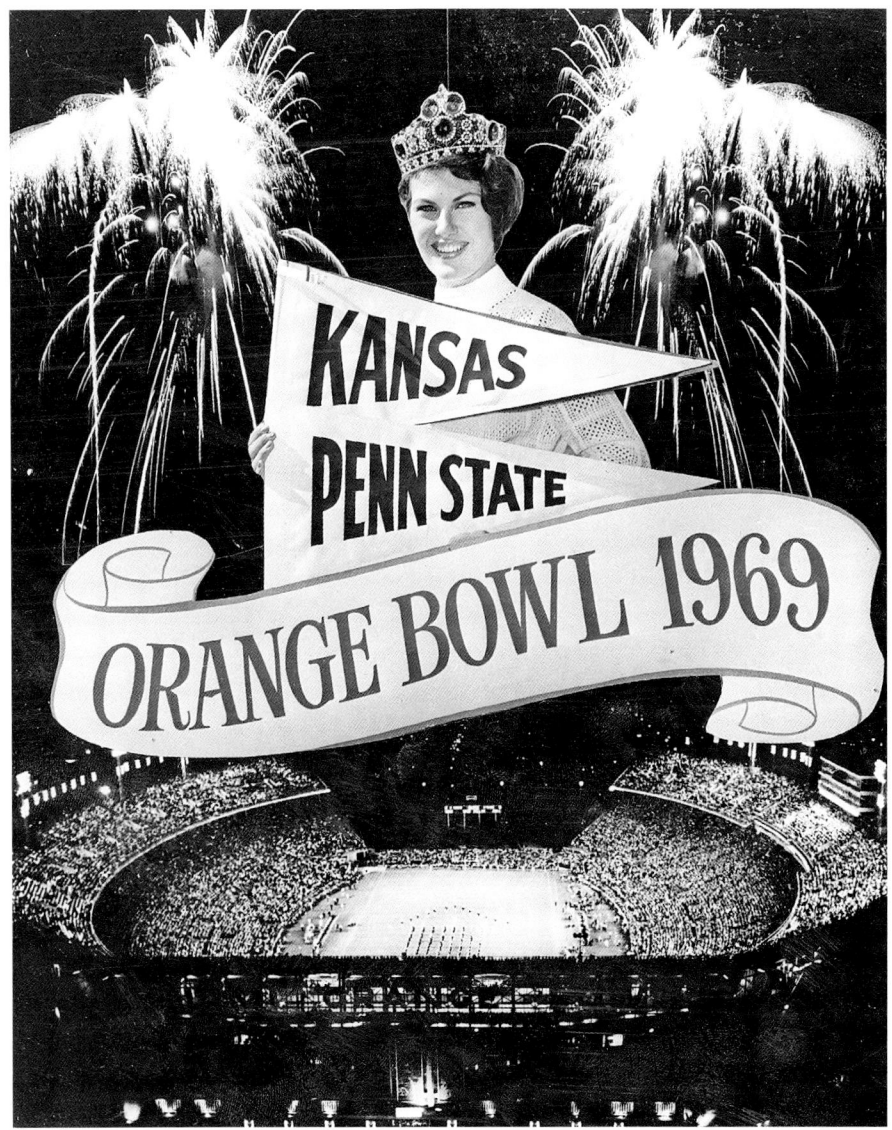

This souvenir poster from the 1969 Orange Bowl depicts Orange Bowl queen Robin Whatley holding the team pennants. P.S.: Penn State won the game. *Penn State University Archives, Pennsylvania State University Libraries*

The Nittany Lions listen to coach Paterno's instructions in the locker room during halftime of the 1969 Orange Bowl. Penn State and Kansas were tied 7–7 after two quarters of play. *Penn State University Archives, Pennsylvania State University Libraries*

The referee signals for the score after Bob Campbell (No. 23) lunged into the end zone on a 2-point conversion in the closing seconds to give the Nittany Lions a thrilling 15–14 win over Kansas in the Orange Bowl on January 1, 1969. *Penn State University Archives, Pennsylvania State University Libraries*

JACK HAM

There was a time when Jack Ham didn't think he had a future in football. Yes, *that* Jack Ham—Penn State All-American, four-time Super Bowl champion, and member of the Pro Football Hall of Fame.

The time was in the 1960s following his high school years in Johnstown, Pennsylvania, and a stint at a military academy in Virginia. In high school, Ham played linebacker, center, and offensive guard.

"I wasn't getting that many scholarship offers," Ham recalled. "I think East Carolina offered me a partial scholarship. So I thought my football career was kind of over."

Penn State to the rescue—specifically George Welsh, the offensive coordinator on Joe Paterno's staff, and Steve Smear, a Penn State defensive lineman and former high school teammate of Ham's.

Welsh asked Smear about his former teammate, and Smear gave Ham great reviews. Welsh decided to follow up with a recruiting trip to Johnstown.

Ham had already been considering going to Penn State and trying to join the football team as a walk-on. Instead, he got the last scholarship in 1966.

"Joe always tells the story of how stupid the coaches were because I was going to come to college and be a student," Ham recalled. "Joe said, 'We could have had him for nothing, and we ended up giving him a scholarship.'"

Ham remembers that life as a freshman football player wasn't always so rosy. "You were kind of cannon fodder or scout teams for the varsity," he said. "But you don't get involved in competing with the varsity until your spring practice of your freshman year."

By that time, Ham started surprising people, especially himself. One day near the end of spring practice, he walked into the locker room and found a blue jersey hanging in his locker.

"Blue means you're on the first team," Ham said. "That shocked me. The other freshmen that went in with me were all on the second and third teams."

Ham joined a strong defensive first squad featuring Smear, Mike Reid, Dennis Onkotz, John Ebersole, Jim Kates, and Paul Johnson.

It was a real turning point for Ham. "I didn't have all that much confidence as a freshman. But . . . Joe Paterno and the coaches had confidence in me, and that's the thing that I remember the most about my inception into the football program."

Ham made key contributions from his linebacker position to some of Paterno's great early teams. He was a big-play performer on the 1968 and 1969 teams that posted perfect records, and he played a part in the school-record, 31-game unbeaten streak during that period.

In 1970, Ham was a unanimous All-American pick after making 91 tackles and 4 interceptions. While making a name for himself, he was also helping to make a name for Penn State: "Linebacker U."

Later, he starred in the National Football League as part of Pittsburgh's famed "Steel Curtain" defense. Ham and the Steelers, one of the NFL's greatest dynasties, won four Super Bowls in the 1970s.

After a great career during which he made the All-Pro team in nine straight seasons, Ham went into private business. He also kept his hand in football by working as a radio analyst for Penn State games and on NFL broadcasts.

For a player who wasn't sure he had a future in football, Ham did all right for himself. After playing at Penn State from 1968 to 1970 and then with the Steelers from 1971 to 1982, Ham was inducted into the Pro Football Hall of Fame in 1988.

"I was very fortunate to play at both Penn State and at Pittsburgh with solid defenses, so I wasn't getting banged around," he said. "Most of my game was speed, so having great defensive lines in front of me was a real positive."

Linebacker Jack Ham was an intimidating presence for opposing quarterbacks from 1968 to 1970. He went on to earn induction in both the College and Pro Football Halls of Fame.
Penn State/Collegiate Images/Getty Images

NIXING THE LIONS

If the Nittany Nation was upset about not earning a national title for the 1968 season, it was livid about what occurred the next year. And this time, Penn State fans had someone directly to blame: the guy living in the White House.

The 1969 season held promise for something very special in Happy Valley. The Lions were returning a slew of experienced players from their 11–0 campaign and Orange Bowl win the year before. Indeed, many of the regulars had never lost a game at Penn State since moving into the starting lineup early in the 1967 schedule.

"It was a combination of superior personnel, experience, and fine young men with tremendous pride," Paterno noted. "They liked each other, played together well, and enjoyed the game. Every one of them was unselfish. They were not concerned with who got the credit."

Nor were they worried about the quality of opposition, although it was significantly better than it had been in the previous perfect season.

Safety Neal Smith (No. 26) is about to pull in one of his school-record 10 interceptions during the 1969 season, this one coming against Colorado in week two. Smith picked off 19 passes during his collegiate career, another Penn State record. *AP Images*

In the first five weeks, Penn State would face three eastern rivals (Navy, West Virginia, and Syracuse), highly ranked Kansas State on the road, and Colorado. The pollsters would have a hard time ignoring the Lions if they handled such opponents.

Paterno's defense would alternate between stingy and downright impenetrable. Onkotz, Reid, and Smith were named first-team All-Americans, and Smear made second team. Ham was establishing his Hall of Fame credentials. The pass rush was formidable, the coverage in the secondary was impeccable, and the linebackers were . . . well, this is Linebacker U, after all. "We were stout," Smear said.

Colorado quarterback Bob Anderson discovered just how miserable an afternoon of dealing with that defense could be.

"I think this was the greatest defensive unit I've ever played against," Anderson said after a 27–3 defeat in which he rushed for a grand total of 4 yards, even though he was considered the best running quarterback in the nation. Anderson also was intercepted three times and fumbled once.

"I think Penn State would be a great team in our [Big Eight] conference, or any other conference, for that matter," Anderson said. "Our coaches told me I would have no more than three seconds to set up and throw. After that, I could expect Reid or Smear on my back."

Anderson credited the depth of the Penn State defense, with strength all the way down the line. "The deployment of their linebackers bothered me. One of them always seemed to be right in the pass route."

All in all, a very frustrating day for the quarterback.

"How do I like playing against Penn State? It's pretty discouraging."

Join the crowd, Bob.

Through the first five contests on the schedule, the Lions allowed an average of just over 10 points. Only Navy, with 22, showed any semblance of offense—and Penn State put 45 on the Navy defense.

The offense really kicked into high gear over the next month, in which the Lions swept five games by averaging 37.6 points. Led by Pittman (another first-team All-American), Burkhart, a solid offensive line, and a pair of developing young backs named Franco Harris and Lydell Mitchell, Penn State made a living in opponents' end zones.

Fran Ganter played fullback for Penn State from 1967 to 1970 before spending 33 years on Joe Paterno's coaching staff and, since 2004, serving as the associate athletic director for football. *Penn State University Archives, Pennsylvania State University Libraries*

All-American tackle Dave Joyner anchored the offensive line for Penn State from 1969 to 1971, during which time the Lions went 29–4. Joyner was also an All-American wrestler, and his sons Matt and Andy both later played football for the Lions. *Penn State University Archives, Pennsylvania State University Libraries*

With back-to-back victories over Kansas and Missouri, Penn State owned the Orange Bowl in the late 1960s. The wins earned them second-place rankings in the national polls following the 1968 and 1969 seasons. *Penn State University Archives, Pennsylvania State University Libraries*

Only once were the Nittany Lions in any real danger of losing. That game, at Syracuse's decaying Archbold Stadium, also provided the biggest source of controversy during the 1969 regular season.

The Lions trailed the Orangemen 14–0 at halftime, putting their 23-game unbeaten string in jeopardy.

"Coach Paterno talked to us about pride," Smear recalled. "He said if we ever had it, we'd better show it now. He told us that losing wouldn't be any disgrace, but the thing that would hurt most would be if we went out and were outplayed and outhit."

Outplay and outhit is exactly what Ben Schwartzwalder's Orangemen had done in the first half and continued to do in the third quarter, even staging a terrific defensive stand when the Lions recovered a fumble at the Syracuse 11.

"It looked kind of bleak," Burkhart admitted.

Bleak, but not hopeless.

With about 10 minutes remaining, Mitchell ran in for a touchdown. The score was set up by a pass interference penalty against Syracuse, a call that enraged Schwartzwalder.

He wouldn't calm down anytime soon.

The Nittany Lions went for the 2-point conversion and failed. Reminiscent of the Orange Bowl against Kansas, though, Syracuse was flagged for a holding penalty. Penn State converted on a second try, and Schwartzwalder fumed some more.

By now, the Orangemen were feeling squeezed. They couldn't move the ball, and a revitalized Penn State was marching down the field, seemingly at will.

The Lions got deep into Syracuse territory and turned to another future legend, Harris. His touchdown and Mike Reitz's extra point made it 15–14 Penn State.

Later, Schwartzwalder let loose with a diatribe questioning just about everyone not wearing a Syracuse jersey.

"My boys said those [Penn State] coaches succeeded in effectively intimidating those officials," Schwartzwalder said. "This was a case of 25 or more bad calls, and it was seemingly unending."

The only thing unending during the 1969 season was Penn State's winning streak. Then, an even more juicy controversy hit.

Paterno's best team yet finished off the schedule in style, going 10–0 for a second consecutive perfect season. But the Nittany Lions were ranked third in the national polls, trailing Texas and Arkansas, both of which were also undefeated heading into their final regular-season game against each other.

The Longhorns and Razorbacks, both members of the vaunted Southwest Conference, would meet on December 6, one week after Penn State ended its schedule with a 33–8 rout of North Carolina State—on the road.

President Richard Nixon, a longtime football fan, decided to attend the Texas-Arkansas game, ostensibly as part of a celebration to cap the 100th anniversary of the sport. He also planned to present a presidential plaque to the winner, the presumed No. 1 team in the land.

The Longhorns won in a 15–14 thriller that included a dramatic 2-point conversion by Texas in the fourth quarter. On national television in the Texas locker room, Nixon handed the plaque to Longhorns coach Darrell Royal, no doubt winning over many voters in the Lone Star State.

Because the polls had yet to be conducted, though, Nixon's actions seemed premature—and, in the eyes of residents of Happy Valley, very biased. Paterno insisted that nothing should be determined until after the bowl games.

(When Nixon later decided to give Paterno a plaque for the nation's longest unbeaten streak, an incensed JoePa declared, "Who needs it?")

Penn State guard/linebacker Charlie Zapiec and others understood that the knock against the Lions was about the perceived level of their competition. "We heard it especially in 1969 from papers and people in Texas," Zapiec said. "To them, a Boston College was nothing. Neither was a team like West Virginia."

This assessment made no sense to Paterno, who knew Texas and Arkansas were playing the likes of Baylor, SMU, and other weaklings from their region.

"We suffer in comparison to the rest of the country," Paterno said. "We don't have the glamour of a conference like the Big Eight, the Big Ten, the Southeastern, or the Southwest."

As an independent, Penn State belonged to the Eastern College Athletic Conference, which, according to Paterno, represented some colleges with different interests and goals in football.

From 1969 to 1971, Lydell Mitchell was a potent force in the Penn State backfield, especially in combination with fellow backs Charlie Pittman in 1969 and Franco Harris for all three seasons. *College Football Hall of Fame*

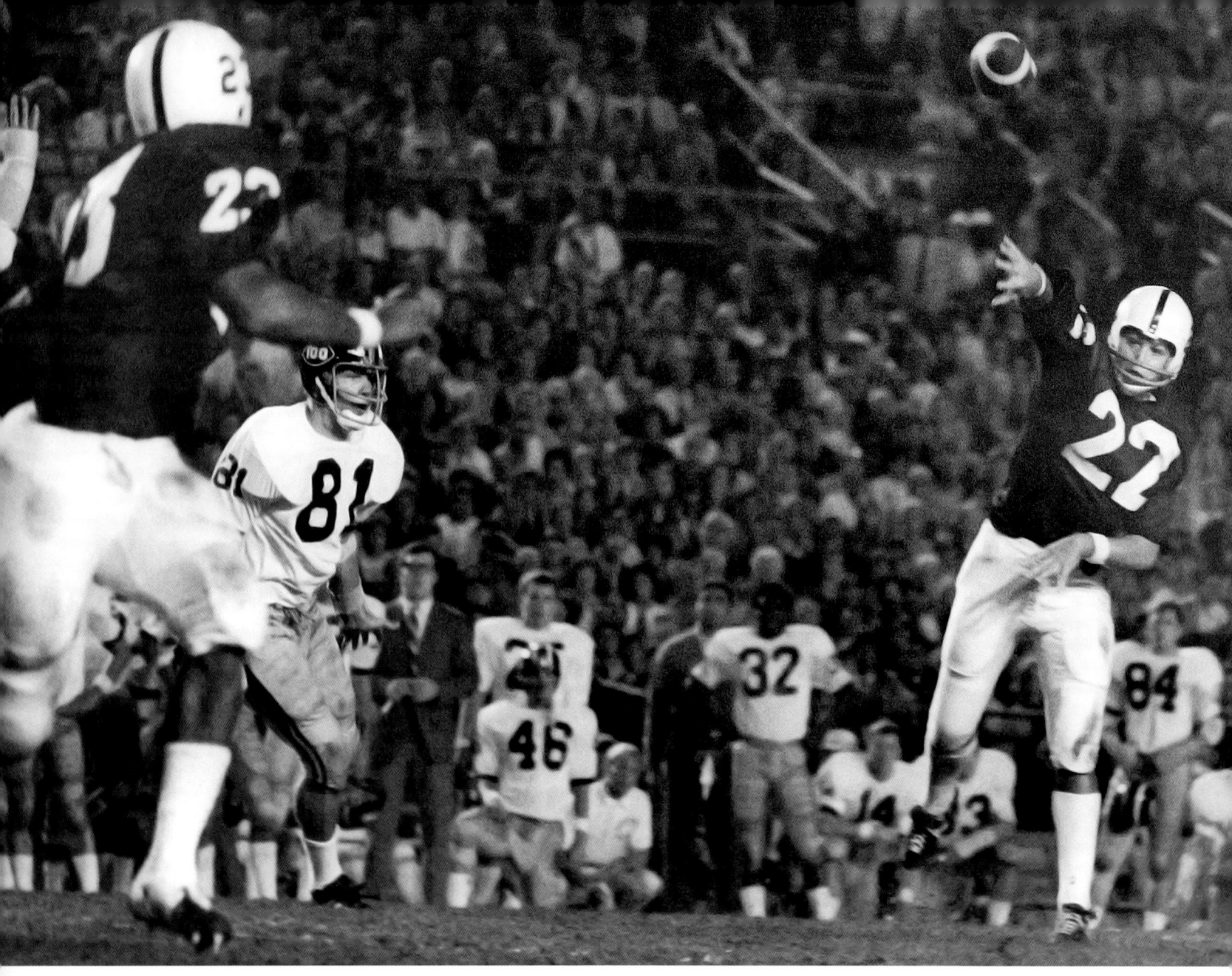

This first-quarter touchdown pass from quarterback Chuck Burkhart (No. 22) to Lydell Mitchell (No. 23) proved to be the game winner in the Orange Bowl on January 1, 1970. The Lions defeated Missouri 10–3. *AP Images*

"We have a commissioner and a public relations man, but they don't spend their time building up the image of eastern football and selling it to our own eastern sportswriters and sportscasters and the rest of the country.

"Our independents play intersectional schedules, and we beat teams from other sections of the country regularly. But we rarely get credit for our accomplishments."

All that Penn State could do was go down to Miami and whip sixth-ranked Missouri in the Orange Bowl. If Texas were to lose in its Cotton Bowl matchup with Notre Dame, then there could be no argument over who deserved the national title: undefeated Penn State.

And if Texas won? Well, the Longhorns did have that presidential decree already.

Paterno and his staff didn't need to look for inspiration heading into the Orange Bowl. If Nixon hadn't provided it, the previous season's disappointment of being overlooked for Ohio State did, as did the comeback win over Kansas a year earlier in Miami.

Pennsylvania governor Raymond Shafer gave the Lions a pregame pep talk in the locker room.

"I don't want you to prove anything to anybody," Shafer said. "You don't have to prove you are number one in the newspapers, to the fans, or even to the president. Just go out and win this game for yourselves."

Which the Lions did by shutting down a strong Missouri offense. Penn State's defense so impressed Tigers coach Dan Devine that he called it "the best I've seen in 20 years in college football." Burkhart hit Mitchell for the only touchdown, a 28-yard pass, and the Lions won 10–3. A very convincing 10–3.

"I can't see how anybody in the country can be any better than Penn State," Devine said. "I might vote a tie [with Texas]. I certainly wouldn't vote Penn State number two."

But that's exactly where the Lions landed after Texas beat Notre Dame 21–17 in the Cotton Bowl. A second straight close call infuriated Paterno, who already had begun a crusade for a playoff—a fruitless crusade that has lasted four decades and counting.

Paterno rarely talked about the polls in those days, but he couldn't hold his tongue when President Nixon stuck his nose in. "The only thing I got upset with was when the president of the United States got involved and went down to the Arkansas-Texas game in order to try to get some sentiment for him in a region that was predominantly Democrat at the time."

Before the Orange Bowl game on January 1, Paterno had talked to his own players about the situation.

"I put an awful lot of pressure on these kids by talking about their right to be rated number one," he said. "I still think we have as much right to be number one as Texas or anybody else.

"We beat a very good team in Missouri. We haven't been beaten in 30 games. We play the games and win."

Paterno insisted it wasn't sour grapes.

"But why should I sit back and let the president of the United States say so-and-so is number one when I've got 50 kids who've worked their tails off for me for three years? If I didn't argue for my team, I'd be a lousy coach."

Forty years later, nobody's calling Paterno a lousy coach—even if fans, coaches, and players alike are still clamoring for a playoff system to determine the national champions, a campaign for which Paterno has been at the forefront.

In December 1985, 15 years after the controversy surrounding Texas and President Nixon, Paterno

Florida's heat and humidity took its toll on the Penn State players during the 1970 Orange Bowl, but they were able to fight through it to secure the second straight postseason win for Paterno's Lions. *Penn State University Archives, Pennsylvania State University Libraries*

Pennsylvania governor Raymond Shafer gets a traditional victory shower from the players after Penn State defeated Missouri in the 1970 Orange Bowl. *Penn State University Archives, Pennsylvania State University Libraries*

stated, "We ought to be doing in our sport what we do in every other sport under NCAA auspices. The 1,500-meter swimming championship is decided head to head. Wrestling, lacrosse, soccer, volleyball, gymnastics—you wouldn't have people looking at gymnasts in different parts of the country and then voting on who's the best."

A HEISMAN WINNER IN HAPPY VALLEY

CHAPTER 7

In 1973, John Cappelletti brought Penn State the first Heisman Trophy in the school's illustrious history, following a second consecutive 1,000-yard season for the running back. Here Cappelletti shakes off Maryland defenders to score a touchdown during the Nittany Lions' 46–16 win in November 1972. *Paul Vathis/AP Images*

Despite falling short on two straight national championships, Happy Valley wasn't exactly a sad place in 1970. The Nittany Lions carried that incredible 30-game undefeated streak into the season, and although graduation had done some damage to the roster, Paterno had talent everywhere.

So it came as a bit of a surprise when the team lost three of its first five contests, including a 41–13 pasting at Colorado in week two that snapped a 31-game unbeaten streak. Something was missing.

"Our defense wasn't as strong," linebacker Jack Ham said, "and we had some guys who were starters for the first time. We were good, but not great."

Texas coach Darrell Royal (left) and Joe Paterno address the media at a news conference prior to the 1972 Cotton Bowl. The Penn State coach had a lot more to smile about after a 30–6 win over the Longhorns. *Penn State University Archives, Pennsylvania State University Libraries*

They got better as the season wore on, winning their final five games, including a 35–15 rout of Pitt, to wind up 7–3.

More importantly, the Lions' future was secured on offense when Paterno turned to John Hufnagel to replace Mike Cooper at quarterback. Hufnagel joined a backfield tandem of Lydell Mitchell and Franco Harris that few schools could match—in all of college football history.

For much of 1971, Mitchell was unstoppable, setting three NCAA marks (29 touchdowns, 26 rushing touchdowns, 174 points) and gaining 1,567 yards on the ground. While Harris was considered a fullback and was a steady blocker for Mitchell, he also was a versatile player. Paterno considered the two interchangeable, used them that way, and they paced Penn State's record-setting attack that scored 481 points.

Except for a 31–11 loss at No. 11 Tennessee, the defense—which included a youngster named John Cappelletti—was formidable. Charlie Zapiec was an All-American at linebacker.

Revenge of a sort from the previous season's affront came on January 1, 1972, when Penn State was matched up against Texas in the Cotton Bowl. Texas couldn't deal with the dual threats of Mitchell and Harris, or the precise passing of Hufnagel. The Nittany Lions routed the Longhorns 30–6 and finished the season ranked fifth.

"That was important for us to show people what we'd done in the previous few years was not a fluke," Paterno said.

Mitchell triumphantly echoed those sentiments. "We finally showed people we could play major college football."

That 1971 season was most memorable for the work of Mitchell and Harris. Paterno even went so far as to compare Mitchell favorably with Lenny Moore, previously the greatest of all Nittany Lions runners.

"I can't believe there is a better all-around back in the country than Lydell," Paterno said. "He runs well, he catches excellently, he blocks. He's a leader."

The coach even called Mitchell the best short-yardage runner in Penn State history, which is ironic because Harris went on to such acclaim in the pros and Mitchell did not. "He's a fierce competitor," said Paterno, "and I mean fierce."

The versatility of backs was another huge asset for JoePa. "Harris was quick enough and had all the

Lydell Mitchell powers for yardage against Texas in the 1972 Cotton Bowl. In his final game as a Nittany Lion, Mitchell rushed for 146 yards and scored a touchdown in the 30–6 win. He was named the offensive MVP of the game. *Penn State University Archives, Pennsylvania State University Libraries*

Fullback Franco Harris (No. 34) teamed with halfback Lydell Mitchell in a formidable backfield tandem in the early 1970s. On three occasions, they each gained 100 yards rushing in the same game. *Penn State University Archives, Pennsylvania State University Libraries*

Joe Paterno and his players whoop it up after the 30–6 victory over Texas in the Cotton Bowl on New Year's Day, 1972. *Penn State University Archives, Pennsylvania State University Libraries*

moves to be a halfback. Mitchell was strong and had the straight-ahead power to be a fullback. You could do so much with them because there was nothing they couldn't do."

By 1973, Harris and Mitchell were in the NFL, but their achievements in Happy Valley were about to be overshadowed by John Cappelletti. With Harris and Mitchell out of the way, Cappelletti could reassume his previous role in the offensive backfield, where he settled in nicely at tailback—and as a star.

There were many significant contributors to yet another perfect season in 1973: tackle Randy Crowder, end Mike Hartenstine, and linebacker Ed O'Neil on defense; blockers Mark Markovich, Charlie Getty, and John Nessel, tight end Dan Natale, and quarterback Tom Shuman on offense.

But this was Cappelletti's club.

Paterno certainly recognized that.

"People keep saying how great Franco Harris is," the coach said, "and Franco is a fine player. But John is faster than Franco and every bit as powerful. If I needed a running back in the pros, John would be my number-one pick. He's got to be the best running back in the country. He's the guy who, when we need to win a game, goes out and wins it."

Paterno sounded in 1973 like he was electioneering for Cappelletti to win the Heisman Trophy, a prize that had eluded Penn State over the years. Cappelletti had rushed for 1,117 yards in his junior year in 1972, but if there was any Heisman buzz going into his senior year, Cappelletti didn't hear it.

Heading into the season, there were more expectations about the team. Penn State had been the fifth-ranked team in 1972, posting a record of 10–2 that included a disappointing 14–0 loss to Oklahoma in the Sugar Bowl.

Quarterback John Hufnagel, posing with his coach, was one of the most efficient passers in Penn State history. As an All-American in 1972, he set school records (since broken) with 2,039 yards passing and 15 touchdown passes. *Penn State University Archives, Pennsylvania State University Libraries*

"We had a strong offensive line, and we had a good junior quarterback [Tom Shuman]," Cappelletti said of the preseason expectations for 1973. "I don't think there were expectations for me as an individual."

Although it is even more so today, back in the early 1970s, the Heisman Trophy was largely a popularity contest, with universities staging huge publicity campaigns to show off their award contenders. That simply was not the Penn State style.

"Being from Penn State, that doesn't put you in the limelight all that much," Cappelletti said. "Back then, Penn State was more of a team concept; you didn't send out press releases on individuals and that kind of stuff."

But Cappelletti had all the ingredients to win any award. He simply had to dominate on the field.

Cappelletti himself carried some doubts into 1973, doubts anchored in having to switch from offense to defense and back again.

"I thought I didn't have it," he recalled. "When I gained some yards against Iowa [in a 27–8 win that boosted the Lions to 3–0], I fumbled a couple of times. I was more concerned about hurting the team than helping it. I was confused about my own ability. I questioned if I could get the job done."

The questions were answered the next week in a 19–9 win over Air Force, when he ran for 188 yards with no miscues.

From there, Cappelletti made 100-yard rushing games a habit. In the second half of the season, he picked up steam with consecutive 200-yard rushing games against Maryland, North Carolina State, and Ohio University. Most memorable was the North Carolina State game, during which Cappelletti carried the ball a Penn State record 41 times and scored three touchdowns. The Lions needed every one of them in a 35–29 victory.

"That was probably the best regular-season, if not the best overall, game that I played in up there," Cappelletti remembered. "It was one of those games when it was 7–0, 7–7, 14–7—you know, back and forth all day until the last score of the game. They had a really strong team that year. They came up just looking to knock us off."

After Cappelletti led Penn State back from a 13–3 halftime deficit to defeat Pitt by a 35–13 score, the Heisman was just about clinched for the Penn State running back. In that game, Cappelletti rushed for 161 yards, more than doubling the yardage total of Pitt's freshman star, Tony Dorsett, as the Lions moved to 11–0.

"He showed his value to this football team," Paterno said of Cappelletti, following the contest.

The coach continued to beat the drums for Cappelletti in the Heisman race, comparing him to other hopefuls, such as Ohio State offensive tackle John Hicks.

"John Hicks could not have won this football game for us. Cappelletti did."

Obviously, the Heisman voters agreed. Cappelletti received 229 first-place votes and 1,057 total points. Hicks was runner-up with 114 first-place votes and 524 points overall.

Cappelletti and crew hardly were done after he became the first Nittany Lion to capture the Heisman Trophy. They had, after all, an unbeaten record to preserve in the Orange Bowl against No. 13 Louisiana State.

Unfortunately, even with a victory, the Lions had no shot at the national crown; they were ranked sixth heading to the bowl game.

By now, JoePa was accustomed to such slights. All he could do was point his players toward Miami and encourage them to finish off Penn State's third perfect season in six years.

Those players were certain they would finish 12–0.

"When there was a tight game, there was calm, there was resolve," said offensive lineman Markovich. "You just knew somehow, some way, you were going to find a way to win."

They knew it even after LSU marched downfield and scored just 3:47 into the Orange Bowl game. Chris Bahr kicked a 44-yard field goal, and after the officials nullified Gary Hayman's 73-yard punt return—Hayman was ruled to have touched his knee to the turf—Shuman connected with Chuck Herd for a 72-yard pass play.

Cappelletti was the focal point of an LSU defense that at times had nine men at the line of scrimmage. The Tigers succeeded in limiting Cappelletti to just 50 yards on 26 carries, although he did score a 1-yard touchdown in the 16–9 victory.

The Lions finished fifth in the polls, but they were No. 1 in their own hearts. Paterno issued his players "championship" rings with the inscription, "No. 1."

"Penn State didn't get a whole lot of respect, and there were some other good teams," Markovich noted. "But I don't remember anyone whining about it. It was the kind of group that it was more important for Coach Paterno to tell us that we were number one than it was for people that didn't know us to tell us."

Tom Shuman (No. 12) runs the ball against Syracuse—a team that Penn State defeated in all three meetings during Shuman's tenure as quarterback (1972–1974), including a 49–6 thrashing in October 1973, midway through the Lions' undefeated season. *Penn State University Archives, Pennsylvania State University Libraries*

John Cappelletti leaps over the LSU defense for a touchdown during the second quarter of the 1974 Orange Bowl. Although the Heisman winner was held to only 50 yards in the game, his TD was the difference in the 16–9 final score. *AP Images*

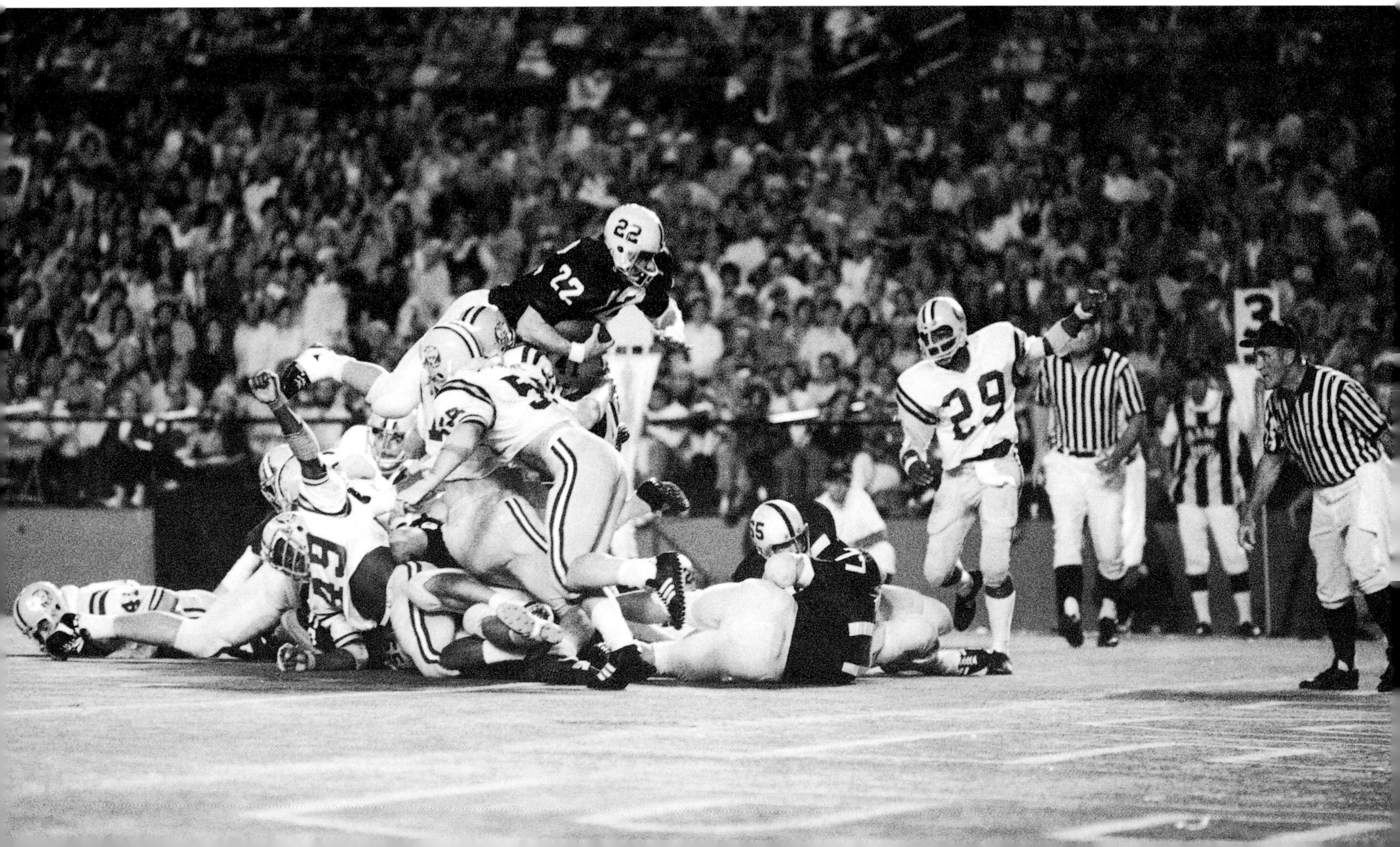

JOHN CAPPELLETTI

"It is a terrific battle out there on the field. Only for me it is on Saturdays, and it's only in the fall. For Joseph, it is all year round, and it is a battle that is unending with him, and he puts up with much more than I'll ever put up with, and I think this trophy is more his than mine because he has been a great inspiration to me."
— *John Cappelletti, accepting the 1973 Heisman Trophy at the Downtown Athletic Club in New York.*

John Cappelletti delivers an emotional speech at the Downtown Athletic Club in New York after receiving his Heisman Trophy in December 1973. Standing at the far right is Vice President Gerald Ford. *College Football Hall of Fame*

Eleven-year-old Joey Cappelletti, who was battling leukemia, wanted something special for his birthday. It wasn't going to be easy for his older brother to deliver.

It was before Penn State's game with West Virginia in 1973, and Joey asked brother John to score four touchdowns against the Mountaineers.

A tall order, even for Penn State's backfield star, but John Cappelletti said he would do his best.

Penn State had a great day against the Mountaineers. The Nittany Lions built up an insurmountable lead, and Cappelletti had scored three touchdowns.

Penn State coach Joe Paterno did not want to run up the score. Out came John Cappelletti.

Sitting on the bench, John was shy by one touchdown for his brother, and it didn't look like he was going to have the chance to score number four.

Teammate Ed O'Neil came to the rescue. A close friend of Cappelletti's, O'Neil knew about the birthday request. He walked over to Paterno, and they had a whispered conference.

Cappelletti was sent out onto the field again. He wasted little time in scoring his fourth TD of the day, as the Lions beat West Virginia 62–14.

Mission accomplished. But there was more to come.

A couple of weeks later, before the Ohio University game, Joey Cappelletti again asked John to score four touchdowns for him.

Cappelletti did just that in a 49–10 Penn State romp. That four-TD day near the end of the season gave Cappelletti a big push for the Heisman Trophy, which he eventually won.

In 1973, Cappelletti wasn't the entire Penn State offense—it only seemed that way. He carried the ball 286 times for 1,522 yards. He scored 17 touchdowns despite missing the Syracuse game with a shoulder separation.

"Cappelletti was fun to watch," said kicker Chris Bahr. "I mean, he seemed to do what he wanted to. It was a very talented team around him, too. It didn't have to be all him, but a lot of times it was."

Cappelletti was supported by a strong offensive line. Several of the linemen were drafted by NFL teams, including Mark Markovich, an ever-present guard that Cappelletti enjoyed following for large gains.

"I'm so used to following Mark around end," Cappelletti said at the time, "that I'm in the habit of following him around campus."

Cappelletti not only won the 39th Heisman Trophy award, he won it with authority—more than doubling the point total of Ohio State lineman John Hicks in the nationwide voting by sportswriters and broadcasters. Paterno added his voice to the landslide vote, endorsing Cappelletti as "unequivocally the best player I've ever been around."

Before Cappelletti brought Penn State its first Heisman Trophy, quarterback Richie Lucas had come closest. He finished second behind LSU halfback Billy Cannon in 1959.

Playing for Penn State was an easy choice for Cappelletti, a star high school running back and quarterback from Upper Darby, Pennsylvania. Paterno sealed the deal by making a visit to the Cappelletti household for Sunday afternoon dinner.

"It was mostly practical reasons," Cappelletti said of his decision to go to Penn State. "Penn State is a football school, and somewhere academically, you really felt like you were going to get an education under Paterno. And all things being equal, being instate and being closer for my parents was certainly a good reason."

John would also be able to see his younger brother on a regular basis. They had formed a special bond, particularly after Joey was diagnosed with leukemia. Joey was John's biggest fan and now would be able to see his brother play on Saturday afternoons at State College when he wasn't undergoing treatment for his illness.

It was a while, though, before Joey Cappelletti saw his brother turn into a star.

Early in his career with the Nittany Lions, Cappelletti played on defense and special teams. With Lydell Mitchell and Franco Harris starting at the running back positions, there was little room for Cappelletti.

John Cappelletti was a tough man for defenses to bring down during his years at Penn State. He was the driving force behind an offense that averaged 40.6 points in 1973. *Penn State/Collegiate Images/Getty Images*

Joey's steady devotion to his older brother, and to Penn State football, motivated John Cappelletti to greater heights. He made that clear in his Heisman acceptance speech on December 13, 1973, a couple of weeks before Penn State wrapped up its 12–0 season with a 16–9 victory over LSU in the Orange Bowl.

Speaking before an audience that included Vice President Gerald Ford, Cappelletti offered highly personal revelations describing how he was guided by a "great father" (John Sr.) and "a very, very strong" mother (Anne) who helped him through the trying times of youth.

"One time, I couldn't walk without tripping," Cappelletti said. "My legs are straight as arrows, and I have no trouble walking now, or running. My mother not only brought me through this, but she brought just about every member of our family through something like this."

Among those who also helped shape Cappelletti were his high school football coach, Jack Gottshalk, and Joe Paterno. Cappelletti remembered when Paterno came to recruit him. When he walked into the Cappelletti house, the Penn State coach saw Joey lying on a couch.

"He was very ill at the time," Cappelletti recalled of his younger brother, "more so than usual. No joke, Paterno was more concerned and talked more about what he could do for my brother than what he could do to get me at Penn State."

A proud JoePa poses with Cappelletti after the running back won the 1973 Heisman Trophy, the first (and to date only) Nittany Lion to win the award. *Penn State University Archives, Pennsylvania State University Libraries*

As a freshman, Cappelletti played three games, "a little bit on both sides of the ball." As a sophomore, he was all over the field—defensive back, special teams, and holding for kicks.

In the spring of his sophomore year, after football season, the 6-foot-1, 220-pound Cappelletti started to make the conversion to running back. Mitchell and Harris were graduating. All of a sudden, the junior wearing No. 22 was a starting running back for Penn State.

It took a while for Cappelletti to get on track. He found it wasn't easy making the transition from defense back to offense.

"I didn't think I had the mental toughness a running back needs to excel," Cappelletti said.

Nevertheless, he had a strong junior season, netting 1,117 yards rushing as the Nittany Lions piled up a solid 10–2 record.

With just about the entire roster coming back, there was reason to be optimistic about the team's chances in 1973.

"There wasn't any reason why we shouldn't do something here," Cappelletti said.

The Nittany Lions did, winning all their games, with Cappelletti as the headline attraction. Highlighting the season were those two four-touchdown games for his brother.

While John Cappelletti was battling for yardage on football fields, Joey Cappelletti was battling for his life. His condition had necessitated spinal taps and chemotherapy, resulting in nausea and headaches, and usually leaving him in a weakened condition. Very often, he was confined to a bed—except on Saturdays in the fall. Somehow, Joey Cappelletti found enough strength to go up to Penn State for football weekends to watch brother John play, and to chat it up with the other players in the Penn State locker room. They had become his buddies.

The trips to Penn State came at a cost for Joey, though. When he came home, he sometimes needed recovery time in a hospital.

Cappelletti's Heisman Trophy and All-American honors earned him celebrity status in 1973. He appeared on Bob Hope's television special shortly after being named the Heisman winner.
John Lent/AP Images

Finally, after citing his brothers and sisters, teammates and other coaches, Cappelletti focused on younger brother Joey, who was sitting in the audience near his parents. With tears streaming down his face and a voice ringing with emotion, Cappelletti announced that he was dedicating the trophy to his sick brother.

"He has leukemia. If I can dedicate this trophy to him tonight and give him a couple of days of happiness, this is everything."

Sobs erupted in the audience as Cappelletti's emotional words gripped those in attendance at the Downtown Athletic Club—and an entire nation.

Up until the day he died, two years later at the age of 13, Joey Cappelletti was the proud owner of the 25-pound Heisman statue. He had lovingly placed it on a shelf alongside a Little League trophy in his home.

The story continued to echo in America's consciousness. Four years after the Heisman ceremonies, the bond between John and Joey Cappelletti was told in a TV movie and young adult book, *Something for Joey*. Students who read the book and people who saw the movie related in letters to Cappelletti how the story had touched their lives and made their own family relations better.

By that time, Cappelletti had gone on to a career in pro football. He and his wife, Betty, started to raise a family, and they named one of their four sons Joey.

John worked with leukemia-related charities such as Ronald McDonald House and continued to be a source of inspiration for many families around the country. Cappelletti, who went into private business following a 10-year NFL career with the Los Angeles Rams and San Diego Chargers, was thrilled that he touched so many lives.

"Having made some small contribution to someone's life," Cappelletti said, "is a lot more meaningful than scoring some touchdowns."

But he would never forget the four he scored against West Virginia as a special birthday present for his younger brother.

RUNNING AT THE NATIONAL CHAMPIONSHIP

After such a momentous season—a third perfect record under Paterno and the school's first Heisman winner—the Nittany Lions refused to rest on their laurels.

Despite losing Cappelletti and so many of his helpers, Penn State couldn't feel sorry for itself. Not with Hartenstine, Natale, and Shuman still on hand, and another strong recruiting class settling in at State College.

But the Nittany Lions were, in Paterno's words, "not quite there." This was evidenced by sloppy losses to Navy in the season's second game and to North Carolina State early in November, as well as a series of close encounters against Stanford, Army, West Virginia, and Maryland.

Still, a 10–2 record that included a 31–10 romp past Pitt and a 41–20 victory over Baylor in the Cotton Bowl made for a nice season.

Shuman nearly ruined it, though, during the bowl game. The quarterback, annoyed that a 64-yard touchdown pass to Tom Donchez was negated by an offensive interference call, picked up the flag and threw it across the field.

A furious Paterno immediately ordered Shuman to apologize to the referee.

By the fourth quarter, tempers had been calmed and the Lions were rolling, scoring 24 points in the final period.

Not a bad way to go into the next season.

But 1975 would be a strange campaign. The defense, led by frenetic linebacker Greg Buttle and sidekick Kurt Allerman, would have nine games in which it yielded 14 points or less. An offense sparked by guard Tom Rafferty and place kicker Chris Bahr was efficient, though hardly spectacular.

Close calls against the likes of Temple (26–25 in the season opener), Kentucky (10–3), and Maryland (15–13) displayed that something was lacking in the 1975 squad. The Lions finished 9–3, including a fortunate 7–6 victory over Pitt in the finale and a 13–6 loss to Alabama in the Sugar Bowl.

That win at Pitt was pretty much handed to the Lions because Panthers kicker Carson Long missed an extra point and three field goals. Long deserved some sympathy, though, because perhaps he had other things on his mind: his wife had given birth that morning.

In 1975, Paterno did something else that would become a staple of his program: he ratcheted up the schedule. A three-game series with Ohio State began with a 17–9 loss at Columbus. Paterno was also

Another bowl game, another postseason victory for JoePa. Paterno and the Lions celebrate after defeating Baylor, 41–20, on January 1, 1975, to complete a 10–2 season. *AP Images*

Above: Quarterback Chuck Fusina posted a 29–3 career record as a starter for Penn State from 1976 to 1978. Here Fusina (No. 14) delivers a touchdown pass to tight end Mickey Shuler during a 21–7 victory over Miami in 1976—one of eleven 200-yard passing games for Fusina in his college career. *Penn State University Archives, Pennsylvania State University Libraries*

Right: Although defensive tackles Randy Sidler (No. 75) and Tony Petruccio (No. 99) were able to bring down Pitt quarterback Matt Cavanaugh on this play, the top-ranked Panthers bested the No. 16 Lions, 24–7, in the 1976 season finale. *AP Images*

looking for other major programs to engage on the field, and he lined up schools from the power conferences or other strong independents. In the ensuing years, the likes of Stanford, Miami of Florida, Houston, Texas A&M, Nebraska, Missouri, Alabama, and Notre Dame would be scheduled.

Paterno had his worst season in a decade as the Nittany Lions went 7–5 in 1976. Penn State's biggest rival, Pitt, won the national championship, led by that western Pennsylvania superstar, Tony Dorsett. Suddenly, the Lions' supremacy in the region was facing a mighty challenger.

The next few years would be critical for JoePa and his program. Not surprisingly, the Nittany Lions responded with not one, but two superb seasons.

Paterno and his assistants aggressively attacked the recruiting trails in the mid-1970s, partly because of how well coach Johnny Majors was faring at Pitt, and greatly because college football itself was evolving. Already having proven his willingness to break racial barriers, Paterno now had to adjust to the more wide-open style of offense permeating the game.

Never a trend-follower—he pretty much ignored the wishbone when it was in vogue—Paterno recognized the absolute need to update his offense. A dedicated proponent of the more classic brand of football featuring strong running games and staunch defenses, Paterno saw that the modern offensive player of the mid-1970s preferred other, more fast-paced modes of attack. If Penn State couldn't offer it, those recruits would wind up elsewhere—including at Pitt, Syracuse, West Virginia, and other top schools in the East.

So Paterno adjusted.

He visited Southern Cal, Cal-Berkeley, and even the Oakland Raiders, and then incorporated what he observed and learned into the Penn State offense.

"We may not be able to move the ball from here to there," he said, displaying a tiny space, "but nobody is going to be bored."

Paterno willingly diversified in large part because of Chuck Fusina. The quarterback from McKees Rocks, Pennsylvania, had the arm, the mobility, the intelligence, and the moxie to handle a more complex, pass-oriented offense. The coach knew it almost from the first day Fusina came to Happy Valley. Paterno proclaimed that Fusina had "the most potential of any of our quarterbacks ever."

THE SUHEYS

At Penn State, one family can claim the title of longest running tradition in football.

No, it's not the Paternos. While Joe Paterno has been coaching at Penn State since 1950, there's another family that predates him at State College by some 35 years.

Meet the Suheys, the original "First Family" of Penn State football—four generations, and counting. When Kevin Suhey joined the Penn State quarterbacking corps in 2006, he became the fourth generation of the Suhey family in the history of Nittany Lions football. In 2007, Joe Suhey followed cousin Kevin into the Penn State fold as a running back, the same position his father, Matt, played at State College in the 1970s.

The Suhey family lineage actually begins with Bob Higgins, who played for Penn State during the World War I era (1914–1917, 1919) and went on to be the Lions' head coach from 1930 to 1948. One of the key players on Higgins' great teams of the 1940s was All-American guard Steve Suhey.

Suhey was a leader on Higgins' legendary 1947 squad, which went 9–0–1 and established itself as one of the great defensive teams in school history. When teammates remember Suhey, what first comes to mind are the size and strength of his hands—and his stoicism.

By 1947, Steve Suhey was not only one of the most popular players on the Penn State roster, but he was also quite popular in the Higgins household. In the early 1940s, he had lived in Higgins' home as a boarder and developed a relationship with Ginger Higgins, one the coach's three daughters. When Suhey went away to serve during World War II, he corresponded with Ginger. The couple married soon after he came back.

Steve and Ginger Suhey went on to have three children: Paul, Matt, and Larry, all of whom played for the Nittany Lions in the 1970s. The three Suhey brothers were immersed in Penn State football for as far back as they could remember. As kids growing up in State College, they would mimic what was going on with the football team.

"We were always rolling around in the grass and playing with a football," Paul Suhey recalled.

When they were old enough, they would go to games and sell programs.

Steve Suhey didn't put any pressure on his sons to follow in his footsteps and play football. They just did what came naturally.

The Suhey boys all sparkled on the State College High School football team. Larry graduated first and signed on at Penn State, although a knee injury limited his playing time.

Paul was next, joining an illustrious group of linebackers at Penn State.

Finally, the youngest, Matt, made it three-for-three when he joined the team as a running back in 1976.

"It was nice," Paul remembered. "I could help Matt, and Larry could help me. We knew a lot of the other guys, so it was an easy transition."

And Kevin and Joe continued the family tradition.

THE BAHRS

When it came to kicking records for Penn State's football team in the 1970s, the Bahrs kept it all in the family.

First, Chris Bahr, who played for the Nittany Lions from 1973 to 1975, set an NCAA record for field goal accuracy. Then along came Matt a couple of years later, setting some records of his own in 1978.

Turns out, they were just getting warmed up. The two brothers were on their way to bright pro careers, each winning two Super Bowls.

And football wasn't even their favorite sport.

"I had said from the beginning if they made me choose a sport, I was going to play soccer," Chris Bahr said of his college days at Penn State.

Fortunately for Penn State football, nobody made either of the brothers choose. Chris and Matt played both football and soccer for the Nittany Lions.

They weren't the only family members on the soccer squad.

Casey Bahr teamed with his brothers on a Penn State soccer team coached by their father. All three brothers went on to play professional soccer, just like their dad, Walter.

The men in the family weren't the only ones with athletic talent. Walter Bahr's wife, Davies, was a champion swimmer, and his daughter, also named Davies, was a top-flight gymnast.

For Chris and Matt, it all started at the Lighthouse Boys Club in Philadelphia, as it did for their father. The Boys Club offered a variety of sports for local kids, but it was mostly known for its soccer program. Walter used the Boys Club as a launching pad to soccer prominence.

The senior Bahr was an all-star in the old All-American Soccer League and helped his team, the Philadelphia Nationals, win four titles. He is also remembered for his play in the 1950 World Cup, helping the United States score a goal to pull off a huge 1–0 upset of England.

Fast-forward to the next generation. The three Bahr brothers always had some kind of a game going, whether at the Lighthouse Boys Club or elsewhere.

"We played more games in the street than you can imagine," Chris said.

Chris' talent was unmistakable, and he was soon invited to join the high school soccer team. He also wound up kicking for the football team.

When Penn State assured him that he could play both soccer and football, he was on his way to State College.

Chris Bahr, No. 99 on your scorecard, was known for booming kicks. Indeed, Chris rarely did anything in a small way. His legs strengthened by all those years playing soccer, he made 50-yarders his specialty. In 1975, he kicked a record three 55-yarders. Through 2008, Chris still was tops at Penn State in making 50-yarders (6 of 15 for 40 percent).

Chris' younger brother Matt raised kicking accuracy to a new level at Penn State. In 1978, he became the first Nittany Lions kicker to boast a perfect extra-point record (31 of 31). He also set a single-season record for field goals, with 22 (tied by Kevin Kelly in 2006). Matt also set a school record with four field goals in a half, against SMU.

Typical of Matt was his performance against Pitt in 1977. He kicked field goals of 34, 31, and 20 yards in icy weather to lead Penn State to a 15–13 victory. Bahr said it was his most memorable game, because of the treacherous conditions.

Their college careers were a sign of things to come.

Chris played on two Super Bowl winners with the Raiders in a 14-year NFL career. Among his most memorable kicks was a 46-yard field goal in Super Bowl XV against Philadelphia.

In 18 NFL seasons, Matt only missed 10 extra points in 482 attempts and connected on a remarkable 73 percent of his field goal tries. He won Super Bowl rings with Pittsburgh and the New York Giants.

Here, the accurate Matt Bahr boots one for the Lions, following in the footsteps of brother Chris. *Penn State University Archives, Pennsylvania State University Libraries*

Quarterback Chuck Fusina (No. 14) and tackle Keith Dorney (No. 71) helped lead the Nittany Lions to back-to-back 11–1 seasons in 1977 and 1978. Dorney, a two-time first-team All-American, earned a spot in the College Football Hall of Fame for his superior blocking skills. *College Football Hall of Fame*

Fusina didn't disappoint.

Few players JoePa ever coached had a better work ethic or grasp of offensive football. By the time Fusina had taken over behind center, the Penn State playbook featured as many as 60 plays from more than a dozen sets. Fusina was called upon to do as much studying for football as for any of his classes.

"I took a projector home and ran game films over and over," he said. "I'd sit there in the dark and watch myself throwing interceptions, and I'd see what I should have been doing instead, and I'd call myself a dummy."

Not that Fusina erred very often in 1977 and 1978. And not that he didn't have lots of help, from tight end Mickey Shuler to receiver/running back Jimmy Cefalo to tackle Keith Dorney to place kicker Matt Bahr. A good, if not great, defense was led by tackles Bruce Clark and Matt Millen, linebacker Paul Suhey, middle guard Randy Sidler, and safety Pete Harris.

Coming off that 7–5 record in 1976, the Lions players carried an extra spur in their egos.

"After we had spring practice," recalled safety Tony Gordon, "we had a meeting before we left to go home. We said that everybody thinks we're going to be terrible, but we're going to work hard, and we're going to win."

And they didn't waste any time backing up those words. The Nittany Lions opened the 1977 season against Rutgers at the newly built Giants Stadium in New Jersey (where Rutgers played some home games) and annihilated the Scarlet Knights, 45–7.

A more worthy test came in the home opener the following week against ninth-ranked Houston; Penn State was ranked 10th at the time. It wasn't close. The Nittany Lions established their credentials as a reborn power with a 31–14 win.

The nation had learned something about this particular Penn State squad, and it was exactly what Paterno was looking for. The Lions could score on anyone, and they could do it with an aerial game they'd never previously possessed.

Outside of a 24–20 upset loss at home to Kentucky, Fusina was stellar that year, setting all kinds of school records. Fusina threw for two touchdowns and 192 yards in a relatively short stint against what was a supposedly stingy Miami of Florida defense. Against a North Carolina State unit that ranked second in America in pass defense, he victimized the Wolfpack defense by completing 22 throws for 315 yards and leading an 83-yard drive in the final minutes for a 21–17 win.

After the flop against Kentucky, the Nittany Lions managed to run off seven straight victories, then won a 42–30 shootout with Arizona State in the Fiesta Bowl—on ASU's home field, no less.

A FAMILY AFFAIR

The Suheys and the Bahrs are not only the families to leave indelible marks on Penn State football. Many other father-son or brother combos have made their presence felt in State College.

The Paternos, of course, include not only longtime coach Joe but also Joe's son, Jay, who played quarterback under JoePa and continued on as an assistant coach under his father.

Charlie Pittman starred in the Penn State backfield in the 1960s, and his son, Tony, was an outstanding cornerback for the Nittany Lions in the 1990s.

Receiver Jim Garrity was generally recognized as Paterno's first recruit back when JoePa was an assistant under Rip Engle in the 1950s. Jim's son, Gregg, made one of the most important catches in Penn State history when he scored a touchdown in the Lions' 27–23 victory over Georgia in the 1983 Sugar Bowl. The win gave Paterno his first national championship.

Jerry Sandusky was a two-way player for Penn State from 1963 to 1965 and a longtime defensive coordinator under Paterno. His sons, E. J. and Jon, later played for Penn State in the 1980s and 1990s.

Dave Joyner, an All-American lineman at Penn State, played on some of Paterno's greatest teams from 1969 to 1971. Sons Matt and Andy followed their dad to Happy Valley.

Before launching a Hall of Fame NFL career, Franco Harris was one of Penn State's top running backs in the early 1970s. Brothers Pete and Giuseppe later stood out as interception leaders for the Lions.

Fran Ganter was a running back for Penn State in the late 1960s before settling in as the Lions' longtime offensive coordinator. Two of Fran's sons, Chris and Jason, followed him to Penn State.

In 2002, Larry Johnson became a 2,000-yard rusher in the Penn State backfield and brother Tony was a star receiver. Larry Johnson Sr. enjoyed watching his sons' successes from the sidelines as a coach.

Right: Defensive end Bruce Clark—seen here bearing down on an unsuspecting Maryland quarterback during a game in 1978—was a two-time All-American at Penn State. In 1978, he became the first junior to win the Lombardi Award as the nation's top defensive lineman. *George Gojkovich/Getty Images*

Penn State finished fifth in the rankings, and everyone in Happy Valley was salivating in anticipation of the 1978 campaign—and perhaps another run at a national championship.

"In 1978, we had the confidence coming out of the '77 season," Suhey said. "We knew that we had some good kids coming back."

Among the returning stars were Fusina, who by now was considered among the best quarterbacks in the country; Millen and Clark, a dominant pair at defensive tackle; Dorney, one of the best blockers Paterno ever coached; and another superb linebacker, Lance Mehl.

With such great expectations can come great failures, and the Nittany Lions nearly stumbled right out of the box. They struggled with Temple before winning 10–7, then beat a mediocre Rutgers team 26–10. Hardly the proper way to tune up for what was next: a visit to the Horseshoe to play Ohio State.

The Buckeyes, coached by legendary curmudgeon Woody Hayes, had recruited, of all things, a skilled passing quarterback in Art Schlichter. Hayes' teams were known for a 3-yards-and-a-cloud-of-dust offense. Now the Buckeyes' opponents had to respect their passing game as well.

But Hayes had kept his choice of starting QB to himself until Ohio State got the ball for the first time against Penn State, deciding between the newbie Schlichter and several upperclassmen.

Out trotted the freshman Schlichter, in the first start of his college career, to a rousing ovation. He then received a less-accommodating welcome from the Penn State defense, which posted the first shutout of the Buckeyes in an opening game at Ohio Stadium in 76 years. The 19–0 verdict wasn't that close, and it spoke—no shouted—volumes to the rest of the college football world: This was a Penn State squad to be reckoned with, on offense, defense, and special teams.

After breaking into the top five in the national polls with the Ohio State win, the Lions had another major obstacle to clear.

"We had lost to Kentucky two years in a row, so I thought that was a jinx," Suhey said. "In my senior year, we went down there to play them. I distinctly remember some of the games we lost to those guys. Usually, we played at one o'clock in those days. But we

Penn State's formidable defense in the late 1970s featured All-American tackle Matt Millen (No. 60), All-American end Bruce Clark (No. 54), and linebacker Ron Hostetler (No. 38), shown here running back an interception. *Penn State University Archives, Pennsylvania State University Libraries*

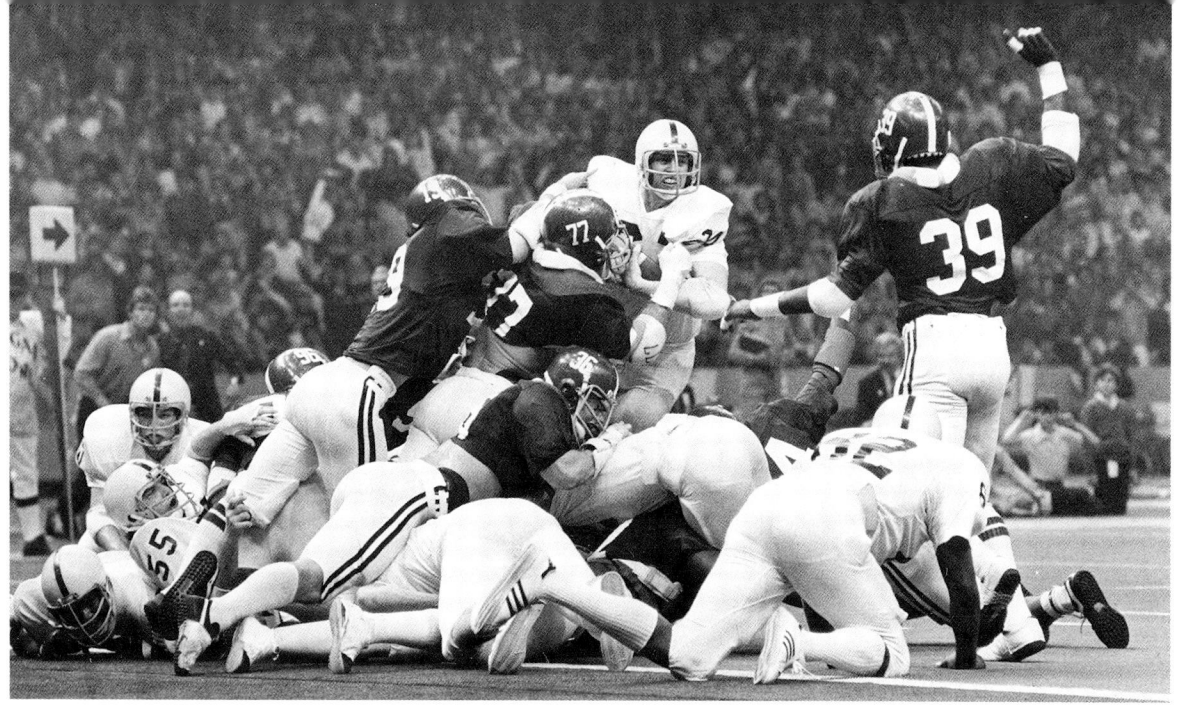

Penn State's perfect 11–0 regular season in 1978 came to a frustrating end on January 1, 1979, when Alabama's defensive line stymied Penn State with a tough goal-line stand to preserve the 14–7 victory for the Crimson Tide. *AP Images*

played a Saturday night game there and put a pretty good thumping on those guys."

What more could you say of a 30–0 wipeout?

"We were confident that we needed to show those guys that they just couldn't come up and beat us any old time."

Nor could anyone else. With Fusina on his way to All-American status—along with Dorney, Bahr, Clark, Millen, and Harris—Penn State ripped through its schedule. In a four-game span, it averaged a margin of 45.5 points to 9.

By November, the Nittany Lions were ranked second. After beating No. 5 Maryland, NC State, and Pitt, they moved up to No. 1 for the first time. Ever.

"It was a great moment for the team and the program," Fusina said, "but we also knew we had our toughest opponent coming up."

That would be Alabama and Bear Bryant, whose team was even more balanced than Penn State's. The Lions had begun to rely too much on their defense late in the year, in part because cold weather hampered some offensive schemes, but mostly because opposing defenses had become more familiar with the wealth of formations and options the Nittany Lions used.

Paterno also understood whom he was matched up against: Bear Bryant was an icon not just in Alabama or the Deep South, but throughout college football. The Bear truly had transcended his sport, something Paterno had not quite done—yet.

"We know this not only will be the most difficult team we've played, but it will be absolutely prepared to play its best game," Paterno said at a news conference leading up to the game. "That's how all of Bear Bryant's teams play."

And how would JoePa's team play?

Poorly.

With yet another shot at a national championship—one that for once would be decided on the field, because this was No. 1 versus No. 2—the Nittany Lions struggled in the Sugar Bowl matchup. Their offense was handcuffed by a quick, fierce, and versatile 'Bama defense. And while Paterno had said before the game that he believed Penn State would win if it held the Crimson Tide to 14 points, he was off in his prediction. The Tide did score 14, but the Lions got only 7.

Penn State was stymied on a late goal-line stand, particularly on a fourth and inches when fullback Mike Guman didn't even get back to the line of scrimmage before being smothered by the Tide.

Alabama went home with the Sugar Bowl trophy and Bryant's fourth of five national titles at Tuscaloosa.

"We knew we were better than them," Suhey said. "They knew we were better than them. We just lost that day. We did not play well."

Not well enough to be national champions, perhaps, but plenty well enough to show that JoePa had the Lions on the right track, the fast track. That track very soon would end at the station Penn State was seeking.

DECADE OF CHAMPIONS

CHAPTER 8

As Penn State prepared for the 1983 Sugar Bowl, it was all so familiar to Mark Battaglia.

For the second time in five years, the Nittany Lions were playing for the national championship in the Louisiana Superdome. As a freshman, Battaglia had dressed for the 1979 Sugar Bowl game and watched from the sidelines in frustration as the Nittany Lions lost 14–7 to Alabama.

"We just couldn't get it in from three yards out," Battaglia recalled of Alabama's magnificent goal-line stand in the final minutes.

So now it was four years later, and Penn State had the opportunity to redeem itself. Once again, the Nittany Lions found themselves playing for the national title, this time against top-ranked Georgia and the Bulldogs' future Hall of Fame running back, Herschel Walker.

Joe Paterno is carried off on a wave of players after winning his first national championship. The Nittany Lions defeated Georgia 27–23 in the 1983 Sugar Bowl to complete an 11–1 season. *Penn State University Archives, Pennsylvania State University Libraries*

Many of the Penn State veterans from the previous year were back, positive they could win a national championship with all that talent.

The Lions had mounted two solid 10–2 seasons in 1980 and 1981, capped by successive wins in the Fiesta Bowl over Ohio State and Southern Cal.

Against Georgia in the Sugar Bowl, it was just another game against a ranked team for Penn State that season. The Nittany Lions had faced more than their share in 1982.

"It was an unbelievable schedule," said Battaglia, an offensive lineman who helped clear the way for running star Curt Warner.

The opposition included such powerhouses as Notre Dame, Alabama, and Nebraska, which was ranked No. 2 in the country when it played No. 8 Penn State.

"That was a huge game and, I must say, one of the most exciting," Battaglia said.

For Kirk Bowman, it was his 15 minutes of fame. Bowman had been a Penn State fan all his life. His father, Wayne, was a center on the 1962 and 1963 Nittany Lions teams.

"I used to sit in the bleachers in the south end zone and watch John Cappelletti," Bowman said. "And it was just very, very special for me, running out on the field my first time as a player."

Bowman, a tight end at Mechanicsburg High School, played the same position at Penn State following experiments at other positions. His main role was usually as blocker. He didn't mind.

"I liked the physical aspect of it," he said. "It's a fun position."

Penn State's all-time leading rusher, Curt Warner, runs for a first down against Cincinnati during the Lions' 52–0 win in September 1981. It was one of 18 games in which Warner gained at least 100 yards in his four seasons at Penn State. *Paul Vathis/AP Images*

Quarterback Todd Blackledge drops back to pass against Miami in October 1981. Blackledge set a school record (since broken) with 358 yards passing in the game while completing 26 of 41 passes. Penn State lost, 17–14. *Ronald C. Modra/Sports Imagery/Getty Images*

Bowman had plenty of fun against Nebraska that day. His first pass reception of the year was a 14-yard TD strike from Todd Blackledge to give the Nittany Lions the lead at 7–0. Penn State led most of the way, before Nebraska rallied to take a 24–21 lead with 78 seconds remaining.

Blackledge started the Lions on a 65-yard drive. With nine seconds left, the ball rested on Nebraska's 2-yard line.

On what would be the last play of the game, Blackledge spotted Bowman at the back of the end zone. He fired a low pass in Bowman's direction, and the receiver plucked it off the grass tops for the winning TD.

Final: Penn State 27, Nebraska 24.

"On my first touchdown catch, there was a little bit of green between the end zones," Bowman said. "The second, I was right in the very back of the end zone. There wasn't any room left."

Fran Fisher, the Penn State broadcaster, called the second reception the best catch he had ever seen.

"It was a low pass," Bowman said, "and catching those kinds of passes is something that we used to do at practice. You actually practiced catching low balls. And it was one where I had to get both arms underneath the ball and was literally six to nine inches off the ground when it got to me."

It was one of 13 times that Todd Blackledge, the "Comeback Kid," had brought Penn State from behind.

The Nebraska thriller set the stage for a top-10 matchup against Alabama in Tuscaloosa the following week. Both undefeated, Penn State was ranked No. 3 and Alabama No. 4.

"It was so hot," Battaglia said. "I don't remember a time I was as hot as I was in that game. We had three of those big fans on our side, one of which was barely spinning. Across the way, on their sidelines, they had six huge air conditioning units, so they had a distinct advantage in climate control."

That's not all Alabama controlled.

"Alabama had a good team, and we had one of those games where we just couldn't do anything right," Battaglia said. "We couldn't control their defensive ends, we were having trouble running the ball. We blocked one of our own punts. We got killed."

Penn State hardly looked like a national-title contender that day, losing 42–21. The players quietly filed into the Penn State locker room, a depressed bunch. Then something happened to change their moods.

That something was Joel Coles. The fiery Penn State fullback stood up and challenged his teammates to rededicate themselves.

"Joel was a very passionate individual," Bowman said. "He just stood up and said, 'It's not over. We're going to win the rest of these games. And we're going to have an opportunity.' That set the tone for the rest of the season."

It was a turning point for Penn State.

"We licked our wounds and came back Monday with purpose," Battaglia said.

Victories followed over Syracuse, West Virginia, Boston College, North Carolina State, Notre Dame, and Pitt. Notre Dame and Pitt were top-10 teams.

A season was salvaged, and suddenly, Penn State was very much back in the championship picture. After six straight victories, the Lions had moved to No. 2 behind top-ranked Georgia and headed to Louisiana for a national-title clash.

That Penn State was in the title game might have been a surprise to SMU. Along with Georgia, the Mustangs were the only other unbeaten team in the country—the only blemish on their record a tie.

But who could argue with Penn State's ferocious schedule? One Penn State player did some research and found that the Nittany Lions had played one of the toughest schedules of any college team in recent memory.

Maybe it was poetic justice that Penn State was in the title game at that. After all, the Nittany Lions had posted perfect records in 1968, 1969, and 1973 but never finished higher than No. 2 in the national polls. In fact, a 12–0 record in 1973 earned the Lions no higher position than No. 5.

Paterno had been long beating the drum for a national championship playoff, but to no avail. This time, at least, his team could settle matters on the field.

Penn State's biggest challenge was Herschel Walker, Georgia's Heisman Trophy–winning halfback. The Nittany Lions had dealt successfully with a Heisman winner before, when they beat Southern Cal and Marcus Allen, 26–10, in the Fiesta Bowl the previous season.

The Nittany Lions' Curt Warner was a pretty good runner in his own right.

"He took pride in the fact that he outgained all the big names," Battaglia said of Warner. Penn State's

Senior linebacker Dave Paffenroth levels Nebraska's Mike Rozier during Penn State's thrilling 27–24 win over the second-ranked Cornhuskers on September 25, 1982. *Rusty Kennnedy/AP Images*

Herschel Walker is brought down by Steve Sefter (No. 41), with help on the way from Scott Radecic (No. 97) and John Walter (No. 86) during the 1983 Sugar Bowl. Georgia's star running back was held to less than 4 yards per carry during the Lions' 27–23 win. *Penn State University Archives, Pennsylvania State University Libraries*

Penn State's running back Curt Warner out-performed Georgia's Herschel Walker in the Sugar Bowl to help Penn State secure its first consensus national championship. *AP Images*

back had overshadowed Allen in the 1982 Fiesta Bowl, gaining 145 yards to Allen's 85 and scoring two touchdowns while the Southern Cal runner failed to cross the goal line.

Battaglia, Warner's first roommate in camp, remembered his driving ambition.

"I was a sophomore, and he was a freshman from Pineville, West Virginia. Back in those days, we stayed in these barracks. We had bunk beds, and Warner was on top and used to talk about his dreams. For a kid from a little town in West Virginia, he knew what he wanted. He talked about wanting to be the leading rusher in Penn State history. He talked about national championships. This kid had dreams and aspirations well beyond anyone that I've ever encountered."

The 1982 season was Warner's senior year. By that point, he was on his way to demolishing Penn State's career running records with a 1,041-yard season.

It was an especially remarkable accomplishment, considering the circumstances. With Blackledge playing at a high level from the start of the season, the Nittany Lions went into a heavy passing mode. The normally conservative Penn State offense had taken the shackles off and suddenly became "Air Paterno."

In the first five games of the season, Warner wasn't getting any more than 15 carries a game. In four of those games, he didn't gain more than 50 yards. He sulked and even cried and started to question his ability.

After a stern lecture from Paterno, Warner grew up in a hurry.

"I decided that if I went around feeling sorry for myself, I wouldn't help the team," Warner said.

Warner started to get more work in the second half of the season, including in the Sugar Bowl game against Georgia.

The Bulldogs were one of the country's top defensive teams, having made 35 interceptions and giving up but six touchdowns through the air.

It didn't bother Blackledge, who completed his first four passes to set up an early touchdown run by Warner.

Warner's second TD run of the game followed a 27-yard catch by Gregg Garrity and made it 20–3 Penn State late in the first half. The Bulldogs responded with a touchdown of their own in the final seconds of the half to cut Penn State's lead to 20–10.

Georgia took the opening kickoff of the second half and returned it 69 yards, and then scored on a short burst by Walker to trim Penn State's lead to just 3 points, 20–17.

Then came "Play No. 643" in the Lions' playbook.

"We ran that play a lot that year," Garrity remembered. "Basically, it was just four guys going out on pass routes. The running back and tight end, Curt Warner and Mike McCloskey, ran down the hashes. Kenny Jackson and myself just ran fly routes on the outside. He was on one side, and I was on the other.

"We were four people, all seams, and someone should be open."

Someone was—Garrity.

Blackledge unleashed a pass down the left side, and Garrity made a sensational, diving grab in the end zone to give the Lions a 27–17 lead.

Georgia came back with a late TD, but it wasn't enough. Penn State hung on to win, 27–23, to secure Paterno's first national title. The Lions had left no doubt they were the class of the country that year. And this time, there was no need for Paterno to issue his players his own version of No. 1 rings.

State College is packed beyond packed as delirious fans welcome back the national champion Nittany Lions following their win over Georgia in the 1983 Sugar Bowl. *Penn State University Archives, Pennsylvania State University Libraries*

DECADE OF CHAMPIONS   **105**

Quarterback Todd Blackledge (No. 14) and defensive tackle David Opfar (No. 67) soak up the good vibes during the Sugar Bowl Victory Parade in downtown State College in January 1983. *Penn State University Archives, Pennsylvania State University Libraries*

"Todd made a great throw, Garrity made a great catch," Paterno said. "It gave us some breathing room."

For the second straight bowl game, Warner had overshadowed a Heisman winner. The Penn State tailback, who played most of the second half with leg cramps, piled up 117 yards on only 18 carries and scored two TDs. Walker could only manage 103 yards on 28 carries.

Blackledge, meanwhile, completed 13 of 23 passes for 228 yards and gained Most Valuable Player honors.

When the game ended, Paterno was lifted onto the shoulders of his players and carried off the field. The beaming coach raised his right hand in celebration, the biggest monkey off his back. (It actually took two tries to carry him off. Paterno was dropped once, breaking his glasses. The second time, the players made it clear across with their precious cargo.)

Battaglia liked to call the 1979 and 1983 contests a "Tale of Two Sugar Bowls." As a fifth-year senior that championship season, he had seen the best of times and the worst of times of the Penn State football program—and it had been mostly good times. In his five years at State College, Penn State had posted a remarkable 50–10 record and victories in four of five bowl games.

DISAPPOINTMENT AND A RETURN TO THE TOP

Penn State's impressive run from 1979 to 1983 would be a hard act to follow for the returning players and the new class of recruits. Over the next two seasons, Penn State teams went a combined 14–9–1, including a mediocre 6–5 season in 1984, Paterno's worst since his first year as head coach in 1966.

After the Nittany Lions allowed 30 points in a win over Boston College and 44 and 31, respectively, in losses to Notre Dame and Pitt in the last three games of the 1984 season, Paterno was desperately unhappy with his team's defense. He sought help from the National Football League, picking up defensive tips from the Chicago Bears, Denver Broncos, and New York Giants.

"The Bears used aggressive man to man and the Broncos a multiple kind of thing with zones," Paterno said. "Out of that, our defensive coaches started to rethink our defense."

In 1985, the defense was better. And even more so in 1986.

By that time, the offense was in the hands of quarterback John Shaffer.

Shaffer had been recruited out of Moeller High School in Cincinnati, a proven winner. Going back to the seventh grade, Shaffer had put together a 54-game winning streak as a starter.

But following a 25–10 loss to Oklahoma in the 1986 Orange Bowl, which cost the Nittany Lions the national championship, Shaffer was hardly the most popular man on campus.

"It was really difficult to deal with," Shaffer recalled. "I rededicated myself to the game. I really didn't feel bad for myself, but more for the guys who were playing their last game and couldn't come back."

Shaffer still had a year left, and there were questions in his mind—particularly after getting booed while playing in the Blue-White game the following spring. Then he read in a newspaper that Penn State fans preferred backup quarterback Matt Knizer over him by a two-to-one margin. This despite Shaffer leading the team to an 11–1 season in 1985 and a berth in the national championship game. The 1985 season was a series of close calls for Penn State. The Nittany Lions won seven games by 7 points or less. They finished strong with a 36–6

GARRITY'S GRAB

Gregg Garrity was full of surprises. Making the Penn State football team as a walk-on was one. Another was making the most important touchdown catch in the history of Nittany Lions football.

At least it could be argued that Garrity's catch in the 1983 Sugar Bowl against Georgia earned that distinction. It gave the Nittany Lions their winning points as they captured their first national championship.

Pulling off big plays in bowl games became a habit for Garrity; he had also scored a TD against Southern Cal to put Penn State ahead for good in the 1982 Fiesta Bowl.

"It seemed like from that point on," Garrity said, "my confidence level and just everything sort of changed."

Garrity had been a star running back, defensive back, and kicker at North Allegheny High in Pennsylvania, but at 5-foot-10, 135 to 140 pounds, he was seemingly too small to play major college football.

He did receive some offers from smaller schools such as Clarion. Al Jacks, a former Penn Stater who coached Clarion, offered Garrity a full scholarship. At the same time, he convinced Garrity that he was good enough to play football for Penn State.

Gregg's father believed that, too. Jim Garrity had been a standout receiver for Penn State in the 1950s, and he talked Paterno into looking at his son. When the Garritys visited State College, Paterno showed them around. One of the stops was the weight room, where gigantic players were working out.

"Here I am a 140-pound kid, and these guys are houses," Gregg said. "I thought, 'What am I doing here?'"

As it turned out, he did plenty.

In 1981, Garrity led the Nittany Lions with an average of 18 yards a catch. He is most remembered for his signature catch against Georgia in the Sugar Bowl, stretching out in the end zone to make a spectacular grab of Todd Blackledge's pass to complete a dazzling 47-yard play.

The catch was immortalized on the front cover of *Sports Illustrated* and is remembered by Penn State fans of that era as "the Catch."

Garrity further proved his worth as a player by going on to a professional football career with the Pittsburgh Steelers and Philadelphia Eagles.

Not a bad resume for a player once considered too small to make an impact in big-time football.

Gregg Garrity makes a dazzling, diving catch against Georgia to win the 1983 Sugar Bowl. *AP Images*

victory over Notre Dame and a 31–0 win at Pitt. But they couldn't get it done in the Orange Bowl against Oklahoma, which featured a big-play offense and a tough defense.

Going into the 1986 season, Shaffer admitted, "My confidence was shaken."

Shaken, but not destroyed.

Shaffer beat out Knizer for the starting quarterback job in 1986 and proceeded to lead Penn State to a 45–15 victory over Temple in the opener.

Victories followed over Boston College, East Carolina, Rutgers, Cincinnati, and Syracuse before the Nittany Lions traveled to Alabama to play the Crimson Tide in one of the landmark games on their schedule. The Tide was unbeaten in 13 games and ranked No. 2 in the country.

Alabama took a 3–0 lead on a field goal in the first quarter. Penn State answered in the second quarter with scores by the Nittany Lions' touchdown twins: a 19-yard touchdown run by D. J. Dozier and a score from 3 yards out by Blair Thomas.

The Penn State defense suffocated the Tide the rest of the way, leading the Lions to a stunning 23–3 win in Tuscaloosa—handing Alabama its most lopsided loss in 10 years.

"I expected a closer game, to be honest with you," said Penn State defensive tackle Bob White. "They're so explosive, you have to expect that."

After rushing past the Tide, the Nittany Lions finished the 1986 season with victories over West Virginia, Maryland, Notre Dame, and Pitt. The defense played an especially critical role in the Maryland and Notre Dame games, helping to stop upset bids in the final minutes. Against Maryland, defensive tackle Pete Curkendall made a key interception to set up a Penn State TD. Against Notre Dame, White and safety Ray Isom made crucial tackles behind the line to save the Lions.

"Any one of us could've made that play," White said of his sack of Notre Dame quarterback Steve Beuerlein, which drove the Irish 9 yards back. "That was just the nature of that group. If you noticed throughout the year, there was always someone who came through in the clutch."

That group included All-American linebacker Shane Conlan, one of 15 players who postponed their jump to the pros for a crack at the national title.

Nittany Lions players celebrate after D. J. Dozier scored the game-winning touchdown in the fourth quarter of the Aloha Bowl on December 27, 1983. Penn State defeated Washington, 13–10. *AP Images*

One of the rare times during the 1986 Orange Bowl that D. J. Dozier found an opening against Oklahoma. The Penn State back was limited to 39 yards rushing as the Sooners squashed Penn State's title hopes by handing the Lions their only loss of the season. *Penn State/Collegiate Images/Getty Images*

"We came up short in the Orange Bowl against Oklahoma," White said. "I think at that point, a lot of the red-shirt guys who could have left ended up coming back for that fifth year because we realized we could get it done.

"When you work that hard and get that close that you can taste something, that taste doesn't leave your mouth."

So now the Nittany Lions had a rare second chance in 1986, just one year after the first. They had climbed to No. 2 in the national polls and would be facing top-ranked Miami for the national championship.

Next stop: The Fiesta Bowl in Tempe, Arizona.

WITHSTANDING A HURRICANE IN THE FIESTA BOWL

It was going to be a war, no doubt about it. That's how players from both sides saw it. Only the top-ranked Miami Hurricanes looked the part. When their plane landed in Tempe, Arizona, many were dressed in Rambo-style combat fatigues. Vinny Testaverde, Miami's Heisman Trophy–winning quarterback, led the charge off the plane wearing wraparound sunglasses, a day's stubble, and gloves.

Players set the tone wearing khaki-colored T-shirts with war-like slogans, such as "Kill a Commie for Mommy," as was displayed on the chest of middle linebacker George Mira Jr.

"The number-one college football team in America arrived at its bowl site looking like the centerfold from *Soldier of Fortune* magazine," one sportswriter said.

It suited the Hurricanes' image as the bad boys of college football, an image they were only too happy to uphold.

"Bad versus good," said Miami running back Melvin Bratton. "We'll take the bad role any time. We feast on that."

The Hurricanes were notorious for their scrapes with the law—which were particularly highlighted when compared to the squeaky-clean image of

Running back Blair Thomas goes airborne over the Rutgers defense. After teaming with D. J. Dozier in the Penn State backfield in 1985 and 1986, Thomas led the team in rushing yardage in 1987 and 1989. He ranks as the school's third all-time rusher, with 3,301 career yards. *Collegiate Images/WireImage/Getty Images*

Penn State. The national championship game was viewed as a morality battle: the good guys in the white helmets versus the bad guys in the black combat boots.

While the Miami players were delighted to go along with the scenario, coach Jimmy Johnson wasn't.

"People have a perception of our team that is off-base," he said. He emphasized that many of his players were involved in charity work, "but no one cares. It's a shame because we've got great young men, and all they can expect is criticism."

Paterno tried to keep things on the light side.

"There are a couple of our kids I wouldn't eat with," Paterno said. "We've been trying to improve their table manners."

Sportswriters certainly couldn't complain about a lack of material. Nothing, however, could match the "Last Supper"—a steak fry that was one of the traditional activities leading up to the Fiesta Bowl game.

Like a celebrity roast, each team prepared to perform skits poking fun at the other.

Penn State went first. Punter John Bruno made a joke about Testaverde's bid for the Heisman Trophy. None of the Miami players smiled.

Nor did they think it was funny when he cracked a joke with racial overtones about Miami's team unity. "Our black players didn't take to that too much," Johnson said. Leading up to the game, some of Miami's black players had been boasting about the team unity among blacks and whites. Yeah, Bruno said, some team unity—the black players get to eat at the training table once a week.

The final blow was a remark about Johnson's meticulously coiffed hairdo.

Next up came Miami's skits, which didn't last long. As they were getting started, Hurricanes defensive tackle Jerome Brown stood up and peeled off his warmup top to reveal camouflage fatigues.

110   CHAPTER 8

He was outraged. He wasn't going to have any more of this nonsense.

"Did the Japanese sit down with Pearl Harbor before they bombed them?" Brown shouted.

When the Miami players answered "No!" Brown started toward the door. His teammates got up and followed him out.

Responding to Brown's Pearl Harbor reference, Bruno had the best quip of the evening: "Hey, didn't the Japanese lose that one?"

Paterno wasn't concerned about the perceived images, only about the style of the game. He did not want a high-scoring shootout.

"We can't let them get us in a position where it's a touchdown contest," he said. "If it's that kind of a game, we're out of our league."

That would mean containing Testaverde, who had torn defenses to shreds with his accurate passing all season. In 10 games, the Miami quarterback completed 175 of 276 passes for 2,557 yards. Testaverde had gone through 116 passes in 1985 and 114 in 1986 without throwing an interception.

Testaverde had an array of great receivers to complement his game. The plan for Penn State: jam the receivers at the line and wallop them in the secondary, making them pay a penalty when they caught the ball.

Defense dominated in the game's early going, before Bratton scored on a 1-yard run for Miami with 6:38 left in the first half. The score followed the recovery of a Penn State fumble on the Nittany Lions' 23.

Shaffer tied it 7–7 when he scored on a 4-yard scramble with 1:14 left in the half. The touchdown capped a 13-play, 74-yard drive highlighted by Shaffer's 23-yard pass to Eric Hamilton on a third and 12.

Paterno's desire for a low-scoring affair held through the third quarter, with neither side putting more points on the board. Early in the fourth period, Miami took the lead back at 10–7 on a 38-yard field goal by Mark Seelig. Minutes later, the Hurricanes seemed to be driving toward another score, when Conlan intercepted a pass by Testaverde for the second time in the game. Despite being hobbled by knee and ankle injuries, he returned it 43 yards to the Miami 5.

Far left: Shane Conlan, one of Penn State's linebacker greats, was an All-American in 1985 and 1986. His interception of a Vinny Testaverde pass was a turning point in the 1987 Fiesta Bowl against Miami. *Penn State University Archives, Pennsylvania State University Libraries*

Left: Before the 1987 Fiesta Bowl, "Dr. Joe" predicted poetically that Penn State would win and replace Miami as the No. 1 team in the country. He wasn't lyin'. *Penn State University Archives, Pennsylvania State University Libraries*

Above: The 1986 team brought Penn State its second national championship. The Lions capped off a perfect 11–0 regular season with a victory over Miami in the Fiesta Bowl. *Penn State University Archives, Pennsylvania State University Libraries*

D. J. Dozier, Penn State's season rushing leader and one of the team's best all-around backs, carried the ball in through a huge hole to make it 14–10 Penn State with 8:13 left.

Back came Miami. The Hurricanes faced fourth and 6 deep in their own territory. Johnson went for it, and Testaverde completed a 31-yard pass to Bennie Blades for the first down, and more.

There was still time left for a comeback by the Hurricanes.

In hardly any time at all, Testaverde had the Hurricanes on the Penn State 13-yard line. It was fourth down with 18 seconds to go.

Testaverde was going to pass. Everyone in the stadium knew it, including the Nittany Lions, who dropped eight men to the goal line.

"We knew in key situations Testaverde would stare at the receiver he was going to throw to," said safety Ray Isom. "On first and 10 he may be the best quarterback in the country. But on third and 8 or fourth and 8, he maybe needs to work on it."

The Hurricanes sent out three receivers. Testaverde looked at one: split end Brett Perrimen. Penn State linebacker Pete Giftopoulos was looking, too.

He stepped in to pick off Testaverde's pass at the 1-yard line, his second interception of the night. It sealed Penn State's 14–10 win.

Giftopoulos cradled the ball and then held it high like a trophy. In fact, it was—the national championship all wrapped up in a leather ball.

Penn State's game plan had worked to perfection.

"They kept talking about how little our defensive backs were," Conlan said in reference to the 5-foot-9 Isom and 5-foot-11 cornerback Duffy Cobbs, "but they'd never been hit by them."

Testaverde's receivers kept hearing footsteps. The All-American quarterback had several passes dropped by his receivers, not to mention the five times he was intercepted.

Penn State's second national title in five years restored pride to Nittany Nation after the letdown in 1985, when the Lions lost to Oklahoma in the Orange Bowl.

"It was just a great culmination of two years, how much hard work had gone into it," White said. "The fact that we had fought back to a position where our fate was completely in our hands was perfect. There was no need for pollsters, or anyone. It was one and two, and if you got it done, you were champion."

Except for the 1988 season, Paterno's first losing year at Penn State, the football program rolled into the 1990s with a succession of bowl visits.

Bowl visits were the norm at Penn State. But the Nittany Lions were about to make a dramatic change in their athletic program.

Left: Penn State's defense put pressure on Miami's receivers and quarterback Vinny Testaverde to take the Hurricanes out of their game plan in the Fiesta Bowl. Here, linebacker Pete Giftopoulos sacks Testaverde (No. 14) from behind in the third quarter. *Rob Schumacher/AP Images*

Below: Coach Paterno gets carried off the field as a national champion for the second time in five years after his Nittany Lions defeated the Miami Hurricanes, 14–10, on January 2, 1987, in the Fiesta Bowl. *Jim Gerberich/AP Images*

CHAPTER 9

BLAZING NEW TRAILS

Joe Paterno had to introduce himself to a new group of rivals in the 1990s when Penn State entered the Big Ten. Paterno greets Michigan coach Gary Moeller following the first conference meeting of the two schools, in October 1993. The Wolverines won 21–13 to hand the Lions their first loss of the season. *Doug Pensinger/Getty Images*

As the "Beast of the East" in college football coming off of two national championships in the 1980s, Penn State didn't seem to be in need of any address changes. And as the premier conference in the sport, the Big Ten appeared set with its current membership.

Yet, the marriage of the Nittany Lions and the Big Ten was hardly a shotgun wedding. It did have its awkward moments, as prized rivalries disappeared and the conference itself now would have 11 schools. But for Penn State and the Big Ten, getting together seemed the natural thing to do.

Even the usually conservative Joe Paterno came around to see the benefits of such an arrangement.

"The world we're in is changing so much. We're going to be very shortsighted if we don't understand that," JoePa said as his university's move from independent to major conference member came to fruition. "I've been concerned from day one whether this is going to be good for Penn State.

"It's not a question of whether it is just good for Penn State football. I've always been a company man, and if the president says it's good for the university, then it's going to be good for our program."

By the end of the 1980s, it had become clear that few schools could prosper as independents in the sport. Joining a conference, especially an elite conference like the Big Ten, meant guaranteed money from bowl tie-ins—the Big Ten splits its bowl revenues among its members—along with lucrative television deals and less scrambling to fill out schedules.

As more independents started looking to form alliances with conferences, Penn State clearly was a prized jewel, and the Big Ten wanted to be sure to beat other conferences to the punch in locking in the Nittany Lions. Big Ten commissioner Jim Delany and his 10 school presidents were well aware that the Big East, ACC, and perhaps others would make a strong pitch to put State College on their conference maps.

So the Big Ten, which also was hoping to sign up Notre Dame for a 12-team super league, pursued PSU for the conference's first expansion since Michigan State came aboard in 1949. Along with a grand sports tradition, Penn State would bring in large television markets (Philadelphia, Pittsburgh, even New York), one of the biggest stadiums in the country, a nationwide fan base, and, yes, JoePa.

"We believe Penn State will make a splendid addition to the conference," said Illinois president Stan Ikenberry, chairman of the Council of 10 that made the decision to accept the Nittany Lions. "We're proud of their academic standing. We're also pleased with the integrity with which they have conducted their intercollegiate programs over a number of years."

Support hardly was unanimous—even within the ranks at Penn State. The decision to join the Big Ten provided the kind of juicy debate usually reserved for quarterback controversies or bowl game matchups.

"I really was against it," offensive coordinator and later associate athletic director Fran Ganter said in a 2006 interview. "Now as I look back, Joe was smart enough [to know] what it would do from a prestige and academic standpoint. The Big Ten is awesome. It really is fun to be in a conference. Now we're playing for a league championship every year. We know these guys, because we've played against them for years."

But what about the guys Penn State played against every season for all those years before? What about the Pitts and West Virginias and Syracuses? What of those longstanding rivalries?

Penn State athletic director Jim Tarman had an answer: "We are launching stimulating series with Ohio State and Michigan and Michigan State and Illinois and the rest of the Big Ten family that will become the important rivalries of the mid-1990s and the next century."

That didn't exactly placate the Panthers or Mountaineers or Orangemen.

"I regret deeply that Penn State University has found it impossible to consider extending the current football series beyond 1992 at this time," Pitt athletic director Ed Bozik said when the Nittany Lions joined the Big Ten. "Traditional rivalries around the country continue to persist even in the face of substantial change. Where there is a will, there is a way."

His insistence that it was Penn State that didn't have the will was somewhat misguided. Both Pitt and

Lou Holtz of Notre Dame and Joe Paterno of Penn State were hot commodities in the early 1990s, as the major football conferences hoped to woo these prestigious programs into their ranks. The two coaching legends shake hands following Notre Dame's 17–16 victory on November 14, 1992. *Mark Elias/AP Images*

BLAZING NEW TRAILS 115

PENN STATE'S LOST RIVALRIES

The revolution that hit college football in the 1990s dealt a cruel blow to some of the nation's great rivalries. No school lost more of them than Penn State.

For decades, the Nittany Lions regularly played instate rivals Pitt and Temple, as well as regional rivals Syracuse and West Virginia. When independents began disappearing from the sport's landscape and the Lions joined the Big Ten, those series either disappeared completely or became now-and-again meetings.

The demise of the annual Pitt-Penn State matchups, the "Battle for Route 22," was a big loss not only for the players on those teams and the fans in the stands, but also for high school players throughout the Keystone State who dreamed of suiting up for the Lions or Panthers and continuing the rivalry.

"It was a big deal," said Jim Sweeney, who played with Dan Marino in the early 1980s on some of Pitt's best teams before a long career in the NFL. "It was one of the great rivalries in the country."

After a few encounters in the 1890s, the two teams met once a year every year beginning in 1900, a tradition that continued until 1931. Following a three-year hiatus, the annual series resumed in 1935 and continued uninterrupted until 1992, with the game holding the juicy spotlight of being the final game on the schedule in most years. The series ended as an annual event in 1992 (with Penn State romping Pitt 57–13) and then resumed for four seasons at the end of the decade (1997–2000), although no longer as the season finale; in 1997, it was the season opener.

The matchup of Penn State University and the University of Pittsburgh is a rivalry that goes back more than 100 years to the teams' first encounter in 1893.

Pitt gladly accepted that much.

"I am thrilled," said then-Panthers coach Paul Hackett. "This is a great development for all parties concerned, but most importantly I am excited for the football fans of Pennsylvania and the entire East."

So was Joe Paterno, even though he had been a driving force behind ending the annual affair in 1992. Embittered by Pitt's decision to join the Big East for basketball years before rather than start a super conference with Penn State, Paterno barely hesitated in dropping the Panthers from the schedule once the Nittany Lions joined the Big Ten.

But he always recognized the meaning of the Pitt-Penn State matchup.

"Some of our kids don't understand how big it is," he said in 1997, just before Pitt visited State College. "I don't know how to explain it. It's like someone taking a team to the first Super Bowl. You don't know what it's like until you get to it."

Since 2000, it has been difficult to keep the excitement of the rivalry alive. Both teams have full conference schedules, and Paterno has insisted that the Lions can't commit to an annual home-and-home series with any non-Big Ten schools.

Unless state legislators intervene successfully—as recently as 2007, State Senator John Wozniak had undertaken such an effort—the rivalry appears dead.

"This is something the taxpayers want," Wozniak said. "Fill up stadiums, bars, restaurants, and sell T-shirts."

Paterno doesn't necessarily buy it.

"We are becoming a national institution," Paterno said. "We have 400,000 living alumni. I go to California and there are 3,500 people living in the L.A. area. You go to San Francisco and there is another 2,500 living up there. You go into Texas and there are over 4,000 people in the Houston area. Everybody wants us to go there.

"Under the present rules, it is going to be tough for us to have an ongoing schedule with anybody except the Big Ten schools."

Penn State leads the series, which began in 1893, 50–42–4. The Panthers defeated the Nittany Lions 12–0 in 2000, their last meeting until at least 2011.

The head-to-head record in Penn State's other longstanding instate rivalry isn't nearly so close: Penn State has won 33 of the 37 meetings with Temple (through 2008), with the Owls' last victory coming in 1941. In fact, the Philadelphia school was kicked out of the Big East after the 2004 season and rarely has challenged the Nittany Lions when they meet.

Because Temple, now in the Mid-American Conference, doesn't make any demands on Penn State—or any other opponents, for that matter—the Owls are in a more favorable position for arranging future games with the Lions.

Plus, it's virtually a guaranteed win for Penn State: Temple has never beaten JoePa.

"We like to play teams in the East, and we feel we have some loyalty to . . . Temple," he said. "I don't make any excuses for playing those people. They're not Division I-AA schools."

Even after Penn State joined the Big Ten, the intensity of its rivalry with Pitt remained heated. Penn State linebacker LaVar Arrington and Pittsburgh safety D. J. Dinkins got into a scuffle during the game in 1999. Arrington's actions earned 30 yards in penalties, but the Lions won the game, 20–17. *George Widman/AP Images*

West Virginia is certainly not in the lower division, and indeed it has become as formidable a football power as, well, the Nittany Lions. Frequent matchups with the Mountaineers could be enticing, but the series that began in 1904 died in 1992, with Penn State holding a dominant 48–9–2 record. Despite the lopsided nature of the rivalry, there were strong ties between the schools.

"With the end of the series, and the fact that we've beaten them so often, it just makes them play a lot harder, it picks them up a lot more," receiver O. J. McDuffie said of the series finale in 1992, which ended with a 40–26 Penn State victory. "A lot of people use Penn State as the game of their season. A lot of people want to knock us off, especially the teams that we've knocked off during the years."

WVU cherished its victories in 1984 and 1988. In 1984, a 17–14 upset was the highlight of the season for the Mountaineers and their first win over the Nittany Lions in 29 games.

"It was just a big thing that hit the whole state of West Virginia," said Rick Dolly, who played defensive tackle at West Virginia. "Not only was I sparked by it, but the whole state was sparked by it."

In 1988, led by All-American quarterback Major Harris, the Mountaineers topped the Lions 51–30 on their way to an unbeaten season.

"Major Harris just killed us, and things were pretty wild there," said McDuffie, recalling that the game never really ended. Fans stormed the field before the final whistle, and game officials never tried to resume it.

"It's kind of an empty feeling if you think about the series ending," Dolly said before the 1992 matchup. "But it's also an exciting feeling about how we're going to have to play and make this last time through the series count. We don't want to be remembered as some little buffed-up team getting beat around."

Sorry, Rick: Penn State 40, West Virginia 26.

Penn State's other big-time Eastern rival was Syracuse, which had its own proud football tradition even before Paterno took over on the Penn State sideline.

In 1955, future Hall of Fame running backs Jim Brown of Syracuse and Lenny Moore of Penn State tried to outdo each other. Paterno remembered that game fondly.

"We won 21–20," he said. "Lenny carried 14 or 15 times for 140 yards, Brown 15 or 16 for 140. We didn't run guys 25 or 30 times in those days. If we had, they both would have gained 300."

In 1959, the Nittany Lions just missed upsetting the undefeated Orange, losing by 2 points.

It was a star-studded series that also featured the likes of Lydell Mitchell, Jack Ham, and Franco Harris doing some of their best work for the Lions, and Floyd Little, Larry Csonka, and Art Monk enhancing their All-American credentials for Syracuse.

"It's sad to be ending," Harris said before the 1990 meeting. "It's always been a big rivalry. It's a big part of Penn State history."

Sure is. The teams met 68 times from 1922 through 1990, with Penn State winning 40 games. The first game was a 0–0 tie at the Polo Grounds in New York.

Among the many games that followed was one that changed football history.

During the 1929 encounter, Penn State was leading 6–0, but early in the fourth quarter, the Orange drove to the 2-yard line. A solid goal-line stand gave the ball back to Penn State, which was caught for a safety rather than deciding to punt after three fruitless running plays.

Because the rules then allowed the team surrendering the safety to keep the ball, Penn State was up 6–2 and did the same thing again. By the time the Lions finally punted, there wasn't enough time for Syracuse to score, and Penn State had a 6–4 victory.

The rules were changed after that, requiring a free kick following a safety.

Fans who miss these historic rivalries got some good news when Penn State and Syracuse resumed relations with a home-and-home series in 2008 and 2009.

The 2008 game ended as expected, with a 55–13 Penn State victory.

Penn State has dominated in its longstanding rivalry with West Virginia. Including this 16–6 victory in 1956, the Nittany Lions have won 48 of the 59 gridiron meetings between the schools. *Penn State University Archives, Pennsylvania State University Libraries*

After an 18-year hiatus, Penn State revived its rivalry with Syracuse in 2008. The Lions crushed the Orangemen, 55–13. *Kevin Rivoli/AP Images*

Syracuse had already moved from independent status to a major conference (the Big East) even before Penn State joined the Big Ten, so those rivalry series were headed for life support anyway.

Some observers from within the Penn State family were skeptical that the Big Ten had the depth of talent that would allow the Nittany Lions to compete against the kinds of elite teams it could as an independent. Linebacker Brian Gelzheiser, who played for Penn State from 1991 to 1994, echoed that sentiment. "Michigan, Ohio State, Michigan State, you know, were the three big schools. [But] Iowa wasn't that good, Indiana and Illinois weren't that good."

The options for postseason bowl games were another big change for the Nittany Lions in joining the Big Ten. As an independent in 1982 and 1986, Penn State was able to choose to play top-ranked teams in a quasi-playoff game, and when the Lions won, they earned the No. 1 ranking and a national crown. In the Big Ten, there would be no such option. While the honor of winning the Big Ten and the prestige of playing in the Rose Bowl were enticing, the opportunities to win the national championship were now more limited.

Joe Paterno was not overly concerned.

"I don't think you ever get anything for nothing in life," Paterno said. "When we moved into the Big Ten conference, we were aware that there were a lot of positives and there might be a negative included, which is true with every conference in the country."

In the end, Penn State opted for the Big Ten rather than joining the Big East or creating a new conference, one that perhaps could entice the likes of Notre Dame, because no other football conference had the history or the reputation the Big Ten enjoyed at the time.

Since the Associated Press began crowning national champions in 1936, and on through various systems employed by the NCAA, 11 Big Ten teams had won the title. The schools had large stadiums, huge followings both locally and nationally, and had employed some of the greatest coaches, from Bernie Bierman and Duffy Daugherty to Woody Hayes and Bo Schembechler. And no conference had more great players attend its schools than the Big Ten, boasting such legendary names as Red Grange, Tom Harmon, "Hopalong" Cassidy, Bubba Smith, and Archie Griffin.

Above: Lou Benfatti was Penn State's starting defensive tackle from 1991 to 1994. He was named team captain in 1994 following an All-American season the year before. *Rick Stewart/Getty Images*

Top: John Sacca was slated to be Penn State's main starter for 1992, but after consecutive losses to Miami (shown here) and Boston College, Paterno handed the reins to Kerry Collins for the last four games of the season. *Gene Sweeney/Getty Images*

Even with the prestige of the Big Ten and the benefits that would come from joining an elite conference, Penn State players and coaches felt much uncertainty about this impending change.

"Obviously, there's a lot of unknowns when you go into something like that," said quarterback Kerry Collins, an All-American in 1994. "You have your opponents you play every year, you know them pretty well. You know what to expect, but obviously our first year [in the Big Ten], a lot of that was new to us. Playing the Michigans and Ohio States and those kind of schools was new. We had to kind of get a feeling for what they're all about, and I think the biggest thing was the unknown of going into it all."

After the Big Ten officially accepted the Nittany Lions into its ranks in December 1989, it would take nearly three years for them to become full-fledged conference members, because much of Penn State's football schedule was already set through the 1992 season.

The Nittany Lions started off their 1990 season with losses to powerful Texas and Southern California teams, but they then reeled off nine straight wins before finishing with a 9–3 record. The streak included victories over Syracuse, West Virginia, and Pitt.

There were no Big Ten opponents on the 1990 schedule, nor on the 1991 ledger, when the Lions went 11–2, including an 81–0 humiliation of Cincinnati in the school's biggest offensive output in the modern era.

"I don't think we got much done," Paterno said after the Cincinnati game. "I don't think anybody gets much out of a football game like this. I just hope the Cincinnati kids don't get too discouraged."

The only losses that year were to USC again, and to Miami. After beating Tennessee in the Fiesta Bowl, the Nittany Lions wound up third in the polls.

The Nittany Lions headed into their Big Ten existence coming off a 7–5 season in 1992 that included a 57–13 thrashing of the Pitt Panthers in what amounted to a grudge game. The rest of the season wasn't nearly as enjoyable for the Lions. They had won their first five games but then fell apart, losing three of their final four.

As the team headed into the 1993 campaign, the Big Ten was still a big unknown, and there was a lot of speculation as to how Penn State would fare in its first year in the new conference.

WELCOME TO THE BIG TEN

The 1993 schedule kicked off with a conference matchup against Minnesota, and the Nittany Lions romped past the Golden Gophers, 38–20. A week later, they blanked Iowa 31–0. Their Big Ten debut had been little more than a stroll through a couple of porous defenses.

But the true indoctrination was coming.

The Minnesota and Iowa victories set up a monumental matchup with Michigan at Beaver Stadium—the Wolverines' first game ever with the Lions. It would be followed two weeks later by Penn State's visit to the Horseshoe in Columbus for a showdown with Ohio State.

Penn State would get the opportunity to not only show it belonged in this new atmosphere, but that it was occupying a stratosphere above where the perennial Big Ten powers existed.

Kerry Collins started four games for Penn State in 1992 and then assumed the regular starting-quarterback role three games into the 1993 season.
Doug Pensinger/Getty Images

And for added drama, the Michigan-Penn State contest would be the Nittany Lions' 1,000th game. And no, JoePa had not been at all of them. But he had seen his share, and Paterno knew a win over the Wolverines would make Penn State a team to beat in the race to the Rose Bowl, no matter how much he played it down.

"Sure, when we were talking about going into the Big Ten, and I would walk around in back of my house, in the woods, I'd dream about being in Pasadena," Paterno said. "But that's a long time ago since I've done any of that stuff. Right now, that's a long way from my thoughts. My thoughts are strictly about figuring how to do a job against Michigan."

Heading into their meeting, Michigan was coming off two early defeats, to Notre Dame and Michigan State. The Nittany Lions were coming off a bye week, were 5–0, and had outscored opponents 191–54.

Both teams' coaches tried to spin the scenario to put greater pressure on the other side. Michigan coach Gary Moeller thought Penn State would have an advantage coming off a bye week. Paterno didn't agree.

"Any advantage we think we might have is offset by the fact that Michigan got licked and will come down here as a very emotional football team," Paterno said of the Wolverines' flop against the Spartans the previous Saturday. "As far as we are concerned, it's still a very, very big football game. It's the first of six straight Big Ten games, a situation we've never been in."

Another difficult situation that Paterno had to deal with was the departure of quarterback John Sacca, who was unhappy after getting benched during the Iowa game on September 18, 1993, and being replaced by Kerry Collins. Sacca quit the team two weeks later. Paterno claimed there was more than football involved, saying, "Academically, he just fell behind."

After passing its first conference test with a 38–20 win over Minnesota, Penn State took on national power USC and defeated the Trojans 21–20. Ki-Jana Carter (No. 32) ran for 104, one of his seven 100-yard games in 1993. *Penn State University Archives, Pennsylvania State University Libraries*

Even after joining the Big Ten, Penn State continued to play some of its traditional eastern foes. In early October 1993, Ki-Jana Carter ran for 159 yards against Maryland, during a 70–7 whipping of the Terrapins.
Ted Mathias/AP Images

Sacca's departure forced Paterno to forgo the plan to red-shirt freshman Wally Richardson, whom he envisioned as Collins' replacement once Kerry used up his eligibility. Richardson now had to suit up to give Paterno a backup at quarterback.

The keys to the contest would be how the defenses handled star running backs Tyrone Wheatley of Michigan and Ki-Jana Carter of Penn State.

Wheatley was hoping to make up for a disappointing performance against Michigan State, which held him to 80 yards overall. Wheatley had led the nation in total offense before the Spartans got stingy. Carter was second in the Big Ten, with nearly 122 yards rushing per game.

Michigan was, in a way, defending the honor of the longtime conference schools against this interloper from central Pennsylvania. This undefeated interloper.

The Wolverines did themselves proud.

Wheatley was virtually unstoppable, rushing for 192 yards. The Michigan defense staged a sensational goal-line stand, and the Woverines' special teams were, well, special in the 21–13 victory.

"We wanted to welcome Penn State to the Big Ten in a Big Ten fashion, and I think we did that today," Michigan center Marc Milia said.

After taking a 14–10 lead, the Wolverines put on a classic display of intensity, resilience, and brute force in a goal-line stand late in the third quarter that carried into the final period and made the difference in the game.

From inside the Michigan 1-yard line, Collins tried a quarterback sneak and was slammed down by defensive lineman Tony Henderson. On second down, from about the same spot, it was a repeat performance by Henderson.

"That wasn't working," Collins noted.

On third down, Carter took a handoff and took off. In midair, he was met by tackle Ninef Aghakhan and knocked straight back.

"It's a mental game at that point," Aghakhan said.

It was now fourth down. Paterno could have chosen to kick a field goal, but all Penn State needed was a few inches to take the lead.

The third quarter ended, leaving the coaches and Collins and Carter plenty of time to discuss the biggest call of the Nittany Lions' short Big Ten existence. With the teams switching end zones, Penn State would be heading directly toward the student section. A very loud, very stoked student section.

Most everyone expected the play to run to the outside, probably with Carter using his speed and athletic skills to get into the end zone. Or possibly a play-action fake by Collins, throwing to a tight end who slipped into the end zone.

But Paterno stayed conservative. Carter took Collins' handoff and surged into the mass of humanity. Jarrett Irons hit Carter high and Shonte Peoples got him low.

No gain. No touchdown.

"When they stopped us," wide receiver Bobby Engram said, "you could feel the momentum change."

Carter injured his hand on that carry, his only one in the fourth quarter. Michigan maintained control the rest of the way.

The Nittany Lions had another bye week before heading to Ohio State. Suddenly, that second idle week was not so enticing. The Lions would have plenty of time to practice for the powerful, unbeaten Buckeyes. They'd also have tons of time to think about their first Big Ten loss—and how they'd been outmuscled by Michigan.

"We have to come out and win the rest of our games," said Carter, a native of Columbus who was eager to heal and go home to make a statement on the Ohio Stadium field. "I have mixed emotions. The beginning of the game will be real hard, but once the game starts, I'll be calmed down.

"We still have a chance to go to the Rose Bowl. It's tough to go undefeated in the Big Ten."

Never mind undefeated. Penn State simply needed to prove it belonged among the Big Ten big boys. Handling Minnesota and Iowa was one thing. Being manhandled by Michigan and, perhaps, also by Ohio State—well, this conference stuff could get awfully rough.

"I think Penn State realizes because of their position, they can ill afford to lose another conference game—whether it's to us or Michigan State or anybody else they might play," Buckeyes coach John Cooper said. "I don't think they need that extra incentive to get fired up for us. They're going to play lights out anyway."

That's what Paterno was counting on for the schools' first meeting since the 1980 Fiesta Bowl, and their ninth overall.

"There are very few places that are more fun to play than Ohio Stadium," Paterno said. Adding, "We have a chance to do something to help ourselves."

Or, they would have a chance to raise more doubts about the decision to enter the conference. The skeptics sure jumped on that train after the third-ranked Buckeyes handed the Lions a 24–6 defeat in a game that wasn't really that close.

Even though Carter rushed for 123 yards on 24 carries, Ohio State forced the Nittany Lions to pass more than they wanted to. Indeed, Collins threw 39 times, completing a mere 13 for 122 yards, and was picked off four times. It was, by far, Collins' worst game as a collegian.

Linebacker Eric Ravotti (No. 94) had to battle Michigan's tough offensive line during a 21–13 loss to the Wolverines in October 1993, but his greatest battle came a few weeks later when he was sidelined after suffering convulsions during the Indiana game. *Doug Pensinger/Allsport/Getty Images*

KERRY COLLINS

In 1994, Kerry Collins owned State College—and possibly the rest of Pennsylvania, as well as all of Nittany Lions Land, wherever it might be found.

By the end of 1998, Collins was an NFL has-been with a litany of off-field woes, ranging from alcohol problems to accusations of racism.

But by the turn of the century, Collins had resurrected his image, his career, his total being.

Collins' saga began not-so-memorably. As a sophomore at Penn State, he was the front-runner for the starting quarterback's job, but he broke a finger in 1992 that sidelined him for most of the season.

Although Collins eventually returned and played in the Blockbuster Bowl that year, he again got hurt and missed much of spring practice. By the start of the 1993 season, John Sacca was getting the start behind center.

"I thought I might be a backup for my whole career," Collins admitted.

But Sacca struggled early in that season, Penn State's first in the Big Ten. By the third game, Joe Paterno had seen enough, and he inserted Collins in the game at Iowa. The Lions won 31–0, and there were no more questions about Collins sitting on the bench.

By the end of that 10–2 season, Collins was sitting pretty, and so were the Nittany Lions.

"We knew we had a really strong team, and we knew a lot of the guys coming back would be even better," Collins said. "We thought the next season would be something special."

It was so special that Penn State went undefeated, powering through the Big Ten and beating Oregon in the Rose Bowl to finish second in the national rankings.

Collins was pretty special, too, putting together the best season a Lions quarterback ever had: 67 percent completion percentage, 2,679 yards in the air, averaging 10.15 yards a throw. The offense gained 520 yards per game, and Penn State scored an astounding 564 points.

"As we were going through the season, and we got a couple of good wins," he recalled, "the possibility of going unbeaten definitely seemed real. And we were able to realize that we could do everything we wanted to do, and we ended up doing it."

Collins rounded out the season by being voted the All-American quarterback.

Although Collins had numerous on-field highlights during his college career, he later talked about how his time at State College was about more than just winning and losing.

"My best memories are just the atmosphere of a game day at Penn State and the excitement of it, and what it means to play in front of all those people," he said. "College and Penn State in itself is just different than anything I've experienced in the pros. That place had a special feeling, especially on a beautiful fall day during the season."

After completing his career as a Nittany Lion, Collins was taken fifth overall in the 1995 NFL draft by the Carolina Panthers. It was a great opportunity—an expansion franchise looking for an identity and for players who would establish that identity. And when Collins guided the Panthers to the NFC championship game in his second season, his future as a pro seemed secure.

But nothing is guaranteed in professional sports.

By that time, Collins already had developed a drinking problem. Some of his Panthers teammates were aware of it, but they couldn't be around to protect him 24/7. The alcoholism led to a charge of driving while intoxicated. Then, one day near the end of training camp in 1997, he used a racial epithet toward a teammate. Collins also was drunk at the time.

"I used a term that was not meant to be used in a malicious way," he said. "In my polluted, altered mind, I believed that, in some sort of way, it would bring forth some sense of camaraderie."

And there was a well-documented incident in which he called coach Dom Capers and asked to be benched, saying he couldn't handle the pressure of being a starting quarterback in the NFL. Teammates labeled Collins a quitter, and instead of benching him, Capers cut him.

From there, Collins went to the New Orleans Saints, a team in dire need of a quarterback. He started the final seven games but played poorly, still plagued by his personal demons.

"I was stupid and idiotic and chemically altered," he said.

But he was so talented that another team, the New York Giants, was willing to take a chance on him. Collins knew he needed to make changes in his life.

He did, and in 2000 came the crowning achievement of his professional career: Collins led the Giants to the Super Bowl. At that Super Bowl in Tampa, Collins staged the most courageous performance of his life—not on the football field, but in a news conference days before the big game.

Collins bared his soul to the media and to the world. "I think I'm a better success story off the field than on the field, because the things I've done off the field have transcended into my professional life," he said. "I had a hard time separating between Kerry Collins the quarterback and Kerry Collins the person. That distinction wasn't very clear until recently, until I realized I had to take care of myself first before I could do anything else.

"I'm very proud sitting at the Super Bowl as the quarterback for one of the teams. I'm more proud of what I do, day in and day out, that makes my life what it is today."

Collins did not back down when confronted with the most difficult questions from the press. When Pat Hanlon, the Giants' director of communications, told Collins he did not have to continue after 30 minutes of questioning, Collins insisted on staying and answering any final queries.

The quarterback later admitted that it was hard to "dredge up all those memories." But, he continued, "The stage being what it is, and the situation being what it is, hopefully, it can have a positive effect on something.

"I'm human, and I have frailties and weaknesses," Collins said. "We all do. Hopefully, people can see me as a role model. Hopefully, they can look at me as someone who realized he had a problem and realized he needed to do something about it."

The future looked bright for Collins when he was selected by the Carolina Panthers with the fifth pick in the 1995 NFL draft, but his journey through the pro ranks would see many ups and downs. *Al Messerschmidt/Getty Images*

Nor were the Nittany Lions much more productive on defense or special teams. Raymont Harris rushed for 151 yards and a touchdown for the Buckeyes, who also blocked a field goal and recovered a fumble.

To add salt to the Lions' wounds, players from the winning side lumped Penn State in with some of the also-rans of the conference.

"It's a great feeling to beat Penn State . . . but it's really no more important to us than a win over Purdue, Northwestern, or any other Big Ten team," Harris said.

As they headed back to State College, the Lions knew they'd be hearing a lot of noise about measuring up in the Big Ten—and about a possible repeat of their 1992 collapse.

"It takes things out of you emotionally," tight end Kyle Brady said. "We're not 18 points worse than this team [Ohio State] by any stretch of the imagination. But I'm sure last year is in the back of all our minds."

If it was, Collins insisted his teammates get rid of it.

"Last year, after being 5–2, we didn't have anything to play for," Collins said. "This year, we can still play in a good bowl. The season's not shot."

Collins was right. If the Lions could straighten out, they could still get to a New Year's Day bowl. But that probably meant sweeping the final four games, all in-conference affairs, including a trip to Michigan State.

Then again, why were they even in the Big Ten if they didn't welcome such a challenge?

Indiana would provide stiff opposition. The Hoosiers, known more for their basketball prowess, were in the midst of a football revival under coach Bill Mallory. They were 7–1, ranked 17th and, unlike Penn State, still in the Rose Bowl hunt.

Paterno said he expected a tight defensive battle, with Indiana coming off consecutive shutout wins. It didn't quite turn out that way.

Penn State, now ranked 19th, twice wasted 14-point margins before Collins hit Engram on a 45-yard touchdown pass with 6:25 left in the game to secure a 38–31 victory on Homecoming Day at State College.

Even in triumph, with a balanced offense and some key defensive plays down the stretch, there was much to be concerned about. Indiana's Thomas Lewis tore apart the Penn State secondary with 12 pass receptions for a Big Ten–record 285 yards and two touchdowns,

Kerry Collins set numerous passing records in his time at Penn State from 1991 to 1994, including most yards passing in a season during the Lions' undefeated 1994 campaign. *Penn State University Archives, Pennsylvania State University Libraries*

including a 99-yarder in the fourth quarter that broke the 38-year-old Big Ten record of 95 yards.

A far more troubling event transpired when Penn State linebacker Eric Ravotti went into convulsions on the sideline during the second quarter and was taken to a hospital. Thankfully, Ravotti was only suffering from a virus and would miss little time in the lineup. (He later went on to play for the Pittsburgh Steelers, from 1994 to 1996.)

One game Ravotti missed was a 28–14 win over Illinois, and when Penn State put a 43–21 licking on Northwestern, the team headed into the season finale at East Lansing with some confidence. A victory against the 24th-ranked Spartans also would secure a January 1 bowl berth and a 6–2 conference record in the Nittany Lions' first Big Ten campaign.

Not much the critics could say about that. Nor could they take much away from the Lions following the barnburner that took place at Spartan Stadium.

With the offense continuing to click—the Lions would score 178 points in their final five games of the season—they scored three unanswered touchdowns against Michigan State to pull out a thrilling 38–37 win. Collins, often operating from a hurry-up offense, hit 23 of 42 passes for 352 yards and three TDs.

"Give Kerry Collins credit," Paterno said. "We didn't want to throw as much as we did. But he hit some clutch throws for us."

The Nittany Lions needed to move the ball quickly, having fallen behind 37–17 late in the third quarter. MSU's Jim Miller was staging target practice until Derek Bochna intercepted a pass, and Collins soon after hit a 40-yard touchdown to Engram with 53 seconds left in the quarter.

After star linebacker Gelzheiser recovered a fumble by Duane Goulbourne, Penn State drove downfield again. Aided by a roughing-the-kicker penalty, the Lions scored on Brian O'Neal's 3-yard run to cut the lead to 37–31. "All of a sudden," Gelzheiser said, "we knew if we got one more stop, we were in great shape."

They got the stop and forced the Spartans to punt. Collins then connected with Engram for 52 yards on the ensuing play, and Craig Fayak's conversion gave Penn State the lead for the first time.

"I can't believe anybody tried to cover Bobby man to man," Collins said of Engram, who had three receptions for 106 yards. "He can get open on anyone that way."

The difference on the scoreboard was a missed extra point by MSU's Bill Stoyanovich. The difference in the standings for Penn State from the end of October and the loss at Ohio State to the end of the regular season was enormous.

With four straight wins to close out the schedule, the Lions headed to the Citrus Bowl in Orlando, Florida, where they routed Tennessee 31–13. A 10–2

Tailback Mike Archie (No. 2) breaks away from the Iowa defense for a touchdown run in September 1994. The Lions trounced the Hawkeyes, 61–21, to earn their third straight victory to open the season. *Penn State University Archives, Pennsylvania State University Libraries*

It was a showdown of football powerhouses when the Ohio State Buckeyes came to Penn State in late October 1994. In front of a capacity crowd at Beaver Stadium, the Nittany Lions handed the Buckeyes their worst loss in nearly half a century. *Doug Pensinger/Getty Images*

record (6–2 for third place in the conference) and a No. 8 final ranking was, all in all, a solid debut in the Big Ten.

"The Big Ten is better than a whole lot of people around Penn State believe," Paterno said. "We have to play at a higher level of intensity every week."

Which is exactly what Penn State would do in 1994, when everyone in the conference and nearly everyone in the nation were chasing the Nittany Lions.

UNBEATEN AGAIN

Expectations should have been high for the Lions entering 1994. Their offense flourished in the final five games of their inaugural conference season. Their defense wasn't quite so stout but had the makings of a solid unit.

Perhaps most significantly, many underclassmen—Collins, Engram, Carter, Brady, Gelzheiser, Jeff Hartings, Vin Stewart, Kim Herring—were experienced and heading into their college primes. In all, 10 starters were coming back.

Paterno certainly was feeling good about all his experienced players returning for the 1994 campaign.

"I had such a great summer," he said, a sly smile creasing his face. "I was down on the beach, and I got a couple of dumbbells. The girls are looking at me now."

Paterno may have been kidding about his build, but he could be smugly satisfied about the shape of his 1994 team. This was surely a team that had the potential to go unbeaten and challenge for the national championship.

Once again, Penn State opened against Minnesota, this time on the road. The size of the rout, 56–3, did not raise many eyebrows, because the Gophers were a tail-ender. Carter ran for 210 yards and three touchdowns, and the Lions had 689 yards of offense.

Next up, just as in the previous season, was Southern California. The Nittany Lions were ranked ninth and USC came east ranked fourteenth.

"They so overwhelmingly dominated Minnesota, you couldn't tell a lot," Southern Cal coach John

Above: In one of its greatest offensive splurges in the Big Ten, Penn State simply demolished Ohio State on October 29, 1994. The game helped the 1994 team set numerous offensive records that year. *Penn State University Archives, Pennsylvania State University Libraries*

Top: Ki-Jana Carter sprints into the secondary during Penn State's 63–14 blowout of Ohio State in 1994. Carter, who scored four touchdowns in the game, was among the returning players for whom the devastating loss to Ohio State a year earlier was still fresh in mind. *Penn State University Archives, Pennsylvania State University Libraries*

Robinson said. "They looked very cohesive, and they executed so exactly on offense."

Paterno, naturally, was in spin-control mode.

"In a game like that, you're never as good as you look, and the other guy is never as bad as he looked," he said about the Minnesota game.

A year earlier, Penn State had edged USC 21–20. The Nittany Lions stymied the Trojans' running game but struggled to stop quarterback Rob Johnson, who was back for his senior season. The rematch would provide an accurate gauge of where the Nittany Lions stood in the college football pantheon.

The answer? Near the top.

Penn State romped, taking a 35–0 lead and coasting to a 38–14 final.

"We were overwhelmed right off the bat by Penn State," Robinson said. "I suppose one could say they can't do that against everybody, but they're 2–0. They look as good a football team as I've seen."

Making the Nittany Lions look so good was an offense that gained 534 yards, with five players scoring TDs, and a first-string defense that hadn't yielded a point in two games.

The next three weeks brought more of the same, with 61–21, 55–27, and 48–21 victories. For the third straight year, Penn State started off 5–0. Once more, a tough, seasoned, highly ranked opponent awaited for game six. This time, it was No. 5 Michigan at the Big House in Ann Arbor.

Whip the Wolverines—and then Ohio State in the next game—and the Lions could start thinking about a special season. Lose both and, well, they would remain in the second echelon of the conference.

Collins understood the challenge, particularly because Michigan had played a far more difficult schedule heading into the encounter. The Wolverines were 4–1, with their only loss coming on a last-second desperation pass by Colorado.

"We haven't been in a tough ballgame with all this riding on it," Collins said, "and I think you need a game like that under your belt to really know what to expect going into a big game. This is the kind of game that could put us back among the top teams in the country, where I don't think we've been for quite a while. In the past four or five years, every time we've had a big game, we seem to go out and lay an egg."

To do that before 106,832 fans (the largest crowd any Penn State team had seen) and a national TV audience would have been devastating. But this group of Nittany Lions was not into egg laying—more like laying waste to the opposition.

"Every time I looked at a tape, the score was 35–0, and the first quarter wasn't over," Wolverines coach Gary Moeller said of Penn State's previous games. "It was like they never changed the scoreboard from game to game."

And the Lions were lighting it up quickly: On 28 of their 38 scoring drives, Penn State needed three minutes or less to put points on the board. Thirteen of those drives took a minute or less.

The memory of the Lions' first Big Ten defeat was also fresh in their minds.

"I'm sure Penn State will be coming in here with a revenge factor in mind," said Wolverines guard Joe Marinaro, who had been recruited by Paterno. "But I'm not sure they need it. They're unbelievable. I saw them on film, and they were pretty much scoring at will."

The Nittany Lions didn't do quite that at Michigan, although they got three field goals and a touchdown pass by Collins on their first four possessions. They were coolly efficient throughout and used one of those fast marches to decide the game. With under three minutes remaining, Collins hit Engram for a 16-yard TD, the quarterback's third touchdown pass of the day, to cap a 55-yard drive in 1:53, securing the 31–24 win. Penn State's 11th straight victory put the Nittany Lions atop the conference at 6–0.

The last time the Nittany Lions started 6–0 was in 1986, when they went on to win the national title.

"For me, this is the biggest game of my life," Carter proudly said after he ran for 165 yards against the Wolverines. "They dominated the Big Ten for so long. I think we just gained respect as a great football team."

You bet. The Nittany Lions moved up to No. 1 in the national polls for the first time since 1986, prompting some wild celebrations back on campus. Thousands of fans swarmed Beaver Stadium, breaking through a gate and climbing barbed-wire fences. They carried an old set of goal posts across campus when they couldn't loosen the posts standing in the stadium. Police detained dozens of students briefly. No injuries were reported.

After that display of enthusiasm, what would the campus be like if the Lions could beat Ohio State? At home? On Homecoming weekend?

Not surprisingly, Paterno was keeping a tight rein on his emotions and those of his players. Their job wasn't nearly done.

"We have to make sure we don't go backwards and maintain the kind of edge you need to have to beat a team like Ohio State," Paterno said as he prepared for another bye before the Buckeyes came calling.

The players loved the idea that they were being hunted.

"The attitude is that everyone is going to be gunning for us now more than ever," center Bucky Greeley said.

Ironically, through the first six games, the Penn State offense had been operating so effectively and efficiently that, in a way, it was making things more difficult for the Penn State defense.

"It was kind of annoying," Gelzheiser explained, "because the average scoring time was less than two minutes to the drive. So needless to say, we were on the field all game long. They would play two minutes and then get a five-minute break. They played two minutes, we played five."

Was he complaining? Hardly. As long as the offense was filling the score sheets, it made life better—if busier—for the defenders.

Life was never easy for the opposing defenses, though, as Ohio State coach John Cooper noted after watching film of the Nittany Lions.

"They're one of the most explosive offensive teams I've seen in all my years as a football coach," Cooper said. "They're just unreal. It's like fireworks going off.

"I don't need to look at any Halloween movies this week. I've been looking at scary pictures all week."

He would need to shield his eyes throughout Penn State's 63–14 annihilation of the Buckeyes, OSU's worst loss in 48 years.

Playing less than three quarters, Carter ran for a career-high four touchdowns and 137 yards. Collins, now the nation's top-rated passer, threw for 265 yards and two touchdowns. Engram added six catches for 102 yards and a touchdown.

After handily defeating No. 21 Ohio State, Kerry Collins and the Lions headed to Indiana to face the unranked Hoosiers. Penn State prevailed with a close, 35–29 victory to stay perfect at 8–0. *Penn State University Archives, Pennsylvania State University Libraries*

Fullback Brian Milne (left, sandwiched by Illini defenders) plunges into the end zone to put the Lions ahead 35–31 in the closing minute against Illinois in 1994. *David Boe/AP Images*

The defense still spent a lot of time on the field, but it overwhelmed Ohio State to the point that it took a late touchdown for the Buckeyes to avoid their worst defeat since 1902.

"I think we made a statement today," Collins said. "We beat a good team, and we won resoundingly."

The Buckeyes were stunned.

"It was absolutely embarrassing," Ohio State cornerback Marlon Kerner said. "Not even in my wildest dreams did I imagine they would put up this big a win."

The big win erased nearly all the big questions in State College—and around the country. Yes, Penn State was for real, as dominant as any school in the nation.

Yes, the offense was nearly unstoppable, with a handful of All-America team contenders and potential first-round NFL draft choices.

And yes, Penn State belonged in the Big Ten.

Remarkably, the AP poll voters didn't feel the Nittany Lions belonged on top, though. When Nebraska beat Colorado 24–7, the Cornhuskers were elevated to the top spot, with Penn State slipping a spot to No. 2—this following a 63–14 win over Ohio State!

With no playoff available to certify the Nittany Lions' status as America's best, there was only one way to approach their situation.

"We're just going to go out there and win every game, and we'll worry about the polls January 3," Carter said.

Echoed guard Marco Rivera: "If we're number two, that's all right with me as long as we're undefeated. If we just keep winning all our games and win the Rose Bowl, the polls will take care of themselves."

Well, maybe. The way the polls worked in the era before the Bowl Championship Series (BCS), margin of victory played a large role in the balloting.

So when the Lions had a close call at Indiana, winning 35–29, they fell behind Nebraska in both the AP and the coaches' polls. And then came a trip to Illinois, where rankings and Rose Bowls had to be placed deep in the equipment shed while the Nittany Lions encountered their toughest test.

Down 21–0 against the bowl-bound Illini, the Lions' quest for a perfect record and all the spoils that go with it was about to be, well, spoiled. Their top-rated offense was sputtering against the second-stingiest defense in the land, and Illinois, sparked by running back Ty Douthard, tight end Ken Dilger, and quarterback Johnny Johnson, was making every big play when it had the ball. When it didn't, Illinois relied on the skills of defensive end Simeon Rice and linebacker Dana Howard, who seemed to be everywhere.

With the capacity crowd of 72,364 at Memorial Stadium in a frenzy, the Illini capitalized on two turnovers and a short Penn State punt to build its 21–0 lead in the first 14:48. There were still a full three quarters to play.

It was time for the Nittany Lions to act like the team they had been all season.

Taking possession on the Penn State 1-yard line, Collins led an inexorable march downfield. He hit Kyle Brady three times for a total of 60 yards on a 99-yard drive, which culminated in Brian Milne's 1-yard touchdown run.

With 3:35 left in the second period, Collins' 38-yard TD pass to Scott cut the Illinois lead to 21–14, but the Illini scored again before halftime to take a 28–14 lead into the dressing room.

In the third period, Carter scored on a 4-yard TD run and Illinois came back with a field goal to make it 31–21.

With 7:59 to go in the fourth quarter, Penn State trimmed the margin to 3 points when Milne scored on a 5-yard run. Collins' 17-yard pass to Engram on fourth down highlighted the drive.

Again, it would require nearly a length-of-the-field drive for Penn State to win the game and cap the biggest comeback of the Paterno era. Taking over at their 4-yard line, the Nittany Lions were primed for one of the most memorable drives in school history— one that would lead them to the Rose Bowl. The alternative would be the sting of a colossal upset that would ruin all they had strived to attain.

"We had 96 yards to go on the nation's best defense," Kerry Collins said. "To say the chips were down is an understatement."

Collins responded by connecting on every one of his seven passes on a 14-play drive. Milne scored his third touchdown of the game on a 2-yard run with 57 seconds remaining. Herring then picked off Johnson's desperation pass to clinch the 35–31 win—and the Big Ten title.

"I think we're afraid to lose," Gelzheiser said. "We've worked so hard to get where we are that we're afraid to lose it."

Clinching the greatest comeback of the Paterno era—and the 1994 Big Ten title—defensive back Kim Herring (No. 3) celebrates after intercepting an Illinois pass in the end zone on the final play of Penn State's 35–31 triumph. *Jonathan Daniel/Getty Images*

Linebacker Brian Gelzheiser blitzes against Northwestern during Penn State's 10th straight win of the 1994 season. Gelzheiser and his defensive mates didn't get much chance for rest during the season, thanks to the team's efficient offense. *Rick Stewart/Allsport/Getty Images*

There were two more games to make sure not to lose, but the Lions weren't about to be ambushed now. They routed Northwestern 45–17 despite missing seven players on defense due to injuries. Their replacements and the holdovers forced four first-half turnovers that led to 28 points. Herring was right in the middle of it all before he was forced out of the game late in the first half with an injury to his left knee. Before he left, he had run back a fumble recovery 80 yards to give Penn State an early 7–0 lead. Then he had intercepted a pass by Northwestern quarterback Steve Schnur and returned it 21 yards to the Penn State 46, setting up another Penn State score and a 14–0 lead with two minutes left in the first quarter. The knee injury kept Herring out of the season's final game.

Despite a battered and bruised roster, the Lions completed the perfect regular season with emphasis—a 59–31 annihilation of Michigan State. Carter scored five touchdowns in the game, emphasizing his Heisman Trophy bid.

Still, Paterno was not about to claim total superiority for his Lions.

"I think we're a great football team," Paterno said to reporters. "I leave it up to you guys to tell the people how great."

Overall, in an 11–0 campaign that led to their first Rose Bowl appearance since 1923, the Nittany Lions were unstoppable. They romped in eight of their victories and outscored the opposition 526–232 overall.

But Nebraska kept on winning, too, and most poll voters felt the Big 8 was a stronger conference in 1994. Even if Penn State handled 12th-ranked Oregon in Pasadena, it would need help from Miami to capture a third national title—the Hurricanes were headed to the Orange Bowl to play the Cornhuskers.

More than 102,000 fans turned out at the Rose Bowl in Pasadena to watch the Nittany Lions take on the Oregon Ducks on January 2, 1995. Penn State reached the Big Ten pinnacle and earned a trip to the Rose Bowl in only its second season in the conference. *AP Images*

With the Orange Bowl scheduled for the day before the Rose, the Lions would know where they stood when they took the field in Pasadena.

"I think it's a crime that it's decided by a bunch of sportswriters and not on the field," Milne said of a system that always has been controversial and sometimes downright unfair.

The Lions' resolve was not diminished, though, after Nebraska beat Miami 24–17. The goals of a spotless season, a record for bowl victories for JoePa, and a Rose Bowl crown remained. They could control that, and they would.

Carter, the Heisman Trophy runner-up to Colorado's Rashaan Salaam, ran for 156 yards and three touchdowns in the 38–20 victory over Oregon. Collins hit 19 of 30 passes in a masterful performance, and Paterno got his 16th postseason win, breaking a tie with Bear Bryant.

But it wasn't enough for the media or coaches' polls. Maybe it was the Lions' lack of balance—Oregon gained 501 yards against the Penn State defense in the Rose Bowl. Maybe it was the desire to see Nebraska's coach, Tom Osborne, finally win a national title; JoePa already had two.

In the final tally, Penn State finished second in the balloting, but many of the Nittany Lions chose to ignore it.

They wore "National Champion" hats after their final game. They planned to get rings commemorating one of the best years in Penn State football history—heck, one of the best in college football history.

"This season shows more than anything that there must be a change," Collins said. "It's really a shame that Penn State couldn't play Nebraska this year. The NCAA has to take a long look at this.

"We had a tougher schedule than Nebraska and came through unblemished. We deserve a split. We're going to know it ourselves that we're national champions. We're going to have a big, fat ring with a [number] one in the middle and lots of diamonds around it."

Although Paterno had long been an outspoken critic of the various flawed attempts to establish a structured plan for deciding the national champion—first the Bowl Coalition, then the Bowl Alliance, and finally, the BCS—he was careful not to insult Osborne and the Cornhuskers, who had an undeniably outstanding year in 1994. Instead, Paterno carefully resumed his campaign for a playoff system in college football.

"It's a shame that we can't have a playoff," he said. "I don't want to take anything from Tom Osborne, who's a good friend of mine. The way they played, I certainly don't think that I would say, 'Hey, we're national champions and they're not.' Because we deserve it as much as they do."

That 1994 team remains one of the best in Penn State history, reaching iconic status with its spectacular offense. There would be highlights through the next five years, but no more conference crowns, no more Rose Bowl trips, and certainly no national-title claims.

Not exactly tough times, but those also were coming in the new century.

Left: Linebacker Thad Brennan leads the cheers after the Nittany Lions defeated the Oregon Ducks in the 81st Rose Bowl game, on January 2, 1995. *Penn State University Archives, Pennsylvania State University Libraries*

Below: Ki-Jana Carter is off and running against the Oregon defense, scoring on an 83-yard touchdown run from scrimmage on Penn State's first offensive play of the game. Carter finished with three touchdowns to lead the Lions to a 38–20 victory in the 1995 Rose Bowl. *Reed Saxon/AP Images*

THE SNOW BOWL

Penn State was prepared for the "Snow Bowl" game with Michigan in November 1995, but not for the blizzard of snowballs that followed from the students. *Penn State University Archives, Pennsylvania State University Libraries*

If one game could sum up the dedication—and the dark side—of Penn State's fandom, it would have to be the contest against Michigan on November 18, 1995, also known as the "Snow Bowl."

As the Wolverines headed to State College for the late-season showdown, a blizzard hit central Pennsylvania. The school was going to have to pull out all the stops to get the field cleared by game time, not to mention making sure that the surrounding roads and on-site parking areas would be cleared enough for those fans who braved the journey to Beaver Stadium.

"It was a Tuesday snowstorm, and there was concern about the game not even being played," recalled Bud Meredith, Penn State's longtime ticket manager. "They were securing students and local folks to shovel; they secured nearly everyone in the athletic department. They also secured penitentiary people to help in the process of removing snow."

Yes, old State Pen helped Penn State.

But despite all the manpower gathered for snow removal, the conditions were hardly optimal for the game. A dusting of snow the day before the contest meant even more work on game day, and the job was not complete until about three hours before kickoff.

Remarkably, about 80,000 fans showed up; 96,677 tickets were sold.

"That's how our fans are," defensive end Terry Killens told the *Collegian* newspaper. "They back us all the way. Rain, sleet, snow, just like the mailman, they're always there for us."

There on this day, and making their presence felt.

"While the bleachers were clear to sit, there was no place to put your legs because all of the snow was packed directly underneath your seat," recalled Dan Perkins, Class of 1999. "When 30,000 students showed up for the game with 10 inches of tightly packed snow under their seats, you can imagine what happened next. It turned into the most wild and all-encompassing snowball fight this university has ever seen."

The snowballs were hurled at everyone, including Nittany Lions players. The main targets, not surprisingly, were Wolverines players and coaches, and the on-field officials. Not to mention classmate against classmate.

"Considering it was a pretty important game . . . it was shocking that, by halftime, the student section seemed half-empty because security ejected a huge amount of students because of all of the snowball fighting," added Perkins.

The players definitely took notice. In fact, Mercury Hayes, the Michigan receiver, took a couple of direct snowball hits to the helmet (courtesy of the student section) as he was split out wide waiting for the snap of the ball.

"It's a shame this happened before the days of video cell phones and YouTube," Perkins said. "This one would be all over the Internet if it happened recently."

Not everyone enjoyed the wintertime shenanigans, however. In fact, the most vociferous protests during and after the game came from Joe Paterno.

The coach did offer his praise to the many people "who did so many great things so that we could play the game under the conditions that we played in." But Paterno, who was battling the flu, scolded the snowball throwers.

"I was disappointed in the crowd," he said. "It was childish; no need for it. It was not fair to the Michigan kids. Michigan has a good football tradition, and for some of our kids to act like a bunch of jerks is embarrassing. We should be better people than that."

The unfortunate Hayes at one point missed making a diving catch in the corner of the end zone, only to be pelted with a barrage of snowballs. He went down to the ground for a short time, and soon Paterno was making another plea to the miscreants—and getting booed.

Following the game, which Penn State won 27–17, there were swift reactions from many members of the student body voicing embarrassment and shame over the conduct of their fellow students. One letter from Melissa Imrich said it all:

"It upsets me that these snowball throwers represented the student body at Penn State in the way that they did on television. It upsets me that even after Coach Paterno yelled at the student section, some students didn't have enough respect for their own team to stop throwing snowballs. Finally, it upsets me that some students didn't have enough respect for their peers to allow them to enjoy the game without the threat of injury."

How did the Nittany Lions players feel about the "Snow Bowl"?

"I just didn't want to take off my helmet," cornerback Brian Miller said.

Following the big blizzard of 1995, Penn State blitzed Michigan in the memorable Snow Bowl game, defeating the Wolverines 27–17. Bobby Engram (No. 10) races down the sideline with Michigan defenders in pursuit. *Penn State University Archives, Pennsylvania State University Libraries*

COOLING OFF, COLLAPSE, AND A COMEBACK

Coach Joe Paterno received an ice-water dousing from his players following Penn State's 38–15 win over Texas in the 1997 Fiesta Bowl. It was the fourth straight bowl victory for Paterno—but the coach soon found himself on the hot seat with impatient fans. *Jeff Robbins/AP Images*

"Joe Must Go."

"Joe Must Stay."

Schizophrenic? For the last decade or so, that's exactly how Penn State football fans have reacted to coach Joe Paterno and the Nittany Lions.

Not that such uneven behavior is unusual for sports fans—the word stems from fanatic, doesn't it? But the tidal wave of emotions surrounding the program carried State College from Happy Valley to Doomsday Country, from euphoria to sheer depression, and back again.

Paterno, the consummate professional, handled the ups and downs with a combination of composure, alarm, and occasionally, self-deprecating humor.

"Hey, if you can't coach, you go sell insurance or do something that you can do," he said.

Paterno coached—and rather well, you might say.

The Lions remained steady winners through the last five seasons of the twentieth century, compiling a 48–14 overall mark from 1995 through 1999, and winning four of five bowl games. They never finished lower than 17th in the rankings, and they produced such All-Americans as linebackers LaVar Arrington and Brandon Short, running back Curtis Enis, defensive end Courtney Brown, safety Kim Herring, and cornerback David Macklin.

Although the Lions didn't get back to the Rose Bowl in that span, Paterno's Powerhouse did post impressive regular-season victories over Michigan, Southern Cal, Ohio State, and Miami, while besting top-20 teams Auburn, Texas, and Texas A&M in the postseason.

But there were signs that trouble was ahead, on and off the field.

New NCAA recruiting limitations and rules were starting to hurt the mainstay football programs like Penn State by preventing the big-time programs from hoarding players. The talent pool was spread out, improving the prospects for many teams that previously had been unable to compete for top-level players.

In addition, colleges from coast to coast in all conferences, and even the independent schools, were getting their games televised. They all had a large presence on the Internet. Recruits knew of the Nittany Lions, but they also knew about Horned Frogs and Utes, about Bearcats and Scarlet Knights. Competition was everywhere, long before the teams even got onto the field.

By 2000, the likes of Paterno, Bobby Bowden of Florida State, Phillip Fulmer of Tennessee, and Lloyd Carr of Michigan no longer ruled the landscape simply by virtue of the reputations of their universities.

The turn of the century brought something else very new to State College: losing.

Beginning with a 29–5 loss to Southern California in the Kickoff Classic at the Meadowlands, the 2000 team spiraled downward. There were such ignominies as a 24–6 home defeat to Toledo, a 12–0 flop at archrival Pitt, a 45–6 humiliation at Ohio State, and a brutal 26–23 loss at Beaver Stadium to Iowa in double overtime.

The 5–7 record marked the most losses for Penn State since 1931, when it went 2–8. For the first time since 1988, Penn State did not earn a bowl invitation.

Although Paterno said at the beginning of the year that he had modest expectations for the team in 2000, criticism still came from all quarters, including, stunningly, a player.

"It's the system," said Larry Johnson, a tailback and the son of defensive line coach Larry Johnson Sr. "We've got coaches who've been here for 30, 20 years. It seems like things never change."

Although Johnson recanted later on, his willingness to speak out reflected a deepening frustration among players because the team wasn't winning. Others spoke out, but none as high profile as Johnson, who later went on to star for the Kansas City Chiefs in the NFL before having off-field woes.

Things didn't get much better for the team in 2001, and the tragedy of the September 11 terrorist attacks hit Paterno particularly hard.

"I'm having a very, very difficult time, because all my background is right around the World Trade Center," said an emotionally drained Paterno, who grew up in Brooklyn and whose father and grandfather worked in Manhattan. "I've walked all those streets many, many times. I have some friends, and we were concerned about one of our football players. I'm not sure we have accounted for everybody that worked in Wall Street."

Paterno's players couldn't help but notice the effect the attacks had on the coach.

"He couldn't get a lot of words out, and when you see an emotional coach we knew something was wrong," linebacker Shamar Finney said. "He spoke to us about the importance of life, not just football. We talked about calling our families just to tell them you love them because you never know when you're going to see them. He told the guys football isn't everything—life is far more valuable than football."

After falling behind 12–7 to Texas in the first half of the 1997 Fiesta Bowl, the Lions charged back to outscore the Longhorns 31–3 in the second half. Curtis Enis (No. 39) rushed for two touchdowns to go with his first-half TD pass reception. *Penn State University Archives, Pennsylvania State University Libraries*

BEAVER STADIUM

It took 13 seasons in the Big Ten before Penn State could claim first place in one area: stadium size.

Always second to Michigan's Big House, Beaver Stadium earned the distinction of the nation's largest venue in 2008, when Ann Arbor lost more than 1,000 seats to comply with government requirements for handicapped access.

Like the Big House, Beaver Stadium has a rich history featuring many renovations that eventually led to a capacity in excess of 100,000.

Beaver Stadium began life at about half its current 107,282 capacity. It opened in 1960 at the current site on the east end of campus after previously existing on the west side.

Named in honor of James A. Beaver, a local lawyer who rose from enlisted man in the Union Army during the Civil War to general, then became a superior court judge and governor of Pennsylvania, the original football home was known as Beaver Field. It opened in 1893 with 500 seats, although weather issues delayed its debut before Penn State routed Pitt (then Western University) 32–0 on November 6.

Sixteen years later, on October 2, 1909, a new, wooden Beaver Field was the site of a 31–0 romp past Grove City. Some major renovations took place in 1936, when the stadium was converted to steel and capacity eventually reached 30,000.

When Penn State joined the Big Ten in the 1990s, the Nittany Lions already had one of the biggest football stadiums in America. This 1995 version of Beaver Stadium seated 93,967 and was soon to be updated. *Penn State University Archives, Pennsylvania State University Libraries*

But the big move came in 1960, when Beaver Field was dismantled in 700 pieces and the materials moved a mile across campus. An additional 16,000 seats were installed to construct Beaver Stadium.

"The opener did not sell out," recalled Penn State ticket manager Bud Meredith. "In the 1950s, with very few exceptions, the games did not sell out."

That stadium was but a shell of what the football team's home looks like today. When the Nittany Lions christened Beaver Stadium on September 17, 1960, with a 20–0 victory over Boston University, there were 46,284 seats, no lights (they came in 1984), and no luxury boxes—it was 2001 before those came.

"I go back to the early 1970s, when we started a master planning for the stadium," said former associate athletic director Herb Schmidt. "We're trying to keep the feel of the stadium so that additions feel like additions. That master planning process has helped us along the way. There are pieces that are still not completed."

As Beaver Stadium has grown in size, demand for tickets had not abated in State College, so the school periodically has increased the capacity by building up and around. Penn State added 2,000 seats in 1969, another 9,000 just three years later, and expanded the bleachers in the south end zone in 1976, bringing capacity to 60,203.

A huge expansion two years later, when the stadium was raised by hydraulic jacks to install more seats, and another expansion in 1980, brought capacity to 83,770. And in 1991, an upper deck in the north end zone added 10,000 seats.

Could Beaver Stadium get even bigger? Of course.

"From a structural standpoint, there are opportunities to enlarge the stadium," Schmidt said. "Some of the things still on our master plan are a new press box back slightly from the current location to allow for seating in front of it, and minor additions could be made."

Infrastructure might become a challenge in the future, though, in terms of accommodating cars and spectator needs if the stadium continues to grow.

"Can we do it? Yeah," Schmidt said. "But can the infrastructure take it? The roads and parking and restrooms and all the other things a football stadium like ours, that has fans coming on Thursday and not leaving until Sunday, must have. We are not in a city with major highways and hotels."

Players, coaches, and school employees—Nittany Lions through and through—carry fond memories of Beaver Stadium. For many, it has been a home away from home.

"I started going to football games in Beaver Stadium probably when I was 12 years old, just after it had been moved," Dave Joyner said. "I can remember climbing the fence and sneaking in as a kid. We didn't watch the games so much, because back then the end zones were open, and there was a lot of grass. I can remember playing football way out of the way, but during breaks getting chased around by the cops."

Perhaps that got Joyner in shape for his three seasons (1969–1971) as a Nittany Lion.

Tailgating is a big-time activity at State College before Penn State games—even the family pet gets into the act. *Penn State University Archives, Pennsylvania State University Libraries*

E. J. Sandusky, son of longtime Penn State assistant coach Jerry Sandusky, recalled the fascination with which the 1978 expansion was viewed, when the stadium was raised up to add more seats. "One of our next-door neighbors, a retired professor in the civil engineering department at Penn State, . . . was always up there taking pictures, because they cut the stadium and raised it up and slid in the concrete . . . like the first 30, 40 rows."

When he was a player, Sandusky witnessed the addition of the first upper deck in the north end zone. "We used to stretch for practice, and the construction workers were up there on the beams, and they'd drop these big rivets, and they'd come falling down and hit the aluminum bleachers. 'BOOM, BOOM!'"

Although Beaver Stadium is one of the hardest places to play in the country, it has been a favored destination even for visiting players and coaches.

"It's a beautiful setting, a classy program," USC coach John Robinson said. "When you go to Penn State to play, they don't hate you, they respect you. It's fun to go there."

TOP-10 BEAVER STADIUM CROWDS (THROUGH 2008)

1.	110,753	September 14, 2002	Penn State 40, Nebraska 7
2.	110,134	October 27, 2007	Ohio State 37, Penn State 17
3.	110,078	September 8, 2007	Penn State 31, Notre Dame 10
4.	110,017	October 18, 2008	Penn State 46, Michigan 17
5.	110,007	October 14, 2006	Michigan 17, Penn State 10
6.	109,865	November 5, 2005	Penn State 35, Wisconsin 14
7.	109,845	November 22, 2008	Penn State 49, Michigan State 18
8.	109,839	October 8, 2005	Penn State 17, Ohio State 10
9.	109,754	October 13, 2007	Penn State 38, Wisconsin 7
10.	109,467	October 29, 2005	Penn State 33, Purdue 15

Beaver Stadium has undergone multiple expansions to accommodate the ever-increasing popularity of the Nittany Lions in the 2000s. Today it can seat well over 100,000 fans, making it one of the largest facilities in the nation. *Ken Rappoport*

The student "white out" has become an annual ritual at Penn State. For designated games, students are asked to dress in white as a show of support for the football team. *Ken Rappoport*

Ultimately, though, the Nittany Lions had to turn back to the field. After a week of mourning, in which nearly every sporting event across the country was postponed or canceled, it became essential to re-create some sense of normalcy in America, including on the football field.

Whether it was a lack of focus after September 11, or a lack of talent overall, the Lions opened the 2001 season 0–4, and the whispers that JoePa had lost his touch grew louder. They couldn't even be drowned out when Paterno passed Bear Bryant for most career victories.

Paterno entered the season needing one victory to tie the legendary Bryant's 323 victories in Division I-A. Normally, that would be no problem. Not in this year.

The Lions lost to Miami of Florida, the second-ranked team in the nation, then to Wisconsin, Iowa, and Michigan. By the time they headed to 22nd-ranked Northwestern on October 20, 2001, it wasn't so much a question of when the 74-year-old Paterno would pass the Bear, but if he could do it in 2001.

But the veteran coach had some new tricks—well, actually, something tested and true—for the Wildcats, who were among the nation's top offensive powers.

Paterno returned to the power-I that had been a staple of his offense—in the 1970s. With a full-house backfield, the Lions went from the most inept offense in the nation to a ground-it-out machine. They rushed for 213 yards against Northwestern, more than in the first four defeats combined, gained 501 yards in all, and rallied behind freshman quarterback Zack Mills to take down the 'Cats 38–35.

It would be fun to report that Paterno did a dance at midfield or was doused with Gatorade after tying Bryant's monumental mark, but not at Penn State. Not for Joe Paterno.

"Sure, it means a lot," Paterno said in his most understated manner. "If I got it, fine. If I didn't get it, I wouldn't have worried about it. I'm just fortunate enough to have coached as many games as I have. I've enjoyed every one of them.

"I'm just excited for this football team. I didn't even think about it until one of the television guys came up to me after the game."

The players were less modest on their coach's behalf.

"He knows everything," running back Omar Easy said. "He can't be stopped."

If he and the Lions couldn't be stopped the next week at home against Ohio State, Paterno would surpass Bryant. In an unguarded moment, he revealed just how meaningful such an achievement would be.

"This is one of the really good ones I've been around. This is one of the really important ones," he said. "I'll go home, probably get in trouble with a good stiff bourbon, take a couple-hour nap, and then look at some Ohio State tape."

LaVar Arrington became the tenth Penn State linebacker to be chosen All-American and only the third to earn the distinction twice (1998 and 1999). Here he sacks Purdue's Drew Brees, causing a fumble that Arrington recovered and ran in for a touchdown in the Lions' 31–25 win in 1999. *Tom Strickland/AP Images*

Following an upset victory over Ohio State on October 27, 2001, Coach Paterno and the Nittany Lions celebrated career win number 324 for JoePa, placing him ahead of Bear Bryant on the all-time list. *Jamie Squire/Allsport/Getty Images*

He couldn't have liked what he saw on those tapes, because the Buckeyes had more talent and more wins—four to Penn State's one. But Ohio State was not playing for history.

Through much of the first three quarters, though, only one team looked like it belonged in the Big Ten, and that was the visitor. Ohio State led 27–9, but Mills led a superb comeback. He connected with Eric McCoo for a 14-yard touchdown pass to give Penn State a 29–27 lead early in the final quarter.

When Bryan Scott blocked a Buckeyes field goal attempt in the closing minutes, the Nittany Lions had their second win of 2001. And JoePa had No. 324.

Paterno even relented to a ceremony after the game at midfield, where he hugged his wife and grandchildren.

"I am overwhelmed right now," Paterno said. "I am struggling here to not say something that sounds stupid—I usually do that when we lose."

A week later, a 7-foot sculpture of the coach was erected outside Beaver Stadium, a lasting tribute to the legend. The sculpture shows Paterno with his hand in the air, index finger raised, and in midstride, leading the Nittany Lions onto the field. The coach is dressed in a blazer, his tie blown to one side, and his pant legs rolled up, of course.

"Looks good," said Sue Paterno. "His pants need to be pressed."

The statue was unveiled the day before the Lions beat Southern Mississippi 38–20 on Homecoming Day. That brought the record to 3–4, but the Lions would split their next four games to finish at 5–6.

Meanwhile, Bobby Bowden was winning enough games at Florida State to run neck and neck with Paterno for the all-time coaching victories record.

"I hope Joe keeps coaching," Bowden said. "He's the only one left older than me."

Bowden's joke would become a sore point for some members of Nittany Nation. They feared that losing records would become a common occurrence in Happy Valley, and that Paterno no longer was the right choice to lead Penn State.

"When you're 0–4 and you end up 5–6, I guess you accomplished something. But 5–6 or 6–5 is not what we're looking for," Paterno said. "We have to get the program back to where it was a couple of years ago."

TROUBLE IN HAPPY VALLEY

Heading into the 2002 season, Paterno believed the Nittany Lions would be special again. Larry Johnson was the most formidable running back he'd had in years. Zack Mills displayed a precociousness as a freshman that could only translate into more success in the near future. Bryant Johnson was outstanding at wide receiver. This team would score.

"Of course, if we had enough people up front, we'd like to just power across the line and shove it down the defense's throat," offensive coordinator Fran Ganter admitted. "But I think those days are over for just about everybody. You've got to start thinking about stretching people out, and that's what we're trying to do."

If Penn State could prevent opponents from lighting up the scoreboard, a bounce-back season seemed likely. And with a defensive line featuring future pros Jimmy Kennedy, Michael Haynes, and Anthony Adams, defensive power wasn't a farfetched notion.

"We have pretty much everyone back from last year's team, and toward the end of the year, we were making a lot of plays," Mills said. "We want to continue to build on that."

They did by winning their first three games, including a 40–7 romp past No. 8 Nebraska. But then the Lions got into their Big Ten schedule, and a 42–35 overtime loss to Iowa marked the first of three conference defeats.

A four-game surge at the end of the season lifted them to 8–4, fourth in the Big Ten. Not exactly where the Lions wanted to be, but hardly discouraging, considering where they'd been the previous two seasons.

The Nittany Lions stayed in the rankings the entire season, peaking at No. 10 before a 13–10 loss to Auburn in the Capital One Bowl. The firestorm that had been building around the program was abating.

Progress was apparent with the 2002 squad, and Paterno told them just that after the bowl loss.

"I said, 'I just hope you guys understand what you did, coming through a period where a lot of people doubted that we'd ever be a competitive football program again,'" he said. "I just hope they don't let this last one distort some of the good things that happened to us."

Unfortunately, a lot more negative things would happen in the next two years, during which time Penn State posted records of 3–9 and 4–7. And with the losing came the rap sheets.

Not that Penn State was squeaky clean in the preceding years; any school that claims it doesn't have disciplinary issues, malcontents, or even criminals is populated by administrators wearing blinders. But in the new millennium, Penn State players—even recruits who never actually got into a game—besmirched the name of the university as well as their own reputations.

The stream of arrests and dismissals from school became steady enough that observers began doubting Paterno's Grand Experiment. The Penn State community was particularly upset to see the program lumped in with universities where academics always took a back seat to athletic performance, and with other prestigious schools suddenly experiencing their own scandals.

Although running back Larry Johnson Jr. had been an outspoken critic of the team's coaching style, he developed into one of Penn State's most potent offensive weapons. In 2002, he set a school record with 2,087 yards rushing. *Penn State/Collegiate Images/Getty Images*

Quarterback Zack Mills emerged as a star during his sophomore season of 2002, leading the Lions to big wins over Nebraska and Wisconsin. He ranks as Penn State's leading passer, with more than 7,200 yards and 1,082 attempts. *Nati Harnik/AP Images*

As one 1999 grad said, "Penn State is not Florida State or West Virginia or some of those other schools that always seem to go on probation. You even see schools like Notre Dame and Stanford having some problems, but you think it won't happen in your backyard. And then it does."

What happened was a number of off-field woes plaguing Penn State early in the new millennium.

Rashard Casey was one of the hottest football prospects in the nation after leading Hoboken to two New Jersey state titles. The state high school player of the year in 1997, he chose to attend Penn State, where Paterno and company envisioned him as the quarterback who could lead them to Big Ten supremacy.

In May 2000, Casey was involved in an incident back home in which an off-duty police officer was beaten up. Casey was charged with assault, but he was not disciplined by the school or the football program. A school judicial committee investigated Casey's involvement, but he was allowed to play for the Lions throughout the 2000 season.

That led to campus protests, particularly one by Justin Leto, a computer engineering major who was charged with trespassing when he helped hang a protest banner outside a National Governors Association reception on campus. Those charges later were dropped, but Leto was placed on deferred suspension by the university.

"We think they're going to bend over backward to find Rashard Casey innocent. But they'll do whatever it takes to find other people guilty," Leto said.

Coach Paterno stood by his player as the storm of controversy swirled around Casey. "You don't expect me to do anything just because something is alleged," said Paterno, who had named Casey as a team captain.

Casey also spoke out in his own defense. "There's nothing anybody can say about me or do to me that will change what I have to do on the field," he said. "I live with it, grow from it. You learn a lot from things that happen in your life."

Paterno's support was criticized until the day a grand jury declined to indict Casey, although it did return a third-degree aggravated-assault charge against Casey's former high school teammate, Desmond Miller. Casey ultimately sued the Hoboken police force, claiming he received hate mail and death threats after being charged. He settled the suit out of court.

But damage had been done to the Nittany Lions' image. And the Casey controversy wasn't the last one to plague the campus.

In 2003, receiver Maurice Humphrey was charged with assault after a fight at an on-campus apartment complex. A year later, after being convicted on those charges, Humphrey was sentenced to nine months in prison for a parole violation.

Receiver Tony Johnson was arrested on a drunken driving charge; so was former player Dethrell Garcia. Five players were cited for underage drinking, and defensive tackle Scott Paxson pleaded guilty to criminal mischief for riding a bicycle that had been reported stolen. Lineman Tommy McHugh was dismissed from the team for allegedly hitting a woman in downtown State College, for harassment, public drunkenness, and underaged drinking, also in 2003.

McHugh's uncle had played for Paterno, which made the dismissal particularly painful for the coach.

"Tommy did a dumb thing. He did it after I had talked to the squad, on the plane, 'Everybody behave,' and the whole bit, and he didn't. And he's got to suffer the consequences," Paterno said. "And I think somewhere along the line the squad has to understand that there's responsibility, and obviously we have some kids that have skirted it here and skirted it there."

In 2004, defensive back Anwar Phillips was charged with sexual assault but ultimately was acquitted, and his arrest was expunged from criminal records. Before his case went to trial, he accepted a two-semester expulsion from the university.

Paterno was excoriated for allowing Phillips to play in the Capital One Bowl on January 1, 2003, but then Phillips was found not guilty.

Even after the Lions turned it around and mounted an impressive 11–1 season in 2005, the team was not without its scandals. Defensive back Paul Cronin was cited by university police for public drunkenness in October and was temporarily kicked off the team. Paterno reinstated him in time to play in the Orange Bowl.

"I watched him. He went on the scout team and worked his butt off, didn't pout, and the coaches thought he should get another shot," Paterno said. "So I gave him another shot."

Defensive tackle Ed Johnson also was expelled for two semesters after violating a university regulation about sexual misconduct. (Years later, Johnson was kicked off the Indianapolis Colts for another legal run-in.)

In 2006, Lavon Chisley, a defensive end who missed his final season due to academic ineligibility a year earlier, was arrested in Maryland on marijuana charges. He previously had been charged with the same offense in Pennsylvania. By far the most chilling crime on Chisley's rap sheet—or on that of any former Nittany Lions player—came in 2007, when he was convicted on murder charges in the killing of a student who was stabbed 93 times. Chisley was sentenced to life in prison.

The 2006 season also saw Paxson plead no contest to disorderly conduct while facing trial on indecent assault charges. A judge also dismissed a sexual assault charge against Paxson.

In 2007, former tight end R. J. Luke was ordered to pay $900,000 to a man who was thrown through

Anwar Phillips was an effective defensive back for Penn State as a starter in 2004 and 2005, but his off-field troubles earned him nearly as many headlines. Here, against Akron, he pulls in one of his team-high four interceptions in 2004. *Carolyn Kaster/AP Images*

a window at an off-campus fraternity house six years earlier. Luke and former linebacker T. C. Cosby had been acquitted of aggravated assault and other counts in a criminal trial in 2002.

Fullback Dan Lawlor was charged with driving under the influence, stemming from an arrest in April 2007.

And in a group action, six players—defensive backs Anthony Scirrotto, Lydell Sargeant, and Justin King, defensive tackle Chris Baker, and linebackers Jerome Hayes and Tyrell Sales—turned themselves in to authorities after being charged with trespassing at a party at an off-campus apartment, where a fight broke out.

In 2008, defensive back Willie Harriott was dismissed from the team after he was arrested for driving under the influence and speeding. Also, defensive tackles Chris Baker and Phil Taylor were kicked off the squad for off-field issues that included fights. Receiver Chris Bell was sent packing after police said he threatened a teammate with a knife in a dining hall. Bell was already suspended at the time for another incident.

In many of these situations, Paterno was proven right to have stood by his players when charges were later dropped or the individuals were found not guilty. Still, the perception of Penn State being something of an outlaw school ran directly contrary to Paterno's mission—a mission that he'd carried out so successfully through the decades.

Overall, according to an ESPN report in 2008, Penn State football players had faced 163 criminal charges since 2002, with 27 players convicted or pleading guilty to 45 counts.

Paterno himself was not immune to off-field turmoil. In October 2007, a motorist complained to university police about a confrontation involving the coach, and although no charges were filed, news of the incident spread quickly on the Internet, and Paterno's actions were portrayed as road rage.

As the coach explained it, a driver ran a stop sign, and Paterno blew his horn at her. He pulled up beside the driver and said, "You went through that sign. Don't do that again, because I took your license number." He hadn't actually taken the license number, but the encounter wasn't over, as suddenly a man came up and knocked on Paterno's window.

"I put the window down, and he says, 'That's my wife.'"

Paterno then told the man, "Boy, that's your problem."

Paterno reflected on the episode after it gained a lot of attention: "I'm not the greatest guy in the world. I make a lot of mistakes, and they want to second-guess my coaching. But, gee, when I was doing what I thought was helpful . . . Now it's a national event."

Coincidentally, on the same day as the traffic incident, Paterno suspended tailback Austin Scott for violating team rules.

Perhaps the most publicized disciplinary action JoePa has taken in recent years came in 2007 following more off-field incidents, including several fights involving football players. Paterno ordered the entire team to clean Beaver Stadium following home games.

"Obviously, he's not happy with the whole situation," co-captain Dan Connor said. "That's understandable, but the mood of the team is we have to overcome things off the field like that. We've got to stay focused."

TURNING THINGS AROUND

As the "Should he stay or should he go?" debate raged on in not-so-Happy Valley, Paterno was more concerned about getting the off-field problems behind him and putting the Penn State football program back on top.

In May 2004, Paterno, then 77, signed a four-year contract extension. There was, of course, much discussion about it—much loud discussion.

"We certainly looked overall and very much felt that we wanted him to continue," athletic director Tim Curley said. "We're really excited about the current squad members and the group that we've got coming in. We don't think we're that far away."

On the other hand, Bill Earley, a retired Wall Street executive and longtime Penn State booster, told the Associated Press: "I'm stunned. I'd have been surprised with two years, but four? I'm flabbergasted. I don't know how anyone could say they did this thinking about the future. The data just doesn't support it. This is a decision not just for the next three to five years, but for five years beyond that."

Paterno was mostly focused on the short-term goal of fielding a competitive team in 2005, but he knew that his long-term status at Penn State was never more endangered.

"It was out there," Paterno said of the criticism. "I didn't pay any attention to it. Oblivious is probably too strong a word. I was not concerned with it. You're not always going to be on top. You've got to be able to take the losses. You shouldn't stay in this business if you can't."

Paterno stayed in the business again and turned the team around, yet again, in remarkable fashion.

The 2005 squad posted Penn State's best record since the perfect 1994 campaign, going 11–1 and trying for the Big Ten championship. They ended the season ranked third in the nation, and JoePa earned his fifth Coach of the Year honor.

Led by the offensive exploits of quarterback Michael Robinson and tackle Levi Brown, plus a staunch defense sparked by All-Americans Tambi Hali at end and Paul Posluszny at linebacker, the Lions did exactly what they had done so many times under Paterno.

"It's a sense of accomplishment and relief," Robinson said. "A lot of people doubted us, a lot of people doubted Joe Paterno, a lot of people doubted this team."

Robinson emphasized how Paterno clearly deserved the Coach of the Year award. "He's worked so hard. He stayed with us. People told him to retire. Now look at him. Nobody's saying to retire and no more 'Joe must go' websites. None of that."

After starting the season 6–0, Penn State's only loss came against Michigan, which scored on the last play of the game for a 27–25 final. The Lions then rolled to victories in their final four games, outscoring the opposition 162–61, to set up a memorable postseason meeting with Bobby Bowden's Florida State Seminoles in the Orange Bowl on January 3, 2006.

For the two legendary coaches, the matchup was irresistible. By this time, Bowden had surpassed Paterno on the all-time wins list; JoePa subsequently would take back the lead in a seesaw contest between "two curmudgeons," as Bowden jokingly referred to them.

"We both have reached the age which, the first time something goes wrong, they say, 'He's too old,'" said Bowden, 76 at the time. "It's been very easy for me to use Joe as a gauge because both of us are experiencing the age factor. Joe was pretty straightforward. He said, 'Don't let it get you. Stay with what you believe. Don't back down.'"

The players also were enamored of the historic nature of the coaching matchup.

"For somebody to say it's not a big deal, I think they'd be lying," Florida State running back Lorenzo

Paterno and company looked to turn things around heading into the 2005 season. Penn State got off to a good start, with six straight victories to open the schedule. *Carolyn Kaster/AP Images*

Linebackers Dan Connor (left, No. 40) and Paul Posluszny (No. 31) converge on Minnesota tight end Matt Spaeth during Penn State's 44–14 thrashing of the 19th-ranked Gophers on October 1, 2005. *Carolyn Kaster/AP Images*

Booker said. "This is like a once-in-a-lifetime deal, and it's not going to happen for another century. We won't be alive, because you have to coach a long time to do what these guys have done.

"It's something you can tell your grandkids, that you actually played for the guy that won the most and played against the guy that was second on the list."

In this case, No. 2 (at the time) outlasted No. 1 (at the time)—until one o'clock in the morning.

Penn State broke away to an early lead on a 2-yard touchdown run by Austin Scott, who carried five times for 57 yards on the scoring drive. The defenses then held each other in check until the final four minutes of the second quarter.

After Florida State scored twice to take a 14–13 lead, the Lions responded with a 25-yard touchdown pass from Robinson to Ethan Kilmer. Kilmer made a great leaping catch with six seconds left in the half.

With 13:36 to play in regulation, Penn State tacked on a safety for a 16–13 lead. At the 4:08 mark, a Florida State field goal tied the score at 16.

After a scoreless first overtime, both teams scored a touchdown—including Scott's second of the night—in the second OT, to set the stage for more drama.

Penn State kicker Kevin Kelly, who earlier missed two short field goals that would have won the contest, ended it in the third overtime with a 29-yarder.

"I still had my confidence," Kelly said after Penn State's 26–23 victory. "I don't think I've ever missed three in a row."

The Lions survived in great part because the Seminoles were even worse in their kicking game—hardly unusual for Florida State.

"When they pick the all-time missed field-goal coach, I'll probably get the award," Bowden said. "We're masters at that."

After the 2005 season, Paterno was a coaching master once more.

Paterno and the Nittany Lions were fired up heading into their historic matchup with Bobby Bowden's Florida State Seminoles in the 2006 Orange Bowl. *Carolyn Kaster/AP Images*

Right: Voted Big Ten Offensive Player of the Year for 2005, quarterback Michael Robinson capped off the season by completing 21 of 39 passes for 253 yards in Penn State's Orange Bowl win over Florida State. *Alan Diaz/AP Images*

Below: After blowing a chance to win the game at the end of regulation, Kevin Kelly delivered this game-winning kick in the third overtime to defeat Florida State, 26–23. *Alan Diaz/AP Images*

PATERNO RISES ABOVE AN INJURY

Some seasons are revered in Happy Valley for long winning strings and convincing victories. Others are marked by defeats and disappointments.

The 2006 campaign had one unforgettable moment: During the November 4 game against Wisconsin, coach Paterno was run down on the sideline by Nittany Lions tight end Andrew Quarless and Badgers linebacker DeAndre Levy.

Levy's helmet struck Paterno's left leg, and down went the coach.

Diagnosis: a broken shinbone and two torn knee ligaments.

Prognosis: For anyone who knew JoePa, he would be one incorrigible patient. But he'd also find a way back to the stadium quickly.

Paterno was still recuperating several days after the incident but was obviously in no mood to sit still.

"He woke up today and asked for the second phase of the game plan and scouting reports on Temple," school spokesman Guido D'Elia told the Associated Press. "He's been on the phone all day. He's still in charge."

Paterno's squad was 7–3, and he knew that wins over Temple and traditional closing rival Michigan State would secure the Nittany Lions a significant bowl bid. Even if he couldn't be on hand, he was going to do his utmost to ensure the team was prepared.

"It was strange not to see him there on the sideline," Posluzny said. "He was just always there. Always."

If Paterno wasn't there physically, his aura still infiltrated Beaver Stadium. One handwritten sign in the student section read: "Roll up your pant legs for JoePa." Another said: "After 41 years, JoePa can still take a hit! Get well soon."

JoePa had a presence outside the stadium, too. The bronzed statue of Paterno was covered with necklaces, pompoms, and, yes, its left knee was bandaged.

Paterno missed a Penn State game for the first time since 1977, when his son David was involved in a serious trampoline accident. He also missed a game in 1955 when his father passed away.

The Nittany Lions blitzed the outmanned Owls 47–0, scoring 21 points in the first quarter and never looking back. At the end of the rout, tackle Levi Brown carried the football off the field with one purpose: "This game ball is going to go to coach Paterno,"
he proclaimed. "Wherever he's at, I'm going to take it to him."

Paterno watched from home.

"What really hit home is when he said, 'Good luck guys, I love you,'" Posluzny said. "Even though he wasn't here, he was definitely with us in spirit."

That spirit would carry the Nittany Lions into their season finale with Michigan State, the annual battle for the Land Grant Trophy. Paterno wasn't about to miss this one, even if it meant coaching from the press box. Watching from his perch up high, he still allowed his assistant coaches to run the team.

Among those assistants was defensive coordinator Tom Bradley. Nicknamed "Scrap," because of his scrappy nature as a player at State College, Bradley joined Paterno's staff directly out of school in 1979. He worked his way up from graduate assistant to recruit-

In a scene that sent chills through the hearts of Nittany Lions fans everywhere, this collision between Wisconsin's DeAndre Levy and Penn State's Andrew Quarless in the game on November 4, 2006, sent Quarless barreling into Joe Paterno. The coach had to be carted off the field with a leg injury. *John Maniaci, Wisconsin State Journal/AP Images*

Defensive coordinator Tom Bradley (center) assumed head coaching responsibilities while Paterno recovered from his leg injury. Bradley led the Lions to an easy 47–0 victory over Temple. *Carolyn Kaster/AP Images*

ing coordinator to position coach and, in 2000, added defensive coordinator to his role as cornerbacks coach.

Penn State's return to the top echelon of the sport was due in great part to Bradley's work as a recruiter. He not only mined the talent-laden ranks of Pennsylvania high schools, but he brought a Nittany Lions presence to other key areas of the country. Thanks greatly to Bradley, Penn State became a major force with high school players from coast to coast.

Dozens of times during more than a quarter-century at Penn State, Bradley entertained offers to become the head coach elsewhere. But he stayed.

"You hear the grass is always greener on the other side," Bradley told *The Sporting News*. "I haven't found that. I just really, sincerely like it here."

And Bradley was liked so much in Happy Valley that it was assumed that if and when JoePa ever decided he had enough, Bradley would take over the program. That was not a subject Bradley, or Paterno, had been eager to broach.

"Whether that's in the cards, I don't know right now. It depends on when I get out of it," Paterno said. "If I'm going to leave tomorrow, I would hope that it's in the cards, but I'm not planning on leaving tomorrow."

Instead, he would be high above the field, watching Bradley and the other coaches lead the Lions against Michigan State in pursuit of victory No. 8 and a spot in the Outback Bowl on New Year's Day in Tampa.

Paterno didn't like what he saw early on, as the Lions lost four fumbles in the first half and trailed 13–7 at halftime. In his way, Paterno let the coaches know about it.

"Joe was up in the box and had observations, saw some things, and it worked," veteran offensive coordinator Galen Hall said. "It was good to have him up there. He was very much involved in the game."

Paterno was up there all right, squirming in his seat until Bradley's defense shut down the Spartans in the second half—Michigan State managed a mere 14 yards rushing all game and barely saw Penn State territory after intermission.

A 6-yard pass from Anthony Morelli to Jordan Norwood put the Nittany Lions in front 14–13, and they added Kevin Kelly's 45-yard field goal for a 17–13 victory.

On to sunny Florida. But where would JoePa coach from?

"It's not like being on the sidelines," said Paterno, making it clear that the press box was not the place for him on game day. "It never will be."

But it would be his station on January 1 when the Lions met Tennessee. At 80 years of age, it's difficult enough recovering from such injuries without manning the sideline for an entire game.

That reality hit Paterno like, well, a couple of players smashing into his leg. At least his players gave him the best get-well wishes they could by holding the Volunteers to 83 yards rushing and finishing off the 2006 campaign in style with a 20–10 victory for JoePa's twenty-second bowl win.

"I have a great staff. . . . They need me like I need a hole in my head," Paterno joked after the game. "All I do is get in the way and yell."

The victory over Tennessee earned the Lions their first win in five games against a ranked team that season. That meant a lot as they looked ahead to 2007.

"We finally proved that we can beat a ranked opponent," Posluszny said. "It's great for the program because now you have all this momentum this season going into the next season."

That next season would be a near repeat of 2006. Despite a 4–4 record in conference play, the Lions' 8–4 overall record was good enough for a trip to the Alamo Bowl, where they defeated Texas A&M 24–17.

Would a more prestigious bowl appearance be in the cards for 2008?

With Joe Paterno coaching from the press box, Penn State defeated Tennessee 20–10 in the 2007 Outback Bowl. Tony Hunt's 158 yards rushing led the way for the offense, while the Lions defense held the Volunteers to a total of 83 yards on the ground. *Steve Nesius/AP Images*

ANOTHER RUN FOR THE ROSES

If Joe Paterno and the Nittany Lions wanted to sneak up on the rest of the college football world and maybe, just maybe, steal away with another national title, they went about it the wrong way in 2008.

While the coach and his players usually preferred to let others grab the national spotlight while the guys from Happy Valley simply went about their business, 2008 was all about making headlines for the Lions. Among those emblazoned across newspapers heading into the season were: "JoePa's Finale?" Or "Penn State Back Among the Elite." Or "Where's Joe? Look in the Press Box."

Indeed, from the summer practices in August through the juicy Rose Bowl matchup with Southern Cal on New Year's Day 2009, the 2008 season was one to remember and cherish.

"When I came here, I wanted to make a difference with the program," receiver Derrick Williams said. "I definitely think I made a difference with my teammates, I guess, putting Penn State back to where we were."

Back on the sideline for the 2008 season opener against Coastal Carolina, Paterno made sure his coaches and players were fully focused. They responded with nine straight wins, while outscoring the opposition by an average margin of 42–11 during that stretch. *Carolyn Kaster/AP Images*

In Penn State's first conference game of 2008, Derrick Williams' 94-yard kickoff return to open the fourth quarter helped the Lions to a 38–24 win over Illinois. *Carolyn Kaster/AP Images*

The Nittany Lions headed into Paterno's 43rd campaign as head coach with a new offense as well as some of the familiar recent headaches. Even before the team gathered in August to prepare for the opener against Coastal Carolina, defensive tackles Chris Baker and Phil Taylor were dismissed from the squad after previously being suspended.

"You're always going to have problems when you're dealing with a lot of kids," Paterno said. "I hope I can always think it through and do what I think is best for the kid."

What was best for the football team on the field was the adjustment to the HD spread offense. With such dynamic performers as quarterback Daryll Clark, running back Evan Royster, and receivers Derrick Williams, Deon Butler, and Jordan Norwood, it was a natural move to open up the attack.

"This is what I've been waiting on," said Clark, a senior who backed up Anthony Morelli for two seasons before getting his chance to shine. "It's been a long time coming. I've been very patient, very quiet about everything."

Clark even consulted Michael Robinson, who ran a similar offense at Penn State before moving on to the San Francisco 49ers, where he was converted to a tailback. Robinson told Clark the key to engineering such an offense is film study; Clark would watch game films three times, each for a different reason, ranging from enjoyment to evaluating the aggressiveness of the defense to analyzing pass coverages.

A true measure of Penn State's strengths and weaknesses would not come too quickly during the 2008 season. As the team prepared for the opener with Coastal Carolina, Paterno reminded his players that Appalachian State had journeyed to the Big House and beaten Michigan in the teams' 2007 debut, and that the Lions could be just as vulnerable.

They weren't, romping 66–10.

Running back Evan Royster left Wolverines defenders in the dust all day long during Penn State's 46–17 win over Michigan in 2008. He ran for 176 yards and one touchdown. *Gene J. Puskar/AP Images*

The Nittany Lions defense held the Buckeyes without a touchdown during their 13–6 victory on October 25, 2008. The fourth-quarter fumble by Ohio State quarterback Terrelle Pryor—caused by linebackers Navorro Bowman (No. 18) and Tyrell Sales (No. 46) and safety Mark Rubin (No. 9)—was a key moment. *Jay LaPrete/AP Images*

The next three non-conference foes put up about the same amount of resistance. Penn State walloped Oregon State (which months later went into its season finale with a shot at the Rose Bowl), Syracuse, and Temple. While it was nice to see the Orange and the Owls, once regular rivals of Penn State, on the schedule, the games were mismatches.

The combined score of the Lions' first four games was 211–40.

These Lions, who roared so loudly in what amounted pretty much to a quartet of preseason games, would get their first real test in the Big Ten opener against Illinois. The Illini were coming off a Rose Bowl appearance the previous season and were among conference favorites in 2008.

"I think we might get some questions answered against Illinois," Paterno said.

One such question was where the coach would station himself during the game. For the Temple game, Paterno moved from the sideline to the press box at halftime, citing pain in his right leg. He sat and watched the Lions dismantle the Owls, and then vowed he would be back on the sideline at Beaver Stadium when the Illini came calling.

Penn State supporters were asked to wear white for the game, something of an annual ritual in recent years. The stadium would look like it was hit by a blizzard come kickoff.

"Prime time, the stage is set so high," Clark said. "And then the 'White House' is what we call it. The big whiteout."

As for Paterno, he was where he promised to be, witnessing one of the greatest individual offensive performances in Penn State history from his normal post on the sideline.

One of the most heralded recruits Paterno ever brought to central Pennsylvania, Williams rarely made highlight-reel plays in his first three seasons at Penn State. As a senior, the year he was also voted a team captain, he was all over the airwaves, particularly in the 38–24 win over Illinois, which helped to establish the Nittany Lions as a potential force in the Big Ten.

Williams scored on Illinois in three ways: a 94-yard kickoff return, a touchdown rushing, and a TD receiving. No one during Paterno's four-plus decades in Happy Valley had ever managed such a feat, and it had both player and coach beaming.

"This is the first time he's really had a chance to break out," Paterno said of Williams. "Derrick's been in tough games and made big plays. . . . When he practices, he carries people with him on the practice field. He can just about do anything you want him to do on the football field. He's a heck of an athlete."

Paterno had dozens of excellent athletes through the years. This group was beginning to have that special look—the look of champions.

Deon Butler—seen here making a touchdown grab against Indiana—became the Nittany Lions' all-time leading receiver in 2008. His 47 catches that year gave him 179 receptions in four seasons at Penn State. *Carolyn Kaster/AP Images*

"Yeah, we think about [a championship]," Williams said with a wide smile. "Why else would you play if you didn't want to be the best at what you do?"

Beating Illinois didn't make the Nittany Lions the best at anything, but it did move them up to No. 6 in the country as they headed to Purdue—and as JoePa headed back up to the press box.

By this time, it had become clear that Paterno was struggling physically when standing on the sideline. With pain in his right hip now added to the 81-year-old coach's maladies, he took a seat upstairs, knowing well that the media would be harping on his health regardless of how the Lions played.

"It is different, but we don't want him to come down there if he's hurt," Royster admitted following a 20–6 victory over the Boilermakers. "We want him to be able to do the best for our team."

The trouble was Paterno himself wasn't sure what would be best for the Nittany Lions from week to week. So he hedged on any pronouncements regarding his intended whereabouts on Saturdays, except for assuring everyone: "I'll be in the stadium."

He was in the press box again for a 48–7 romp at Wisconsin, a prime-time masterpiece that the entire football nation took notice of. Perhaps Paterno played it safe because he was thinking back to two years earlier, when he tore left knee ligaments in a sideline collision with a Badgers player.

For the first time in 2008, Penn State put all the elements together against a formidable opponent. Williams again was a highlight machine, contributing a 63-yard punt return for a touchdown; Clark ran for two touchdowns and passed for one; and cornerback Lydell Sargeant nabbed two interceptions.

The Lions were performing so well that they were able to end their recent jinx against Michigan with no trouble, ending a nine-game losing streak against the Wolverines—the most any team ever hung on JoePa's squads. A coaching change in Ann Arbor had sunk the Wolverines into the morass at the bottom of the league, and the Lions doled out a 46–17 rout that could have been even worse. Clark led his fellow Penn State students in cheers following the game at Beaver Stadium.

Royster rushed for 174 yards on 18 carries, including a 44-yard TD run, and the Lions outscored the Wolverines 32–0 in the second half. The stage was set for a battle for the Big Ten lead at Ohio State the following Saturday.

Paterno was getting used to coaching from the press box—to a point. While he admitted he had a better view of the game, his preference obviously was to coach from the sidelines.

"I'll never like it," Paterno said of his perch high above the field.

Nevertheless, he remained up there for the rest of the schedule.

Up there also could have referred to Penn State's place in the national polls. The Nittany Lions were ranked third as they headed to the Horseshoe in Columbus. If they passed this test, an undefeated season and possibly a spot in the BCS title game would be in reach.

The Buckeyes had dominated the Big Ten for most of the decade, won a national championship, and played for two more. They would have a record 105,000 fans rocking the building.

But the 10th-ranked Buckeyes would be virtually powerless against Penn State's miserly defense.

Although they limited the Buckeyes to two field goals through the first three quarters, the Lions managed only one field goal of their own and trailed 6–3 in the fourth quarter. Things appeared dire, with Clark sidelined with a head injury. Then came the

The Lions clinched a trip to the 2009 Rose Bowl with a 49–18 win over Michigan State in the regular-season finale. Quarterback Darryl Clark had a stellar day, throwing for 341 yards and four touchdowns and running for one TD. *Carolyn Kaster/AP Images*

Although the Nittany Lions scored 482 points en route to an 11–1 regular season and a Big Ten championship in 2008, the offense didn't have enough on January 1, 2009, falling to USC in the Rose Bowl, 38–24. *Jeff Gross/Getty Images*

biggest play of Penn State's season, as defensive back Mark Rubin forced Ohio State quarterback Terrelle Pryor—a Pennsylvania product who spurned Penn State for OSU—to fumble.

From the Buckeyes' 38-yard line, backup quarterback Pat Devlin guided the Nittany Lions to the winning score, which came on his own 1-yard run. A field goal by Kevin Kelly with just over a minute left in the game rounded out the scoring in the 13–6 final.

How momentous was the victory? It was Paterno's first at Ohio Stadium since the Lions joined the Big Ten in 1993. It put the Nittany Lions in command of the conference, making the Rose Bowl—at the very least—easily attainable.

Perhaps most importantly, it also confirmed what the players and coaches felt all along, even if they refused to say so publicly: Penn State was a pretty darn good football team.

"You have to prepare yourself for the worst, expect the worst, and pray that something good happens," safety Anthony Scirrotto said after the Ohio State win. "There are ups and downs. You

have to pull through the adversity, and that shows the character of your team and what kind of team we really are."

With just three games left on the schedule, Paterno's main concern was a letdown against Iowa in the final road game of the season. Beat the Hawkeyes, and the debate would rage whether Penn State belonged in the national-title race with Alabama, Florida, Texas, Oklahoma, Texas Tech, and USC.

JoePa was having none of it.

"I haven't got the slightest idea what the BCS—is it the BCS or the BSC? I don't know," Paterno said. "I'm telling you what I'm concerned about; I'm concerned about Iowa. Period."

Coachspeak? Sure.

Prescient? Unfortunately.

Penn State held a 23–14 lead heading into the final quarter against Iowa, but the Lions couldn't stop Shonn Greene, one of the nation's best rushers, who gained 117 yards in the game. Early in the fourth, Greene scored his second touchdown of the day to cut the score to 23–21. Penn State couldn't hold back Iowa's last-ditch drive, and Daniel Murray's 31-yard field goal with one second remaining won the game for the Hawkeyes, 24–23.

Penn State was victimized by its carelessness, lack of energy, and just maybe, by looking too far down the road.

"I want to apologize to the whole Penn State nation for my game play today," Clark said.

He could have been speaking for the entire team.

Even if a national championship was now out of reach, other prizes remained: winning the conference, and going to and winning the Rose Bowl.

The Lions took care of the Big Ten in the same style they began the year: with blowouts.

Penn State 34, Indiana 7. Penn State 49, Michigan State 18.

Pasadena, here we come.

"Everything is perfect," Williams said, clutching a red rose after routing the Spartans.

Leading Penn State to its second Rose Bowl appearance since joining the Big Ten, Paterno was headed to Pasadena complete with a new hip—he underwent surgery after the season ended—as well as a contract extension, signed just as he turned 82.

"There's no reason for me not to think that I can go for a while," he said. "Now how long is a while? I don't know.

"We've got too many people who worked too hard for me to back away. Our coaches have really worked hard, and we're on the verge of having some success in a lot of areas I think I have to be involved in, and I want to do it."

The contract extension was for three seasons, which didn't surprise son and assistant coach Jay Paterno.

"He's talking two years from now, will we need X number of linemen, and X number in the secondary?" Jay Paterno said. "He's still talking about two, three, four years down the road in recruiting meetings."

Any long-term goals took a back seat to the January 1 meeting with Southern Cal, considered by many the most talented team in the nation. The Trojans were college football's most successful school throughout the decade, and Paterno made certain his players recognized the challenge facing them in the Rose Bowl.

"I hope we can go out there and be competitive with them. I'm a little bit nervous," said Paterno, who was selected as Big Ten Coach of the Year. "This is a very, very impressive football team, Southern Cal. They do everything well."

Too well, as it turned out. The Trojans' speed and diversity on offense, combined with the nation's most fearsome defense, was more than the Nittany Lions could handle. USC broke away from a 7–7 tie to build a 31–7 halftime lead on the way to a 38–24 victory.

It was not the way JoePa and the Lions wanted the season to end. Paterno again stayed in the press box, a headset covering his ears, a scowl covering his face, as Southern Cal pulled away.

But moments after the game, Paterno was looking ahead.

"Before the operation, every day was an ordeal, physically, regardless of football or what," Paterno said. "It was tough to concentrate, and then coming out here, where I was hoping to be on the sideline, and I was disappointed I couldn't be. That's all behind me now.

"It was a good year, a productive year. But I'm glad for me that it's over."

On to a new season.

NO ORDINARY JOE

CHAPTER 11

Before joining the coaching staff at Penn State, Joe Paterno played football at Brown under Rip Engle. Here, Joe hands off to his brother George for a publicity shot. *Penn State University Archives, Pennsylvania State University Libraries*

For more than four decades, Penn State football has been defined largely by coach Joe Paterno. He has been a fixture on the sidelines (and, nowadays, in the press box), as well as in the hearts and minds of the Nittany Nation since 1966.

Through the 2008 season, he has led the team to 383 victories—more wins than any coach in the history of Division I-A football. Paterno's Lions have posted five perfect seasons and earned two national championships. In the Paterno regime, bowl visits became a way of life, and JoePa holds the coaching record for most bowl victories (23) and most bowl appearances (35). He is the only college football coach to notch wins in each of the four traditional major bowls: Rose (once), Sugar (once), Cotton (twice), and Orange (four times). He has won numerous Coach of the Year awards and was inducted in the College Football Hall of Fame in December 2007.

But the won-loss records, the bowl appearances and championships, the individual honors are only a part of the story of JoePa's impact on Penn State and its football program. Since the very beginning, his Grand Experiment emphasized the student-athlete, encouraging academic as well as athletic excellence. Major football program or not, Paterno felt that academics should share equal time with sports, and the result has been one of the highest graduation rates in Division I.

"We want our players to enjoy football, but we also want them to enjoy college," Paterno said. "We want them to learn about art and music and all the other things college has to offer."

The Paternos have also contributed millions of dollars to educational facilities at Penn State, most notably for the school library that now bears his name, and he has worked tirelessly with charities.

Coach Paterno has been deeply involved in the lives of his players and has imparted in them many valuable lessons that served them well, far beyond the football field.

"I think Joe had a tremendous effect on me," said Kerry Collins, Penn State's All-American quarterback who forged a solid pro career after leaving Happy Valley. "His values and his approach to not only the game but to life, and to the things that come your way, have done a lot for me on and off the field."

Like many other fresh-faced recruits who arrive at Happy Valley to play football, it took Matt Joyner a while to figure out the ways of Joe Paterno.

Joyner, who played safety and on special teams for Penn State from 1995 to 1998, had heard about the "Paterno Experience" from his father, Dave, who had been an All-American at Penn State in both football and wrestling in the 1970s. Dave hoped to pass on to his own children the lessons he learned while playing offensive tackle for Paterno from 1969 to 1971.

"There are these little snippets that you get from Joe, and those are the kind of things I talked to my kids about a lot, probably ad nauseam," said the elder Joyner. "It probably drove them insane."

Matt learned from his dad about the intense preparation needed to be a part of a Paterno team, the zealous work habits that were expected of each and every member of the roster. But hearing about Paterno and getting a first-hand taste of the legendary coach are entirely different experiences.

As a freshman, Matt found out how tough Paterno could be when he was late for team meetings. Other character-building lessons such as picking up pieces of trash, taking your hat off inside a building, and never taking shortcuts were emphasized by Paterno.

Shown here in 1960, young Joe Paterno worked as an assistant coach to Rip Engle from 1950 to 1965, before taking the top spot on the staff. *Penn State University Archives, Pennsylvania State University Libraries*

"Discipline is self-motivating," Dave continued. "When you walk around and you see a piece of trash on the ground, you pick it up. You're not just helping to clean up; you're helping your internal self-discipline. To this day, I can't walk by a piece of paper and not pick it up."

Neither can Matt.

"At first, you have no idea what Paterno is talking about," said Matt. "Then in your junior year, the light starts to go on. OK, I'm not learning about football, I'm learning about life."

Welcome to Football 101, as taught in Paterno's exclusive finishing school.

Actually, Life 101.

Some of the key "Paterno Platitudes" that the coach passes on to his charges are:

- Take care of the little things, and the big things will take care of themselves.
- Don't cut corners.
- Keep plugging and something good will happen.
- Respect your peers and elders.

Walking across the grass when there is a path is also a no-no according to the Paterno Rules. The Penn State coach equates that with taking shortcuts in life.

Then there's Paterno's tuck rule—in games or practices, the players' jerseys must be tucked into their uniform pants. No hangovers. And a coat and tie are required at team meetings.

PATERNO STANDARD TIME

One of the lasting lessons that Nittany Lions players under Joe Paterno carry on after leaving Penn State is an appreciation for promptness. They all had to adjust to State College's local time zone, known as "Paterno Standard Time" (PST). That means setting your watch 15 minutes ahead of normal time for practices, team meetings, and road trips. Paterno doesn't just want you there early; he wants you there earlier than that.

As a freshman, safety Matt Joyner got the message soon enough. Early in the 1995 season, the Nittany Lions were playing Rutgers at the Meadowlands.

"It was my first year traveling," Joyner remembered. "I knew you had to be five minutes early to team meetings at home. Nobody told me it was 15 minutes when you were on the road."

When Joyner came down to the hotel lobby after spending some time with his parents in their room, he headed for the conference room for the team meeting. Uh, oh. It was already underway.

Joyner was the only one missing.

There was something else missing. All of a sudden Joyner realized that he wasn't wearing a tie.

"You had to wear a coat and tie," Joyner said. "Joe is very strict about that."

Joyner turned on his heels to go back to the room for a tie. Too late. He heard footsteps behind him.

It was Paterno. JoePa screamed at Joyner as he chased him across the hotel lobby. Joyner tried to hide, but Paterno found him.

"He came around the corner and started shaking me," Joyner recalled.

Paterno's voice resounded in the meeting room, in the lobby, and beyond.

"I was so embarrassed," Joyner said.

After that, Joyner made sure he was always on Paterno Standard Time.

Mark Tate, a cornerback at Penn State from 1993 to 1996, was another player impacted by Paterno Time.

"At Penn State, the meeting starts at nine and everybody's in his seat at 8:45," he said. "It's like you're afraid to ever be late. It's a good habit, and I'm definitely grateful. I'm always 15 to 20 minutes early [for meetings at work], and everybody knows it's just a habit from my football days at Penn State."

From the sideline at Beaver Stadium, JoePa checks his watch to make sure Paterno Standard Time is running smoothly. *Carolyn Kaster/AP Images*

Paterno's players say he is fanatical about their appearance both on and off the field.

"We couldn't wear T-shirts to class; we had to wear collared shirts, tucked in, and we had to wear socks," said Tony Gordon, a safety from the 1970s.

His players might contend that Paterno could have used some fashion advice in his own daily dress habits.

Said Penn State defensive tackle Jimmy Kennedy in 2002: "He's the only cat I know who will roll out of bed and put on royal-blue pants and a green sweater vest. We can tell as soon as he shows up to practice whether Sue [Paterno] was around to dress him that day or not."

Beginning early in his coaching career, Paterno was making personal fashion statements. As the story goes, Sue Paterno was upset that he would come home from games with the bottom of his pants caked with mud. Paterno's solution: cuff the pants a couple inches higher.

Fans and the media took note of the shortened pants, which accented his white socks and looked almost comical. The so-called "floods" had caught everyone's attention.

Paterno has always been a stickler for the length of his players' hair, too.

"The white guys' hair couldn't be more than an inch below the ear," Gordon recalled. "Joe would measure it. If it was longer, he would cut it. With the black guys, you'd get the ruler."

Gregg Garrity, a receiver for Penn State in the late 1970s and early 1980s, knew about Paterno's rules governing hair thanks to his father, Jim, who played end for Penn State in the early 1960s.

"I remember before I went up there for my freshman year, I tried to grow a mustache," said Gregg Garrity. "My dad said, 'You better get the facial hair off your face. You're not allowed to have anything on your face.'"

Gregg Garrity also recalled the coach's eagle eye when it comes to execution on the football field. If a player did something wrong in practice, Paterno could spot it, even when working on an adjoining field 100 yards away.

"He would run 100 yards, yelling as he was running at you, get in your face, and yell at you some more," Garrity said. "It was ruthless, but it worked."

Fashion was never one of JoePa's strong points, but his rolled-up pant legs are as much a part of the Paterno Way as the thick-rimmed glasses—and the winning attitude.
George Gojkovich/Getty Images

Joe's wife, Sue, has been by his side throughout his half-century-plus working at Penn State. Here the couple revels in Penn State's victory over Texas in the 1972 Cotton Bowl. *AP Images*

Though the 5-foot-3 Paterno is dwarfed physically by most of his players, he has been a strong presence on the field ever since he started as an assistant coach under Rip Engle in 1950. Always the teacher, always the perfectionist.

Dave Joyner remembered one particular spring when Paterno really gave him a hard time. Paterno didn't like the way Joyner was attacking the seven-man sled in practice.

"It was such a subtle concept," Joyner recalled. "He wanted you to hit through the man, not to the man. That was the old principle. And evidently, I was hitting to the man on this sled."

Joyner recalled how Paterno had a great joy in riding that sled, blowing his whistle, and screaming at the linemen.

"And every time I'd go, he'd just scream at me because I never got it right," Joyner said.

By the end of spring practice, Joyner was doing things the Paterno way and on his way to All-American recognition.

Charlie Pittman, a star running back for Penn State in the 1960s, also recalled Paterno's drive to help his players succeed. "He dictates the whole show," Pittman said of his former coach. "He's driving you so hard, you don't want to lose."

Paterno doesn't stop yelling once the games get underway. Tramping up and down the sideline in a constant state of agitation, he chalks up almost as much yardage as his football team.

Many times, Paterno seems to be reprimanding his coaches during games. Not true, according to long-time assistant Fran Ganter.

"When there's a penalty or something goes wrong, he would always come over to me. 'What happened? Who missed that block?' He's yelling at me to find out upstairs who he can go get. He just wanted to know who it was, so he could get the kid when he came off."

Paterno deals with coaches more discreetly, Ganter said.

"He would never yell at a coach in front of 110,000 people," Ganter emphasized. "He'll get on you on Sunday morning, and he'll get on you in the office. He'll second-guess you [in the office], which is his job, but never in public. Now the kids, he would let them have it."

Ganter recalled that, when Paterno was starting out as head coach, he did little things to build camaraderie within the coaching staff.

"Every Thursday during the season, we would go to one of our houses. . . . Everybody would go over there and bring something to eat, and we'd have a couple of beers, tell a couple of stories."

Then the group would go downtown, and Paterno would treat everyone to sandwiches at the Tavern, a popular State College restaurant.

"That went on for ten, fifteen years, as I recall," Ganter said.

Ganter, who spent 37 years with Paterno as a player and coach before moving into administration, found him to be "a great leader."

"He just commands a certain respect, and you can see it in the way the officials handle him."

The same respect is offered by opposing coaches and players as well.

"I see so many times our opponents break their huddle and wait for our team to come out of our huddle," said Ganter, "and they'll look over at the bench and try to find Joe. They want to see this guy. That's as close as a lot of them have been. It's amazing."

Paterno also displays an amazing ability to remember game details, no matter how small or how many seasons in the distant past. Associates say his total recall is downright scary.

"When you bring up a game, he'll bring up the down, the distance, the official's name who made the call in 1987," Ganter said. "He knows who scored what touchdown to beat us; he knows who was out of position, who dropped the interception."

Matt Joyner remembered when he attended a charity dinner with his father and sat at the same table with Paterno. Leaning over to Matt, Paterno asked casually, "So, did your dad teach you how to hold like him yet?" Paterno still remembered a costly holding call against Dave Joyner three decades earlier in the Orange Bowl.

Paterno has always been an enthusiastic cheerleader on the sidelines. Here he rejoices in a Penn State touchdown in the late 1960s. *Penn State University Archives, Pennsylvania State University Libraries*

OLD FAITHFULS

Any way you measure it, the Creamery tells the story: Having a flavor named after you at Penn State's famous ice cream parlor is the honor of honors. There's "Peachy Paterno," honoring the Nittany Lions' coach. During his time at Penn State, longtime defensive coordinator Jerry Sandusky had a flavor named after him, too. What else but "Sandusky Blitz"?

The Creamery has since been renamed and renovated, but Jerry Sandusky's longtime loyalty has not been forgotten. Nor has Fran Ganter's. He's the other bookend of the two most prominent assistant coaches historically on Joe Paterno's staff—Sandusky on defense and Ganter on offense.

Following the 1999 season, Sandusky retired from the Penn State staff after 35 years. Ganter left the sidelines after three decades in 2003 to take the post of associate athletic director. It wasn't long after Ganter left coaching that Paterno started missing him.

"It's amazing how many times things will pop up, and I am always thinking, 'What would [Fran] have done there?'" Paterno said.

Growing up in western Pennsylvania near Pittsburgh, Ganter was a big Penn State football fan. He recalled listening to Nittany Lions football games on the radio with his dad.

Ganter's future was true blue, first as a Penn State running back in the late 1960s, then as a coach. In 1994, the Lions produced their greatest offensive team in history. They finished with a 12–0 record, capping the season by beating Oregon in the Rose Bowl. Score one for Ganter.

For Sandusky, the high point had to be the 1980s, when the Lions won their first two national championships behind one of the toughest defenses in the nation. The defensive coordinator devised a scheme to bottle up Heisman Trophy–winner Herschel Walker in the 1983 Sugar Bowl, and the Nittany Lions gained a 27–23 victory for their first title. In the 1987 Fiesta Bowl, the Lions frustrated another Heisman winner, Miami quarterback Vinny Testaverde. Penn State prevailed, 14–10, for its second national championship in five years.

Like Ganter, Sandusky had played at Penn State before turning to coaching. Sandusky was a receiver from 1963 to 1966.

Under Sandusky's coaching, Penn State developed a reputation as "Linebacker U." By the time he retired, Sandusky had turned out nine first-team All-Americans and a number of other great players at the position.

Jerry Sandusky, one of Joe Paterno's top aides, gets some love from the Penn State fans upon his retirement after 32 years on the staff. *Penn State University Archives, Pennsylvania State University Libraries*

Joe Paterno confers with offensive coach Fran Ganter on the sideline. Paterno's assistant made a big impact on the Penn State football program. *Penn State University Archives, Pennsylvania State University Libraries*

Although Paterno's long tenure at Penn State has seen many ups and downs, the loyal fans always show their support for their beloved coach, never more so than when he was laid up by a knee injury during the 2006 season. *Carolyn Kaster/AP Images*

While the Paterno of today represents a father figure to many of the Penn State players, Jim Garrity recalled a different kind of Paterno.

Garrity is widely regarded as Paterno's first recruit, back when JoePa was an assistant under Engle in charge of the offense. He wasn't much older than many of the players.

"He was a really young guy, and he could relate well with us," Garrity said. "During the course of my time at Penn State, Joe was kind of one of the guys. We played basketball together, we played handball together. He was young enough to do that with us."

Paterno was also a counselor in charge of a football dorm, a first—and last—at Penn State. He lived with the players and tried to control them. Big mistake.

"It was never done before and would never be done again," Garrity said. "It was absolutely bonkers, really wild, and Joe tried to control us. He learned a big lesson that year."

Paterno's Penn State journey hasn't been without its sidetracks and setbacks.

In the 1970s, Paterno was becoming restless. His first 10 years as head coach had produced a brilliant 94–10 record (a .903 winning percentage). He had made his mark in bowl games against the toughest competition in the country. What more could he do, other than win a national championship?

One of Paterno's sons showed him a book stating that only three college football coaches—Knute Rockne and Frank Leahy of Notre Dame and George Woodruff of Penn, Illinois, and Carlisle—had better records in their first 10 years.

"Honestly, I don't pay attention to that kind of stuff," Paterno said. "But it got me to thinking about my coaching, and I began to wonder if maybe, subconsciously, I wasn't being over-conservative just to protect my record. If I was, then I was taking all the joy out of the job."

BOBBY AND JOEPA

Their names sit atop the success list of college football, and probably will remain there for a very long time.

For years, Bobby Bowden and Joe Paterno staged an unofficial race for winningest coach in Division I-A that was marked as much by humor and self-deprecation as by tackles and touchdowns. And when the College Football Hall of Fame wanted both of them inducted even though they were still active, the Hall simply changed its rules.

"I wasn't expecting it because I thought you had to die first—and I didn't want to volunteer for that," Bowden said of the 2006 announcement. "They might have changed the rules to get me and Joe in. But I'm very excited about it."

Two legendary coaches—Bobby Bowden and Joe Paterno—share a light moment with the media prior to their showdown in the 2005 Orange Bowl. Through their combined 100-plus years of coaching, the two have remained good friends—and rivals for the title of winningest coach in Division I football history. *J. Pat Carter/AP Images*

Bowden and Paterno were to be enshrined together in 2006, but only Bowden went in that year because Paterno was recovering from a broken leg sustained from a sideline collision with a player during a game.

"Well, I beat Joe to something," Bowden joked at the time. "I'd right rather have him be here. I feel like it's kind of been a Bobby and Joe show, and without him it feels like something is missing."

A year later, Paterno was enshrined, to which Bowden said, "I can't think of anyone more deserving than Joe. He is everything that is good about college football."

JoePa's response to getting into the Hall a year after Bowden was more lighthearted: "I'd rather do it now than when I'm dead."

For Paterno, the sport is as much about the friendships you develop and cultivate as it is about Xs and Os. Being associated with his fellow coaching icon has been something special for him.

"I appreciate the fact that people have said to us, 'Hey, you've been an asset to college football, and we want to acknowledge that,'" Paterno said. "I think we're all very privileged to belong to something that is as meaningful to young people as college football."

While longevity plays into the incredible win totals put up by these two men—two of the greatest coaches in sports history—neither would have lasted so long in their jobs if they weren't brilliant tacticians and leaders.

For most of their careers, Bowden and Paterno have benefited from their reputations, their ability to adapt to changes in the landscape—athletically and socially—and their ability to attract top football talent. While Bowden has a down-home style and Paterno is a bit more straightforward, both have managed to deliver the same message, with only a slight variation between them: "Florida State is the place for you, son," or "Penn State is the place for you, son."

Despite the competition for top recruits and for the top spots in the national polls, the two coaches have grown closer over the years. "As we've grown older, there ain't nobody else left," Bowden said. "Everybody has been fired or is gone or retired. So we naturally gravitate to each other."

Although these two legends have coached more than 1,000 college football games between them, Paterno and Bowden have faced each other on the field only eight times. Overall, Penn State is 7–1 against Bobby Bowden teams—two of them with Bowden coaching the Seminoles and the other six, all Penn State wins, against the Bowden-led West Virginia Mountaineers.

The two coaches first met in 1962, when Paterno was an assistant coach to Rip Engle at Penn State and Bowden was head coach at Samford (then known as Howard College).

"You can imagine our budget," Bowden said. "I think they gave me $55 to go to Pennsylvania so I could watch Penn State. I said, 'I'm going to go up there and see if I can learn something.'"

Bowden even hitchhiked part of the way and slept at a fraternity house before meeting the Penn State coaches.

The first time Paterno and Bowden coached against each other was in 1970, when the Nittany Lions defeated the Mountaineers 42–8. The win was part of a 25-game winning streak by Penn State over West Virginia, including six with Bowden at the helm.

Bowden moved to Florida State in 1976, and the two schools have never scheduled a regular-season meeting in all that time. Bowden and Paterno did go head to head at the 1990 Blockbuster Bowl, which Florida State won, 24–17.

In 2005, when Paterno received several national Coach of the Year honors, Bowden expressed his own pride in his friend's accomplishments.

"It's a real credit to Joe—and to us old boys," Bowden said.

The "old boys" had to stay up extra late on January 3, 2006, when Penn State and Florida State faced off in the Orange Bowl—the most recent meeting of the two coaches, and the most classic. That game had just about everything. The coaches kidded about it maybe needing a curfew, too.

It had three overtimes, four key field goal misses, and almost five hours of football before Kevin Kelly's 29-yard kick gave Penn State a 26–23 victory.

"I kept saying to myself, 'When is this going to end?'" Paterno said afterward. "I was looking at my watch. It's 12:30, quarter to one. I'm usually asleep three hours at that time."

JoePa was glad he stayed up. So was Bowden, who took inspiration from his elder's work that season.

Before Paterno led Penn State to an 11–1 record in 2005, the team was coming off a rough stretch of four losing seasons in five years, and critics were calling for the coach's head. Bowden wasn't getting a lot of love at Florida State, either, with four losses in the 2005 season.

"We've caught a lot of heck this year," Bowden said at the time. "I've caught a lot of heck."

Still, he could point to his old buddy for comfort.

"I can look at Joe's program and say, 'Just be patient. Look what'll happen.' . . . It just substantiates my feeling that nobody's going to win forever. You can have a bad year. You can have a bad series of years. You can have a bad cycle, but that's not the end, because you can come back."

Working alongside son and assistant coach Jay Paterno (left) has been a special thrill for JoePa. Here father and son confer during preseason practice in August 2008. *Carolyn Kaster/AP Images*

Paterno could think of two options other than staying at Penn State: go to another school and turn a losing program into a winner, or coach in the pros.

Paterno, who had earlier rejected overtures from the pros, agreed to terms with the New England Patriots in 1972 after long and agonizing soul searching. After a sleepless night, he changed his mind.

He told his wife, Sue: "You went to bed with a millionaire and woke up with a pauper."

He ultimately decided it would be more satisfying for him to mold college kids. Paterno did make a change, all right, but he did it within the structure of the Penn State program. Admittedly conservative on the field and criticized in some quarters for that style, Paterno opened up his offense in the mid-1970s. The change paid off, and the team amassed a 106–25–1 overall record from 1977 to 1987, winning two national titles in the process.

As losing seasons became more common for Penn State in the early 2000s—and as the doubters questioned ever more loudly whether the septuagenarian coach was past his prime—Paterno righted the ship yet again. He returned the Lions to the elite of college football, while continuing to set new coaching milestones.

In 2007, Paterno reached a landmark with his 42nd season as head football coach at Penn State, eclipsing Amos Alonzo Stagg's mark of 41 years at the University of Chicago.

If anything, Paterno has been stubbornly consistent. Noted Dave Joyner: "I was here for my tenure and my sons', and I watched how the program worked. The very core issues of the program didn't change at all. I'm not saying that Joe and the coaches and the kids didn't change and adapt to a new world. They did, and that's appropriate. But the very core never changed, and to me, that was very reassuring."

While Paterno's football philosophy has changed over the years to keep up with the times, not much else has changed about the man. He still retains traces of his Brooklyn accent, acquired while growing into manhood in Flatbush, as well as his baseball allegiances. Like most baseball fans in Brooklyn, he loved the Dodgers and hated the rival New York Yankees.

Old loyalties die hard. Before a recent game at Beaver Stadium, Paterno was introduced to a youngster, who was wearing a Yankees' cap. Paterno smirked, pulled the cap off the youngster's head, and threw it on the ground—all in jest, of course.

Another remainder of days gone by is his colorful language, which can only be described as "Paternoisms." Phrases like "willy-nilly," "outta whack," and "loosey goosey" sprinkle his conversation, just as they did decades ago.

"He's basically the same," Dave Joyner said, "and that's good, because that means that love him, hate him, agree with him, don't agree with him, you pretty much know what you get."

The story of Jimmy Kennedy perhaps sums up the Penn State experience under Paterno as well as any.

Kennedy grew up in Yonkers, New York, where he wasn't much of a student. But he sure could play ball, which probably could have gotten him into any college football factory. Once there, Kennedy would have survived on his ability to make tackles, and if he foundered, he would have soon been forgotten by those very people who brought him to that school.

It's a common and sad story in college sports.

It didn't happen to Kennedy. Not with JoePa watching over him.

"If not for Joe Paterno, who knows where I would be today," Kennedy said in 2002. "I've been in and out of Special Ed classes since the tenth grade, and then I made the dean's list last September. That's because of the Paternos, Joe and his wife, Sue. Mrs. Paterno would show up some nights at 11 o'clock to tutor me on vocabulary, literature, anything I had trouble with."

In the end, that is what Paterno would like the Penn State football legacy to be.

"I grew up in his house and heard the same thing he tells players," said Joe's son Jay, the team's quarterbacks coach. "It's not important whether you like me now. It's important whether you like me when you're 35, you have a job, and you're married with a family.'"

The Paterno way. The Penn State way.

An ailing leg forced Paterno to give up his coaching position on the sidelines, but he continued to monitor the team from his elevated perch of the press box, as shown during the game against Temple in September 2008. *Gene J. Puskar/AP Images*

APPENDIX

THE PENN STATE FOOTBALL ALL-TIME RECORD BOOK

TOP 30 GAMES IN PENN STATE FOOTBALL HISTORY

November 16, 1912: During the Nittany Lions' undefeated season of 1912, the team mounted a historic 37–0 upset of Ohio State at Columbus. The game ended in a massive brawl involving spectators, as Buckeyes players walked off the field with nine minutes left to play.

October 22, 1921: Penn State fought mighty Harvard to a 21–21 tie in a battle of national powers. The game featured a spectacular 59-yard gallop by "Lighthorse" Harry Wilson, one of the early Penn State greats.

January 1, 1923: In the school's first postseason bowl game, Penn State lost 14–3 to Southern Cal in the Rose Bowl, but the team gained plenty in national exposure.

January 1, 1948: The Nittany Lions' undefeated 1947 season was capped by a 13–13 tie with powerful SMU in the Cotton Bowl, raising Penn State's football profile considerably.

October 23, 1948: Penn State and Michigan State played to a spectacular 14–14 tie in front of a standing-room-only crowd of 23,000, more than 5,000 over capacity, at Beaver Field. The game sparked Penn State's decision to expand Beaver Field to nearly twice its size.

September 27, 1952: Penn State rallied to tie Purdue 20–20 in the second game of the season, helping to counter some of the bias against eastern schools. A late interception by Don Eyer sparked the comeback. Coach Rip Engle considered this game one of the turning points in establishing the Lions as a national powerhouse.

November 22, 1952: Pittsburgh appeared to be headed for the Orange Bowl until the Panthers' plans were curtailed by Penn State's 17–0 win in the final game of the regular season. Rip Engle called the upset a key moment in Penn State's resurgence.

September 25, 1954: Penn State opened its 1954 season with a 14–12 upset win at Illinois, which boasted the "nation's fastest backfield," consisting of J. C. Caroline, Mickey Bates, and Abe Woodson. Illinois was ranked No. 1 in the preseason polls.

November 5, 1955: Featuring a great running duel between the Nittany Lions' Lenny Moore and the Orangemen's Jim Brown, the Lions prevailed over Syracuse, 21–20.

October 20, 1956: Penn State knocked off an undefeated Ohio State team 7–6 at Columbus, shocking the crowd of 83,000 at Ohio Stadium in what coach Rip Engle called "undoubtedly one of our biggest upsets." Milt Plum's 72-yard punt set up the winning score for the Lions.

December 19, 1959: Penn State wrapped up an 8–2 regular season with its first bowl victory, a 7–0 win over Alabama in the Liberty Bowl. It was the only time Penn State would beat a Bear Bryant team. The game's lone touchdown came on a screen pass from Galen Hall to Roger Kochman.

November 7, 1964: Facing second-ranked Ohio State in Columbus as 21-point underdogs, the Nittany Lions trounced the Buckeyes, 27–0.

November 11, 1967: A 13–8 upset win over undefeated and third-ranked North Carolina State gave Joe Paterno his first victory against a ranked opponent during his head coaching career. Later that year, the Lions earned their first bowl invitation under Paterno, largely because of the win over the Wolfpack.

January 1, 1969: Penn State closed out its perfect season in 1968 with a thrilling 15–14 win over Kansas in the Orange Bowl. With time running out, the Lions won it on a second-chance 2-point conversion after the Jayhawks were penalized for having too many men on the field.

January 1, 1970: A 10–3 win over Missouri in the 1970 Orange Bowl further established Penn State as a national power. The Lions were in the midst of a 31-game unbeaten streak.

January 1, 1972: Making its fourth bowl appearance in five seasons, Penn State topped Texas, 30–6, in the Cotton Bowl—a particularly impressive win considering the game was played in the Longhorns' own backyard. The victory was also sweet revenge for the Lions, who had been beaten out for the No. 1 spot by Texas two years earlier.

November 28, 1981: After falling from first to thirteenth in the rankings with losses to Miami and Alabama, Penn State finished the 1981 regular season with a flourish, posting big wins against Notre Dame and Pitt in the final two weeks. The Lions' 48–14 domination of Pitt in the finale knocked the Panthers from the No. 1 spot.

January 1, 1982: The Lions completed their season with a 26–10 win over No. 8 Southern Cal in the Fiesta Bowl. Penn State's defense dominated, allowing only three offensive points. Penn State's Curt Warner outplayed USC's Heisman Trophy–winning running back, Marcus Allen.

January 1, 1983: Penn State won its first national championship with a victory over Georgia in the Sugar Bowl. The Lions' "Magic Defense" pretty much bottled up Heisman Trophy–winner Herschel Walker. On the offensive side, Gregg Garrity's touchdown grab helped spark the 27–23 win and became known as "the Catch" in Penn State lore.

January 2, 1987: Penn State claimed its second national title in five years by beating Miami 14–10 in the Fiesta Bowl. The Lions intercepted five passes by Heisman winner Vinny Testaverde, including one by Pete Giftopoulos at the goal line with nine seconds left that slammed the door on the Hurricanes.

October 27, 1990: Penn State whipped Alabama 9–0 at Tuscaloosa, limiting the Crimson Tide to its lowest rushing output in history (six yards). It was the first time an Alabama team had been shut out in 31 games.

November 17, 1990: Penn State won a thriller against top-ranked Notre Dame in South Bend, 24–21, with Craig Fayak's 34-yard field goal in the final minute providing the game-winner. The victory was the highlight of Paterno's 25th season as head coach.

October 29, 1994: The Lions set numerous offensive records during the perfect 12–0 season in 1994—averaging nearly 48 points and 520 yards per game—but the most impressive was the 63–14 pasting of No. 21 Ohio State. It was the worst defeat suffered by a Buckeyes team since 1946.

November 12, 1994: In a season full of convincing victories, Penn State's close call at Illinois in week nine was probably the biggest win. After falling behind 21–0, the Lions rallied to beat the Illini 35–31 in the greatest comeback of the Paterno era. The win also clinched Penn State's first Big Ten title.

October 27, 2001: The 29–27 comeback win—triggered by quarterback Zack Mills' 69-yard touchdown run—over Ohio State was more than just another victory over a conference opponent for Paterno. The Penn State coach surpassed Bear Bryant as the all-time Division I-A leader in victories with number 324.

September 14, 2002: Before a national television audience and an overflow record crowd of 110,753 at Beaver Stadium, Penn State polished off Nebraska 40–7 in an unexpected lopsided victory.

January 3, 2006: Penn State wrapped up an 11–1 season with a thrilling triple-overtime victory over Florida State in the Orange Bowl. With Paterno on one sideline and Bobby Bowden on the other, the contest matched the two winningest coaches in college football history. After two consecutive field goal failures, kicker Kevin Kelly finally connected in the third overtime to give Penn State the 26–23 edge.

October 18, 2008: Making up for past disappointments against Michigan, Penn State pounded the Wolverines 46–17 in one of the highlights of the 2008 season. The Lions rallied from a 17–14 deficit in the first half to beat Michigan for the first time in 10 games.

October 25, 2008: The Lions held Ohio State without a touchdown en route to a 13–6 triumph in front of a record crowd of 105,711 at Ohio Stadium—Penn State's first win at Ohio State in 30 years. Backup Pat Devlin, filling in for injured starter Daryll Clark, scored the go-ahead touchdown on a quarterback sneak from the one-yard line with 6:24 remaining.

November 22, 2008: Penn State completed an 11–1 regular season with a solid 49–18 win over Michigan State at Beaver Stadium. The victory clinched a Rose Bowl berth for the Lions, sending them to Pasadena for the first time since the 1994 season. It also marked Penn State's 800th victory, making it only the sixth college football team to achieve that mark.

PENN STATE FOOTBALL BOWL HISTORY

Date	Bowl	Result	
January 1, 1923	Rose	USC 14, Penn State 3	L
January 1, 1948	Cotton	Penn State 13, SMU 13	T
December 19, 1959	Liberty	Penn State 7, Alabama 0	W
December 17, 1960	Liberty	Penn State 41, Oregon 12	W
December 30, 1961	Gator	Penn State 30, Georgia Tech 15	W
December 29, 1962	Gator	Florida 17, Penn State 7	L
December 30, 1967	Gator	Penn State 17, Florida State 17	T
January 1, 1969	Orange	Penn State 15, Kansas 14	W
January 1, 1970	Orange	Penn State 10, Missouri 3	W
January 1, 1972	Cotton	Penn State 30, Texas 6	W
December 31, 1972	Sugar	Oklahoma 14, Penn State 0	L
January 1, 1974	Orange	Penn State 16, LSU 9	W
January 1, 1975	Cotton	Penn State 41, Baylor 20	W
December 31, 1975	Sugar	Alabama 13, Penn State 6	L
December 27, 1976	Gator	Notre Dame 20, Penn State 9	L
December 25, 1977	Fiesta	Penn State 42, Arizona State 30	W
January 1, 1979	Sugar	Alabama 14, Penn State 7	L
December 22, 1979	Liberty	Penn State 9, Tulane 6	W
December 26, 1980	Fiesta	Penn State 31, Ohio State 19	W
January 1, 1982	Fiesta	Penn State 26, USC 10	W
January 1, 1983	Sugar	Penn State 27, Georgia 23	W
December 26, 1983	Aloha	Penn State 13, Washington 10	W
January 1, 1986	Orange	Oklahoma 25, Penn State 10	L
January 2, 1987	Fiesta	Penn State 14, Miami (Fla.) 10	W
January 1, 1988	Citrus	Clemson 35, Penn State 10	L
December 29, 1989	Holiday	Penn State 50, BYU 39	W
December 28, 1990	Blockbuster	Florida State 24, Penn State 17	L
January 1, 1992	Fiesta	Penn State 42, Tennessee 17	W
January 1, 1993	Blockbuster	Stanford 24, Penn State 3	L
January 1, 1994	Citrus	Penn State 31, Tennessee 13	W
January 2, 1995	Rose	Penn State 38, Oregon 20	W
January 1, 1996	Outback	Penn State 43, Auburn 14	W
January 1, 1997	Fiesta	Penn State 38, Texas 15	W
January 1, 1998	Citrus	Florida 21, Penn State 6	L
January 1, 1999	Outback	Penn State 26, Kentucky 14	W
December 28, 1999	Alamo	Penn State 24, Texas A&M 0	W
January 1, 2003	Capital One	Auburn 13, Penn State 9	L
January 3, 2006	Orange	Penn State 26, Florida State 23 (3 OT)	W
January 1, 2007	Outback	Penn State 20, Tennessee 10	W
December 28, 2007	Alamo	Penn State 24, Texas A&M 17	W
January 1, 2009	Rose	USC 38, Penn State 24	L

Overall Record: 26–13–2

PENN STATE ALL-AMERICANS

Name	Position	Year
W. T. "Mother" Dunn	center	1906
Bob Higgins	end	1915, 1919
Percy "Red" Griffiths	guard	1920
Charley Way	halfback	1920
Glenn Killinger	halfback	1921
Harry Wilson	halfback	1923
Joe Bedenk	guard	1923
Leon Gajecki	center	1940
Steve Suhey	guard	1947
Sam Tamburo	end	1948
Sam Valentine	guard	1956
Richie Lucas	quarterback	1959
Bob Mitinger	end	1961
Dave Robinson	end	1962
Roger Kochman	halfback	1962
Glenn Ressler	center/middle guard	1964
Ted Kwalick	tight end	1967, 1968
Dennis Onkotz	linebacker	1968, 1969
Mike Reid	defensive tackle	1969
Charlie Pittman	halfback	1969
Neal Smith	safety	1969
Jack Ham	linebacker	1970
Dave Joyner	tackle	1971
Lydell Mitchell	halfback	1971
Charlie Zapiec	linebacker	1971
Bruce Bannon	defensive end	1972
John Hufnagel	quarterback	1972
John Skorupan	linebacker	1972
John Cappelletti	halfback	1973
Randy Crowder	defensive tackle	1973
Ed O'Neil	linebacker	1973
John Nessel	tackle	1974
Mike Hartenstine	defensive end	1974
Chris Bahr	kicker	1975
Greg Buttle	linebacker	1975
Tom Rafferty	guard	1975
Kurt Allerman	linebacker	1976
Keith Dorney	tackle	1977, 1978
Randy Sidler	middle guard	1977
Matt Bahr	kicker	1978
Bruce Clark	defensive tackle	1978, 1979
Chuck Fusina	quarterback	1978
Pete Harris	safety	1978
Matt Millen	defensive tackle	1978
Bill Dugan	tackle	1980
Sean Farrell	guard	1980, 1981
Curt Warner	tailback	1981, 1982
Walker Lee Ashley	defensive end	1982
Kenny Jackson	flanker	1982, 1983
Mark Robinson	safety	1982
Michael Zordich	strong safety	1985
Shane Conlan	outside linebacker	1985, 1986
Chris Conlin	tackle	1986
D. J. Dozier	halfback	1986
Tim Johnson	defensive tackle	1986
Steve Wisniewski	guard	1987, 1988
Andre Collins	inside linebacker	1989
Blair Thomas	tailback	1989
Darren Perry	defensive back	1991
O. J. McDuffie	wide receiver	1992
Lou Benfatti	defensive tackle	1993
Kyle Brady	tight end	1994
Ki-Jana Carter	running back	1994
Kerry Collins	quarterback	1994
Bobby Engram	wide receiver	1994
Jeff Hartings	guard	1994, 1995
Kim Herring	free safety	1996
Curtis Enis	tailback	1997
LaVar Arrington	outside linebacker	1998, 1999
Courtney Brown	defensive end	1999
Brandon Short	middle linebacker	1999
Michael Haynes	defensive end	2002
Larry Johnson	tailback	2002
Jimmy Kennedy	defensive tackle	2002
Tamba Hali	defensive end	2005
Paul Posluszny	outside linebacker	2005, 2006
Dan Connor	linebacker	2006, 2007
A. Q. Shipley	center	2008
Aaron Maybin	defensive end	2008

PENN STATE PLAYERS AND COACHES IN THE COLLEGE FOOTBALL HALL OF FAME

Hugo Bezdek	coach	1918–1929
Pete Mauthe	halfback	1909–1912
Dexter Very	end	1909–1912
Shorty Miller	quarterback	1910–1913
Dick Harlow	coach	1915–1917
Glenn Killinger	quarterback	1918–1921
Bob Higgins	coach	1930–1948
Harry Wilson	halfback	1921–1923
Steve Suhey	guard	1942, 1946–1947
Rip Engle	coach	1950–1965
Richie Lucas	quarterback	1957–1959
Dave Robinson	end	1960–1962
Glenn Ressler	center/guard	1962–1964
Joe Paterno	coach	1966–present
Mike Reid	defensive tackle	1966, 1968–1969
Ted Kwalick	tight end	1966–1968
Dennis Onkotz	linebacker	1967–1969
Jack Ham	linebacker	1968–1970
Lydell Mitchell	running back	1969–1971
John Cappelletti	halfback	1971–1973
Keith Dorney	offensive tackle	1975–1978

ALL-TIME COACHING RECORDS

	W–L–T	Pct.	Bowl Record
Joe Paterno, 1966–2008 (active)	383–127–3	.751	23–11–1
Rip Engle, 1950–1965	104–48–4	.679	3–1
Bob Higgins, 1930–1948	91–57–11	.607	0–0–1
Hugo Bezdek, 1918–1929	65–30–11	.665	0–1
Tom Fennell, 1904–1908	33–17–1	.657	0–0
Bill Hollenback, 1909, 1911–1914	28–9–4	.732	0–0
Dick Harlow, 1915–1917	20–8–0	.714	0–0
George Hoskins, 1892–1895	17–4–4	.760	0–0
Pop Golden, 1900–1902	16–12–1	.569	0–0
Samuel Newton, 1896–1898	12–14–0	.462	0–0
Jack Hollenback, 1910	5–2–1	.688	0–0
Daniel A. Reed, 1903	5–3–0	.625	0–0
Joe Bedenk, 1949	5–4–0	.556	0–0
Sam Boyle, 1899	4–6–1	.409	0–0

INDIVIDUAL CAREER RECORDS

Most Points, Total Offense
- 425 Kevin Kelly, 2005–2008 (183 PAT, 78 FG, 1 TD, 1 2-pt.)
- 282 Craig Fayak, 1990–1993 (132 PAT, 50 FG)
- 276 Brett Conway, 1993–1996 (141 PAT, 45 FG)
- 258 Travis Forney, 1996–1999 (117 PAT, 47 FG)
- 246 Lydell Mitchell, 1969–1971 (41 TD)

Most Yards, Total Offense
- 7,796 Zack Mills, 2001–2004 (7,212 pass, 584 rush)
- 6,000 Tony Sacca, 1988–1991 (5,869 pass, 131 rush)
- 5,300 Kerry Collins, 1991–1994 (5,304 pass, –4 rush)
- 5,168 Michael Robinson, 2002–2005 (3,531 pass, 1,637 rush)
- 5,162 Chuck Fusina, 1975–1979 (5,382 pass, –220 rush)

Most All-Purpose Running Yards
- 5,045 Larry Johnson, 1999–2002 (2,953 rush, 681 rec., 1,411 ret.)
- 4,982 Curt Warner, 1979–1982 (3,398 rush, 662 rec., 922 ret.)
- 4,512 Blair Thomas, 1985–1987, 1989 (3,301 rush, 477 rec., 734 ret.)
- 4,231 Tony Hunt, 2003–2006 (3,320 rush, 799 rec., 112 ret.)
- 4,043 Bobby Engram, 1991, 1993–1995 (155 rush, 3,026 rec., 682 ret.)

Most Rushing Yards
- 3,398 Curt Warner, 1979–1982
- 3,320 Tony Hunt, 2003–2006
- 3,301 Blair Thomas, 1985–1987, 1989
- 3,256 Curtis Enis, 1995–1997
- 3,227 D. J. Dozier, 1983–1986

Most Rushing Attempts
- 654 Tony Hunt, 2003–2006
- 649 Curt Warner, 1979–1982
- 633 Matt Suhey, 1976–1979
- 624 D. J. Dozier, 1983–1986
- 606 Blair Thomas, 1985–1987, 1989

Highest Rushing Average
- 7.2 Ki-Jana Carter, 1992–1994
- 6.4 Larry Johnson, 1999–2002
- 6.2 Lenny Moore, 1953–1955
- 6.1 Bob Campbell, 1966–1968
- 5.8 Lydell Mitchell, 1969–1971

Most 100-Yard Games
18	Curt Warner, 1979–1982
17	Blair Thomas, 1985–1987, 1989
17	Ki-Jana Carter, 1992–1994
17	Curtis Enis, 1995–1997
15	Lydell Mitchell, 1969–1971
15	Tony Hunt, 2003–2006

Most Rushing Touchdowns
38	Lydell Mitchell, 1969–1971
36	Curtis Enis, 1995–1997
34	Ki-Jana Carter, 1992–1994
30	Charlie Pittman, 1967–1969
29	John Cappelletti, 1972–1973
29	Richie Anderson, 1989–1992

Most Passing Yards
7,212	Zack Mills, 2001–2005
5,869	Tony Sacca, 1988–1991
5,382	Chuck Fusina, 1975–1978
5,304	Kerry Collins, 1991–1994
5,275	Anthony Morelli, 2004–2007

Most Pass Attempts
1,082	Zack Mills, 2001–2005
824	Tony Sacca, 1988–1991
821	Anthony Morelli, 2004–2007
692	Wally Richardson, 1992, 1994–1996
665	Chuck Fusina, 1975–1978

Most Pass Completions
606	Zack Mills, 2001–2005
460	Anthony Morelli, 2004–2007
401	Tony Sacca, 1988–1991
378	Wally Richardson, 1992, 1994–1996
371	Chuck Fusina, 1975–1978

Highest Completion Percentage (min. 200 attempts)
56.3	Kerry Collins, 1991–1994 (370/657)
56.0	Anthony Morelli, 2004–2007 (460/821)
56.0	Zack Mills, 2001–2005 (606/1,082)
55.8	Chuck Fusina, 1975–1978 (371/665)
55.7	Mike McQueary, 1994–1997 (171/307)

Passing Efficiency
145.57	Mike McQueary, 1994–1997
140.83	John Hufnagel, 1970–1972
137.33	Kerry Collins, 1991–1994
136.68	Tom Shuman, 1972–1974
132.48	Chuck Fusina, 1975–1978

Most Passing Yards per Attempt
8.89	Mike McQueary, 1994–1997 (2,730/307)
8.69	John Hufnagel, 1970–-1972 (3,545/408)
8.09	Chuck Fusina, 1975–1978 (5,382/665)
8.07	Kerry Collins, 1991–1994 (5,304/657)
7.91	Tom Shuman, 1972–1974 (2,886/365)

Most 200-Yard Passing Games
16	Kerry Collins, 1991–1994
16	Zack Mills, 2001–2005
11	Chuck Fusina, 1975–1978
11	Tony Sacca, 1988–1991
11	Anthony Morelli, 2004–2007

Most Passing Touchdowns
41	Todd Blackledge, 1980–1982
41	Tony Sacca, 1988–1991
41	Zack Mills, 2001–2005
39	Kerry Collins, 1991–1994
37	Chuck Fusina, 1975–1978

Most Interceptions Thrown
41	Todd Blackledge, 1980–1982
39	Zack Mills, 2001–2005
32	Chuck Fusina, 1975–1978
25	Tony Rados, 1951–1953
24	John Shaffer, 1983–1986
24	Tony Sacca, 1988–1991
24	Rashard Casey, 1997–2000

Lowest Interception Percentage (min. 200 attempts)
2.05	Wally Richardson, 1992, 1994–1996 (14/682)
2.31	Anthony Morelli, 2004–2007 (19/821)
2.31	John Sacca, 1991–1993 (5/216)
2.82	Pete Liske, 1961–1963 (10/355)
3.20	Kerry Collins, 1991–1994 (21/657)

Most Receptions

179	Deon Butler, 2005–2008
167	Bobby Engram, 1991, 1993–1995
161	Derrick Williams, 2005–2008
158	Jordan Norwood, 2005–2008
125	O. J. McDuffie, 1988–1992

Most Receiving Yards

3,028	Bobby Engram, 1991, 1993–1995
2,771	Deon Butler, 2005–2008
2,015	Jordan Norwood, 2005–2008
1,988	O. J. McDuffie, 1988–1992
1,837	Jack Curry, 1965–1967

Most 100-Yard Games, Receiving

16	Bobby Engram, 1991, 1993–1995
9	Joe Jurevisius, 1994–1997
8	Bryant Johnson, 1999–2002
7	O. J. McDuffie, 1988–1992
6	Kenny Jackson, 1980–1983
6	Freddie Scott, 1993–1995
6	Deon Butler, 2005–2008

Most Receiving Touchdowns

31	Bobby Engram, 1991, 1993–1995
25	Kenny Jackson, 1980–1983
22	Deon Butler, 2005–2008
16	O. J. McDuffie, 1988–1992
15	Joe Jurevisius, 1994–1997
15	Terry Smith, 1988–1991

Most Field Goals Made

78	Kevin Kelly, 2005–2008
50	Craig Fayak, 1990–1993
47	Travis Forney, 1996–1999
45	Brett Conway, 1993–1996
40	Massimo Manca, 1982, 1984–1986

Most Field Goals Attempted

107	Kevin Kelly, 2005–2008
80	Craig Fayak, 1990–1993
63	Travis Forney, 1996–1999
61	Matt Bahr, 1976–1978
61	Brett Conway, 1993–1996
61	Robbie Gould, 2001–2004

Best Field Goal Accuracy (min. 25 attempts)

77.6%	Nick Gancitano, 1981–1984 (38/49)
74.6%	Travis Forney, 1996–1999 (47/63)
73.8%	Brett Conway, 1993–1996 (45/61)
72.9%	Kevin Kelly, 2005–2008 (78/107)
70.7%	Herb Menhardt, 1978–1980 (29/41)

Most Consecutive Games, Field Goal Made

31	Kevin Kelly, 10/14/2006–11/15/2008

Most Consecutive Games, Field Goal Attempted

41	Kevin Kelly, 10/29/2005–11/15/2008

Most 50-Yard Field Goals Made

6	Chris Bahr, 1973–1975 (long 55)
3	Massimo Manca, 1982, 1984–1986 (long 53)
3	Kevin Kelly, 2005–2008 (long 53)
2	Brett Conway, 1993–1996 (long 52)
2	Robbie Gould, 2001–2004 (long 51)

Most Extra Points Made

183	Kevin Kelly, 2005–2008
141	Brett Conway, 1993–1996
132	Craig Fayak, 1990–1993
117	Travis Forney, 1996–1999
115	Robbie Gould, 2001–2004

Most Extra Points Attempted

185	Kevin Kelly, 2005–2008
142	Brett Conway, 1993–1996
139	Craig Fayak, 1990–1993
121	Travis Forney, 1996–1999
121	Robbie Gould, 2001–2004

Best Extra Point Accuracy (min. 50 attempts)

100%	Herb Menhardt, 1978–1980 (59/59)
99.3%	Brett Conway, 1993–1996 (141/142)
98.9%	Kevin Kelly, 2005–2008 (183/185)
98.9%	Massimo Manca, 1982, 1984–1986 (86/87)
98.0%	Brian Franco, 1980–1981 (49/50)

Most Consecutive Extra Points Made

119	Brett Conway, 1994–1996

Most Punts
251	Jeremy Kapinos, 2003–2006	
241	Doug Helkowski, 1988–1991	
225	Ralph Giacomarro, 1979–1982	
204	John Bruno, 1984–1986	
193	David Royer, 1999–2002	

Most Punting Yards
10,476	Jeremy Kapinos, 2003–2006
9,402	Ralph Giacomarro, 1979–1982
9,391	Doug Helkowski, 1988–1991
8,508	John Bruno, 1984–1986
7,782	Pat Pidgeon, 1996–1999

Most Yards per Punt
43.02	Jeremy Boone, 2007–2008 (4,216/98)
43.00	George Reynolds, 1981–1983 (3,096/72)
41.84	Pat Pidgeon, 1996–1999 (7,782/186)
41.79	Ralph Giacomarro, 1979–1982 (9,402/225)
41.74	Jeremy Kapinos, 2003–2006 (10,476/251)

Most Punt Returns
109	Bruce Branch, 1998–2001
86	Calvin Lowry, 2003–2005
84	O. J. McDuffie, 1988–1992

Highest Punt Return Average (min. 15 returns)
17.6	Ron Younker, 1953–1954
16.5	Wally Triplett, 1946–1948
15.9	Don Jonas, 1958–1961

Most Punt Return Touchdowns
4	Bruce Branch, 1998–2001

Most Kickoff Returns
67	Kenny Wilson, 1996–2000
59	Larry Johnson, 1999–2002
50	Derrick Williams, 2006–2008

Highest Kick Return Average (min. 15 returns)
29.6	Larry Joe, 1946–1948
28.8	Curt Warner, 1979–1982
28.4	Charlie Pittman, 1967–1969

Most Kick Return Touchdowns
3	Curt Warner, 1979–1982

Most Interceptions
19	Neal Smith, 1967–1969
15	Pete Harris, 1977–-1978, 1980
15	Darren Perry, 1988–1991

Most Interception Return Yards
299	Darren Perry, 1988–1991
275	Dennis Onkotz, 1967–1969
269	Alan Zematis, 2002–2005

Most Interceptions Returned for a Touchdown
3	Dennis Onkotz, 1967–1969
3	Darren Perry, 1988–1991

Most Tackles
419	Dan Connor, 2004–2007
372	Paul Posluszny, 2003–2006
343	Greg Buttle, 1973–1975

Most Solo Tackles
227	Dan Connor, 2004–2007
210	Paul Posluszny, 2003–2006
186	Shane Conlon, 1983–1986

Most Tackles for Losses
70	Courtney Brown, 1996–1999
51	Brandon Short, 1996–1999
45	Larry Kubin, 1977–1980

Most Sacks (since 1975)
33	Courtney Brown, 1996–1999
30	Larry Kubin, 1977–1980
25.5	Michael Haynes, 1999–2002

Most Blocked Punts
4	Jack Ham, 1968–1970
4	Andre Collins, 1986–1989

INDIVIDUAL SINGLE-SEASON RECORDS

Most Points, Total Offense
- 174   Lydell Mitchell, 1971
- 140   Larry Johnson, 2002
- 138   Ki-Jana Carter, 1994
- 122   Curtis Enis, 1997
- 119   Pete Mauthe, 1909

Most Yards, Total Offense
- 3,156   Michael Robinson, 2005 (2,350 pass, 806 rush)
- 2,874   Darryl Clark, 2008 (2,592 pass, 282 rush)
- 2,660   Kerry Collins, 1994 (2,679 pass, –19 rush)
- 2,638   Anthony Morelli, 2007 (2,651 pass, –13 rush)
- 2,618   Zack Mills, 2002 (2,417 pass, 201 rush)

Most All-Purpose Running Yards
- 2,655   Larry Johnson, 2002 (2,087 rush, 349 rec., 219 ret.)
- 1,831   O. J. McDuffie, 1992 (133 rush, 977 rec., 721 ret.)
- 1,772   Blair Thomas, 1987 (1,414 rush, 300 rec., 58 ret.)
- 1,754   Lydell Mitchell, 1971 (1,567 rush, 154 rec., 33 ret.)
- 1,743   Ki-Jana Carter, 1995 (1,539 rush, 123 rec., 81 ret.)

Most Rushing Yards
- 2,087   Larry Johnson, 2002
- 1,567   Lydell Mitchell, 1971
- 1,539   Ki-Jana Carter, 1994
- 1,522   John Cappelletti, 1973
- 1,414   Blair Thomas, 1987

Most Rushing Attempts
- 286   John Cappelletti, 1973
- 277   Tony Hunt, 2006
- 271   Larry Johnson, 2002
- 268   Blair Thomas, 1987
- 264   Blair Thomas, 1989

Highest Rushing Average (min. 100 attempts)
- 7.96   Lenny Moore, 1954 (1,082/136)
- 7.77   Ki-Jana Carter, 1994 (1,539/198)
- 7.70   Larry Johnson, 2002 (2,087/271)
- 6.62   Ki-Jana Carter, 1993 (1,026/155)
- 6.47   Eric McCoo, 1998 (822/127)

Most 100-Yard Games
- 10*   Ki-Jana Carter, 1994
- 9*   Lydell Mitchell, 1971
- 9*   Blair Thomaas, 1989
- 8   John Cappelletti, 1973
- 8   Larry Johnson, 2002
- 8*   Tony Hunt, 2006

(* includes bowl game)

Most Rushing Touchdowns
- 26   Lydell Mitchell, 1971
- 23   Ki-Jana Carter, 1994
- 20   Larry Johnson, 2002
- 19   Curtis Enis, 1997
- 18   Richie Anderson, 1992

Most Passing Yards
- 2,679   Kerry Collins, 1994
- 2,651   Anthony Morelli, 2007
- 2,592   Daryll Clark, 2008
- 2,488   Tony Sacca, 1991
- 2,424   Anthony Morelli, 2006

Most Pass Attempts
- 402   Anthony Morelli, 2007
- 386   Anthony Morelli, 2006
- 335   Wally Richardson, 1995
- 333   Zack Mills, 2002
- 321   Daryll Clark, 2008

Most Pass Completions
- 234   Anthony Morelli, 2007
- 208   Anthony Morelli, 2006
- 193   Wally Richardson, 1995
- 192   Daryll Clark, 2008
- 188   Zack Mills, 2002

Highest Completion Percentage (min. 100 attempts)
- 66.7   Kerry Collins, 1994 (176/264)
- 63.2   John Hufnagel, 1971 (86/136)
- 59.8   Daryll Clark, 2008 (321/192)
- 58.2   Anthony Morelli, 2007 (234/402)
- 57.9   Tony Sacca, 1991 (169/292)

Passing Efficiency
172.86 Kerry Collins, 1994
151.84 John Hufnagel, 1971
149.76 Tony Sacca, 1991
148.04 John Hufnagel, 1972
146.38 Chuck Fusina, 1977

Most Passing Yards per Attempt
10.15 Kerry Collins, 1994 (2,679/264)
9.44   John Hufnagel, 1972 (2,039/216)
9.03   Chuck Fusina, 1977 (2,221/246)
9.00   Milt Plum, 1956 (675/75)
8.71   John Hufnagel, 1971 (1,185/136)

Most 200-Yard Passing Games
10* Kerry Collins, 1994
7*   Todd Blackledge, 1982
7*   Michael Robinson, 2005
7   Anthony Morelli, 2007
6   Tony Sacca, 1991
6   Mike McQueary, 1997
(* includes bowl game)

Most Passing Touchdowns
22 Todd Blackledge, 1982
21 Tony Sacca, 1991
21 Kerry Collins, 1994
19 Doug Strang, 1983
19 Anthony Morelli, 2007
19 Daryll Clark, 2008

Most Interceptions Thrown
15 Vince O'Bara, 1950
14 Jack White, 19965
14 Todd Blackledge, 1981
14 Todd Blackledge, 1982
13 Todd Blackledge, 1980

Lowest Interception Percentage (min. 100 attempts)
1.46 Kerry Collins, 1992 (2/137)
1.71 Tony Sacca, 1991 (5/292)
1.79 Wally Richardson, 1996 (8/279)
1.94 John Sacca, 1992 (3/155)
1.96 John Shaffer, 1986 (4/204)

Most Receptions
63 Bobby Engram, 1995
63 O. J. McDuffie, 1992
55 Terry Smith, 1991
55 Derrick Williams, 2007
52 Bobby Engram, 1994

Most Receiving Yards
1,084 Bobby Engram, 1995
1,029 Bobby Engram, 1994
977   O. J. McDuffie, 1992
973   Freddie Scott, 1994
917   Bryant Johnson, 2002

Most 100-Yard Games
6* Bobby Engram, 1993
6* Bobby Engram, 1995
5* O. J. McDuffie, 1992
5   Freddie Scott, 1995
5   Joe Jurevicius, 1996
5   Bryant Johnson, 2001
(* includes bowl game)

Most Receiving Touchdowns
13 Bobby Engram, 1993
11 Bobby Engram, 1995
10 Joe Jurevicius, 1997
9   O. J. McDuffie, 1992
9   Freddie Scott, 1994
9   Deon Butler, 2005

Most Field Goals Made
22 Matt Bahr, 1978
22 Kevin Kelly, 2006
21 Massimo Manca, 1985
21 Travis Forney, 1999
20 Travis Forney, 1998
20 Kevin Kelly, 2007 and 2008

Most Field Goals Attempted

34	Kevin Kelly, 2006
33	Chris Bahr, 1975
29	Travis Forney, 1998
27	Matt Bahr, 1978
26	4 times; most recent: Kevin Kelly, 2007

Best Field Goal Accuracy (min. 10 attempts)

83.3%	Brett Conway, 1994 (10/12)
83.3%	Kevin Kelly, 2008 (20/24)
82.6%	Ray Tarasi, 1989 (19/23)
81.5%	Matt Bahr, 1978 (22/27)
80.9%	Nick Gancitano, 1983 (17/21)

Most Consecutive Field Goals Made

13	Craig Fayak, 1992

Most 50-Yard Field Goals Made

4	Chris Bahr, 1975
3	Massimo Manca, 1985
2	Robbie Gould, 2002
2	Kevin Kelly, 2008
1	shared by 12 players

Most Extra Points Made

62	Brett Conway, 1994
60	Kevin Kelly, 2008
59	Alberto Vitiello, 1971
49	Kevin Kelly, 2005
44	Travis Forney, 1999
44	Kevin Kelly, 2007

Most Extra Points Attempted

63	Brett Conway, 1994
62	Alberto Vitiello, 1971
60	Kevin Kelly, 2008
50	Kevin Kelly, 2005
46	Craig Fayak, 1991

Most Extra Point Attempts w/out a Miss

60	Kevin Kelly, 2008

Most Punts

79	John Bruno, 1984–1984
71	David Royer, 2001
71	Ralph Giacomarro, 1979
68	George Reynolds, 1983
68	Doug Helkowski, 1988
68	Jeremy Kapinos, 2003

Most Punting Yards

3,273	John Bruno, 1984
2,899	George Reynolds, 1983
2,880	David Royer, 2001
2,850	Jeremy Kapinos, 2003
2,822	Ralph Giacomarro, 1979

Most Yards per Punt (min. 30 punts)

43.55	Ralph Giacomarro, 1981 (2,395/55)
43.31	Ralph Giacomarro, 1980 (2,252/52)
43.03	Jeremy Boone, 2008 (1,678/39)
43.02	Jeremy Boone, 2007 (2,538/59)
42.92	John Bruno, 1985 (2,575/60)

Most Punt Returns

41	Bruce Branch, 1998
41	Bruce Branch, 1999
41	Bryant Johnson, 2002

Highest Punt Return Average (min. 5 returns)

21.4	Don Jonas, 1960
19.2	Gary Hayman, 1973
17.6	Kevin Baugh, 1980

Most Punt Return Touchdowns

2	Jimmy Cefalo, 1977
2	O. J. McDuffie, 1991
2	Bruce Branch, 1999

Most Kick Returns

26   Kevin Baugh, 1983
22   Gary Brown, 1988
22   Chris Eberly, 1997
22   Kenny Watson, 1999
22   A. J. Wallace, 2007

Most Kick Return Yards

581   A. J. Wallace, 2007
522   Kenny Watson, 1999
515   Derrick Williams, 2008

Highest Kick Return Average (min. 8 returns)

43.0 Gary Brown, 1990
35.0 Curt Warner, 1980
32.6 Larry Joe, 1947

Most Kick Return Touchdowns

2   Curt Warner, 1980
2   Chuck Peters, 1940
2   Derrick Williams, 2008

Most Interceptions

10   Neal Smith, 1969
10   Pete Harris, -1978
8   Don Eyer, 1952
8   Jack Sherry, 1952
8   Neal Smith, 1968

Most Interception Return Yards

207   Alan Zematis, 2003
179   Dennis Onkotz, 1967
155   Pete Harris, 1978

Most Interceptions Returned for a Touchdown

2   Dennis Onkotz, 1967
2   Jeff Hite, 1974
2   Scott Radecic, 1982
2   Darren Perry, 1991
2   Rich Gardner, 2002

Most Tackles

165   Greg Buttle, 1974
145   Dan Connor, 2007
144   Shawn Mayer, 2002

Most Solo Tackles

86   Greg Buttle, 1974
85   Shawn Mayer, 2002
76   Greg Buttle, 1975

Most Tackles for Losses

29   Courtney Brown, 1999
23   Larry Kubin, 1979
23   Courtney Brown, 1998
23   Michael Haynes, 2002

Most Sacks (since 1975)

15   Larry Kubin, 1979
15   Michael Haynes, 2002
13.5 Courtney Brown, 1996–1999

Most Blocked Punts

3   Jack Ham, 1968
3   Andre Collins, 1989

INDIVIDUAL SINGLE-GAME RECORDS

Most Points	36	Harry Robb, vs. Gettysburg, 10/6/1917 (6 TD)
Most Touchdowns	6	Harry Robb, vs. Gettysburg, 10/6/1917 (6 rush); Michael Robinson, at Illinois, 10/22/2005 (4 pass, 2 rush)
Most Yards, Total Offense	418	Zack Mills, vs. Ohio State, 10/27/2001 (280 pass, 138 rush)
Most All-Purpose Running Yards	341	Curt Warner, at Syracuse, 10/17/1981 (256 rush, 20 rec., 65 ret.)
Most Rushing Yards	327	Larry Johnson, at Indiana, 11/16/2002
Most Rushing Attempts	41	John Cappelletti, vs. NC State, 11/10/1973
Highest Average Rushing Yardage	44.0	Blair Thomas, vs. Syracuse, 10/18/1986
Longest Run	92 yards	Blair Thomas, vs. Syracuse, 10/18/1986
Most Rushing Touchdowns	6	Harry Robb, vs. Gettysburg, 10/6/1917
Most Passing Yards	399	Zack Mills, vs. Iowa, 9/28/2002
Most Pass Attempts	54	Kerry Collins, at BYU, 10/31/1992
Most Pass Completions	33	Wally Richardson, vs. Wisconsin, 9/30/1995
Highest Completion Percentage	91.7	Pete Liske, at Oregon, 9/21/1963
Longest Pass Play	92	Harold Hess to Bob Higgins, at Pittsburgh, 11/29/1919
Most Touchdown Passes	5	Tony Sacca, vs. Georgia Tech, 8/28/1991; Rashard Casey, vs. Lousiana Tech, 9/9/2000
Most Interceptions Thrown	4	Shared by four players; most recently, Zack Mills, vs. Boston College, 9/11/2004
Most Receptions	13	Freddie Scott, vs. Wisconsin, 9/30/1995
Most Receiving Yards	216	Deon Butler, vs. Northwestern, 9/30/2006
Most Receiving Touchdowns	4	Bobby Engram, vs. Minnesota, 9/4/1993
Most Field Goals Made	5	Brian Franco, at Nebraska, 9/26/1981; Massimo Manca, vs. Notre Dame, 11/16/1985; Travis Forney, vs. Michigan State, 11/28/1998
Most Field Goals Attempted	6	Massimo Manca, vs. West Virginia, 11/1/1986; Travis Forney, at Minnesota, 10/10/1998; Travis Forney, vs. Michigan State, 11/28/1998
Longest Field Goal	55 yards	Chris Bahr, at Temple, 9/6/1975; at Ohio State, 9/20/1975; at Syracuse 10/18/1975
Most Extra Points Made (kick)	10	Charles Atherton, vs. Gettysburg, 10/13/1894; Travis Forney, vs. Akron, 9/4/1999
Most Extra Points Attempted (kick)	10	Charles Atherton, vs. Gettysburg, 10/13/1894; Travis Forney, vs. Akron, 9/4/1999
Most Punts	14	Joe Colone, at Cornell 10/17/1942
Most Punting Yards	453	Doug Helkowski, at Alabama, 10/22/1988
Highest Punting Average	54.8 yards	Ralph Giacomarro, at Syracuse, 10/17/1981 (4 punts, 219 yards)
Longest Punt	89 yards	Coop French, at Iowa, 11/15/1930
Most Punt Returns	9	Bruce Branch, at Illinois, 10/30/1999
Most Punt Return Yards	145	Matt Suhey, vs. North Carolina State, 11/11/1978
Highest Punt Return Average	31.7 yards	Derrick Williams, vs. Temple, 11/11/2006 (3 ret.)
Longest Punt Return	100	Jim Boring, vs. Johns Hopkins, 11/11/1933
Most Kick Returns	7	Gary Brown, at West Virginia, 10/29/1988
Most Kick Return Yards	201	Gary Brown, vs. Texas, 9/8/1990

Highest Kick Return Average	47.5 yards	A. J. Wallace, vs. Akron, 9/2/2006 (2 ret.)	
Longest Kick Return	101	Chuck Peters, vs. NYU, 11/16/1940	
Most Interceptions	4	Mike Smith, vs. Ohio U., 11/14/1970	
Most Interception Return Yards	108	Mark Robinson, at Pittsburgh, 11/28/1981	
Most Interceptions Returned for a Touchdown	2	Jeff Hite, vs. Maryland, 11/2/1974	
Longest Interception Return	98	Wayne Berfield, at Boston U., 10/18/1958	
Most Quarterback Sacks	4	Terry Killens, vs. Indiana, 10/28/1995; Jimmy Kennedy, at Wisconsin, 10/5/2002; Tambi Hali, vs. Wisconsin, 11/5/2005	

TEAM SINGLE-SEASON RECORDS

Most Yards, Total Offense	5,722	1994		Fewest Fumbles Lost	4	1994
Fewest Yards, Total Offense	2,914	1960		Most Points	526	1994
Most Total Plays	886	1978		Fewest Points	67	1925
Fewest Total Plays	637	1960		Scoring in Consecutive Games (all games)	138	1973–1984
Most First Downs	277	2002				
Most Rushing Yards	3,347	1971		Scoring in Consecutive Games (regular season)	190	1966–1984
Fewest Rushing Yards	1,317	2001				
Most Rushing Attempts	643	1973		Most Touchdowns	71	1994
Highest Rushing Average	6.1 yards	1994		Fewest Touchdowns	21	1963
Lowest Rushing Average	3.44 yards	2001		Most Rushing Touchdowns	45	1994
Most Passing Yards	2,962	1994		Fewest Rushing Touchdowns	11	1989
Fewest Passing Yards	914	1960		Most Passing Touchdowns	23	1991, 1994
Most Pass Attempts	424	2006		Fewest Passing Touchdowns	1	1969
Most Pass Completions	226	2006		Most Touchdown Returns	7	1967
Fewest Pass Completions	68	1970		Fewest Touchdown Returns	0	1966, 1976, 1993
Highest Completion Percentage	64.9	1994		Most Field Goals	22	1978; 2006
Lowest Completion Percentage	41.8	1966		Fewest Field Goals	2	1970
Most Interceptions Thrown	19	2004		Most Shutouts	6	1947
Most Punts	79	1984		Most Consecutive Shutouts	3	1940, 1947
Fewest Punts	36	1963		Fewest Points Allowed	27	1947
Most Penalties	88	1991		Most Interceptions Made	28	1971, 1978
Fewest Penalties	36	1963, 1996		Most Sacks	54	1999
Most Penalty Yards	776	1978		Longest Unbeaten Streak	31	1967–1970
Fewest Penalty Yards	287	1996		Longest Winning Streak (single season)	12	1973, 1986, 1994
Most Turnovers	36	1972				
Fewest Turnovers	11	1994		Longest Winning Streak (multiple seasons)	23	1968–1970
Most Fumbles	40	1965				
Fewest Fumbles	8	2001		Longest Home Winning Streak	50	1889–1908
Most Fumbles Lost	25	1972		Longest Losing Streak	7	1931

TEAM SINGLE-GAME RECORDS

Most Points	109	vs. Lebanon Valley, 10/23/1920
Most Points Since 1920	82	vs. Susquehanna, 9/25/1926
Most Yards, Total Offense	711	vs. Susquehanna, 9/25/1926
Most Total Plays	99	at West Virginia, 10/22/1966
Most First Downs	38	vs. West Virginia, 11/10/1962
Most Rushing Yards	622	vs. Lebanon Valley, 9/27/1924
Most Rushing Attempts	83	vs. West Virginia, 10/11/1975
Most Passing Yards	399	vs. Iowa, 9/28/2002
Most Pass Attempts	54	at Brigham Young, 10/31/1992
Most Pass Completions	33	vs. Wisconsin, 9/30/1995
Highest Completion Percentage	91.7	vs. Oregon, 9/21/1963
Most Punt Returns	12	vs. Rutgers, 9/18/1982
Most Punt Return Yards	256	vs. Rutgers, 9/18/1982
Most Penalty Yards	142.5	at Pittsburgh, 11/19/1966
Most Interceptions Made	7	at Boston College, 10/10/1970
Most Sacks	11	at Illinois, 10/30/1999
Most Opponent Points	106	at Lehigh (Penn State 0), 11/11/1889
Most Opponent Points Since 1920	55	at Navy (Penn State 14), 10/7/1944

INDEX

A

Adams, Anthony, 142
Aghakhan, Ninef, 122
Alabama, University of ('Bama), 58, 91, 99, 100, 102, 103, 161
Albright, Ed, 52
Allen, Bobby, 52
Allen, Marcus, 103
Allerman, Kurt, 70, 91
Anderson, Bob, 76
Appalachian State, 155
Archie, Mike, 126
Arizona State University, 96
Arkansas, University of, 79
Arnelle, Jesse, 49, 52
Arrington, LaVar, 70–71, 117, 136, 141
Auburn University, 137, 143

B

Bahr, Casey, 94
Bahr, Chris, 87, 88, 91, 94, 99
Bahr, Davies, 94
Bahr, Matt, 94, 96
Bahr, Walter, 94
Bailey, Don, 49
Baker, "Ironsides," 33
Baker, Christopher, 146, 155
Barclay, Watson Levret, 9, 11
Bates, Mickey, 49
Battaglia, Mark, 100, 101, 103, 104
Baugh, Sammy, 61
Baylor University, 91
Beaver, James A., 59, 138
Beaver Field, 10, 12, 16, 20, 23, 28, 35, 40, 45, 47, 54, 59
Beaver Stadium, 6, 7, 8, 50, 61, 62, 64, 127, 135, 137, 138–140, 142, 151, 157, 159, 173
Bebout, "Red," 20
Bedenk, Joe, 6, 25, 27, 30, 31, 33, 36, 37, 39, 46
Bell, Chris, 146
Benfatti, Lou, 119
Berryman, Robert "Punk," 20
Beuerlein, Steve, 108
Bezdek, Hugo, 23, 24, 25, 26, 27, 28, 30, 31, 33, 34, 36
Bierman, Bernie, 119
Blackledge, Todd, 102, 105, 106, 107
Blades, Bennie, 112
Blue Ridge College (Maryland), 48
Bochna, Derek, 126
Booker, Lorenzo, 147, 149
Boston College, 79, 103, 106
Boston University, 139
Bowden, Bobby, 137, 142, 147, 149, 170–171
Bowman, Kirk, 101, 102
Bowman, Navorro, 157
Bowman, Wayne, 101
Bozik, Ed, 115
Bradley, Dave, 69
Bradley, Tom "Scrap," 151–152
Brady, Kyle, 125, 127, 131
Bratton, Melvin, 109, 111
Brees, Drew, 71, 141
Brennan, Thad, 134
Brown, Courtney, 71, 136
Brown, Jerome, 110–111
Brown, Jim, 50, 118
Brown, Leo, 54
Brown, Levi, 147
Brown University, 47, 62
Bruce, Earl, 48, 52
Bruno, John, 110
Bryant, Bear, 48, 57, 58, 99, 133, 141, 142
Bucknell, 10, 39
Buell, Charley, 28
Burkhart, Charlie "Chuck," 72, 73, 76, 78, 80, 81
Butler, Deon, 155, 158
Buttle, Greg, 70, 91

C

Camp, Walter, 15, 17, 25, 27
Campbell, Bob, 63, 72, 73, 74
Campbell, Don, 33
Cannon, Billy, 57
Capers, Dom, 124
Cappelletti, Betty, 90
Cappelletti, Joey, 88–90
Cappelletti, John, 7, 57, 82, 83, 85, 86, 87, 88–90, 91, 101
Carlisle, 169
Caroline, J. C., 49
Carr, Lloyd, 137
Carter, Ki-Jana, 121, 122–123, 127, 128, 130, 134
Casey, Rashard, 144
Cassidy, "Hopalong," 119
Cefalo, Jimmy, 96
Cenci, Aldo, 38
Chicago, University of, 26, 173
Chisley, Lavon, 145
Cincinnati, University of, 101
Clark, Bruce, 96, 98, 99
Clark, Daryll, 155, 158, 161
Clark, Don, 55
Clark, John, 20
Cleaver, Nelson E., 9, 11
Coastal Carolina, 154, 155
Cobbs, Duffy, 112
Coles, Joel, 103
Colgate University, 24, 41, 48
Collins, Andre, 70
Collins, Kerry, 7, 70, 119, 120, 121, 122, 124, 125, 126, 127, 128, 129, 130, 131, 133, 163
Colone, Joe, 41
Colorado, University of, 76, 82
Conlan, Shane, 70, 108, 111, 112
Connor, Dan, 70, 146, 148
Cooney, Larry, 44, 45
Cooper, John, 123, 129
Cooper, Mike, 83
Cornell University, 8, 16, 20, 37
Cosby, T. C., 146
Cronin, Paul, 145
Crowder, Randy, 85
Csonka, Larry, 118
Curkendall, Pete, 108
Curley, Tim, 146
Czekaj, Ed, 40, 42, 44, 45

D

Dartmouth College, 26
Daugherty, Duffy, 119
Delany, Jim, 115
D'Elia, Guido, 151
Devine, Dan, 81
Devlin, Pat, 160
Dilger, Ken, 131
Dinkins, D. J., 117
Dolly, Rick, 117, 118
Donato, Sam, 37
Donchez, Tom, 91
Dorney, Keith, 95, 96, 98
Dorsett, Tony, 86, 93
Douthard, Ty, 131
Dozier, D. J., 108, 109, 110, 112
Drazenovich, Chuck, 39, 41
Drazenovich, Joe, 40, 44
Dunn, William Thomas "Mother," 15, 17
Durkota, Jeff, 40, 41

E

Earley, Bill, 146
East Carolina University, 75, 108
Easy, Omar, 141

Ebersole, John, 75
Economos, John, 37
Eisaman, Jerry, 57
Engle, Lloyd "Dad," 8, 20
Engle, Rip, 6, 7, 15, 17, 22, 25, 45–50, 52–55, 57, 59, 61–65, 67, 68, 96, 162, 163, 166, 171
Engram, Bobby, 122, 125, 126, 127, 129, 131, 135
Enis, Curtis, 136, 137
Episcopal Academy of Philadelphia, 11
Ewing, Stan, 23
Eyer, Don, 51

F

Farkas, Jerry, 60
Fayak, Craig, 126
Fennell, Tom, 9, 15, 18
Finney, Shamar, 137
Fisher, Fran, 101
Fitts, Roscoe, 28
Florida, University of, 60, 161
Florida State University, 68, 81, 137, 142, 147, 149, 150, 171
Forbes Field, 26
Ford, Gerald, 88, 89
Fordham University, 39
Forkum, Carl, 16
Franklin Field, 21
Fulmer, Phillip, 137
Fusina, Chuck, 92, 93, 95, 96, 98, 99

G

Gajecki, Leon, 38
Gann, Stan, 60
Ganter, Chris, 96
Ganter, Fran, 77, 96, 115, 142, 167, 168
Ganter, Jason, 96
Garcia, Dethrell, 145
Garrity, Gregg, 48, 96, 105, 106, 107, 164
Garrity, Jim, 48, 51, 96, 107, 169
Gelzheiser, Brian, 70, 119, 126, 127, 129, 131, 132
Georgia, University of, 100, 101, 103–106
Georgia Tech, 29, 54, 59, 60, 100
Getty, Charlie, 85
Gettysburg College, 15, 23, 26, 34
Giants Stadium, 96
Giftopoulos, Pete, 112, 113
Gilmore, Bruce, 54
Golden, William "Pop," 13, 14
Gordon, Tony, 96, 164
Gottshalk, Jack, 89
Goulbourne, Duane, 126
Grange, Red, 61, 119
Greeley, Bucky, 129

Greene, Shonn, 161
Grier, Roosevelt, 49, 52
Griffin, Archie, 119
Grimes, Burleigh, 24
Grove City, 138
Guman, Mike, 99
Gurksy, Al, 61

H

Hackett, Paul, 116
Haines, Hinkey, 27
Hali, Tambi, 147
Hall, Galen, 58, 59, 152–153
Ham, Jack, 7, 65, 68, 69, 70, 71, 75, 82, 118
Hamilton, Eric, 111
Hanlon, Pat, 124
Hansen, Albert, 20
Harlan, Judy, 29
Harlow, Dick, 22, 23, 24, 26, 47, 48
Harmon, Tom, 119
Harriott, Willie, 146
Harris, Franco, 68, 75, 78, 79, 83, 84, 85, 88, 89, 96, 99, 118, 125
Harris, Giuseppe, 96
Harris, Major, 117, 118
Harris, Pete, 96
Harris, Raymont, 123
Hartenstine, Mike, 85, 91
Hartings, Jeff, 127
Harvard University, 28, 30
Hayes, Jerome, 146
Hayes, Mercury, 135
Hayes, Woody, 53, 98, 119
Hayman, Gary, 87
Haynes, Michael, 87, 142
Heisman, John, 25
Henderson, Elmer "Gloomy Gus," 31, 33
Henderson, Tony, 122
Herd, Chuck, 87
Hermann, Dutch, 6, 18, 24
Herring, Kim, 127, 131, 136
Hess, Bill, 27
Hess, Frank, 28
Hewitt, Earl. E., 16
Hicks, John, 86, 88
Higgins, Bob, 23, 25, 27, 34, 36, 37, 38, 42, 44, 45, 46, 48, 65
Higgins, Virginia, 37
Hildebrand, Charles C., 9, 11
Hirschman, Heff, 16
Hoak, Dick, 52, 59
Hoggard, Dennie, 42, 43, 44
Hollenback, Bill, 8, 9, 16, 18, 19, 22

Hollenback, Jack, 9, 19
Holtz, Lou, 115
Hope, Bob, 90
Hoskins, George W., 12, 13
Hostetler, Ron, 98
Houston, University of, 96
Howard, Dana, 131
Hudson, Don, 61
Hufnagel, John, 83, 86
Humphrey, Maurice, 144
Hunt, Tony, 153

I

Ikenberry, Stan, 115
Illinois, University of, 49, 125, 131, 157
Imrich, Melissa, 135
Indiana University, 125, 130–131, 161
Iowa, University of, 120, 126, 143, 161
Irons, Jarrett, 122
Isom, Ray, 108, 112

J

Jacks, Al, 107
Jackson, John Price, 9, 11, 105
Jaffurs, John, 38
Johnson, Bryant, 142
Johnson, Ed, 142
Johnson, Jimmy, 110, 112
Johnson, Johnny, 131
Johnson, Larry Jr., 96, 137, 142, 143
Johnson, Larry Sr., 96, 137
Johnson, Paul, 75
Johnson, Rob, 128
Johnson, Tony, 96, 145
Jones, Casey, 37
Joyner, Andy, 78, 96
Joyner, Dave, 69, 78, 96, 139, 163, 166, 167, 173
Joyner, Matt, 78, 96, 163, 167

K

Kane, Billy, 52
Kansas, University of, 69, 72–73, 74
Kansas State, 76
Kates, Jim, 75
Kearns, Mike, 51
Kelly, Kevin, 94, 149, 150, 153, 171
Kennedy, Jimmy, 142, 164, 173
Kentucky, University of, 48, 91, 96, 98
Kerner, Marlon, 130
Kerns, John, 38
Kessler, Charles Milton, 9, 11
Killens, Terry, 135
Killinger, Glenn, 25, 26, 27, 29

Kilmer, Ethan, 149
King, Justin, 146
Knizer, Matt, 106, 108
Kochman, Roger, 58, 59, 60, 61
Kremblas, Frank, 55
Krouse, Len, 38
Kulka, John, 69, 72
Kwalick, Ted, 64, 65, 66, 68, 69

L

Lafayette College, 34
LaFleur, Bill, 36
Lamb, Levi, 20
Lawlor, Dan, 146
Leahy, Frank, 169
Lehigh University, 37
Leonard, Bill, 49
Leto, Justin, 144
Levy, DeAndre, 151
Lewis, Art, 50
Lewis, Thomas, 125
Leyden, Harry R., 9, 11
Lightner, Joe, 27
Linsz, George H., 9, 11
Liske, Pete, 19, 60
Little, Floyd, 118
Long, Carson, 91
Louisiana State (LSU), 86, 87, 89, 100, 103
Louisiana Superdome, 100
Lucas, "Riverboat" Richie, 56, 57, 88
Luke, R. J., 145–146
Lungren, Cy, 34
Luther, Bill, 36, 42

M

Macklin, David, 136
Majors, Johnny, 93
Mallory, Bill, 125
Marinaro, Joe, 129
Marino, Dan, 116
Markovich, Mark, 85, 87, 88
Marquette University, 55
Martin, Bill, 24
Maryland, University of, 22, 37, 61, 67, 82, 86, 91, 96, 99, 122
Mason, H. D. "Joe," 11
Mattioli, Rudy, 49
Mauthe, Pete, 8, 19, 20, 21, 22
McCloskey, Mike, 105
McCoo, Eric, 142
McCoy, Ernie, 45
McCreary, I. P., 10, 11
McDuffie, O. J., 117, 118

McHugh, Tommy, 145
McIlveen, "Irish," 16
McLean, Harvey B., 9, 11
McLeary, Bull, 16
Meadowlands, 137, 164
Meek, George, 15
Mehl, Lance, 70, 98
Meredith, Bud, 135, 139
Miami, University of (Florida), 68, 92, 96, 102, 109–113, 119, 141
Michigan, University of, 114, 121, 122, 123, 128, 129, 135, 136, 138, 141, 147, 155, 156
Michigan State (MSU), 45, 121, 122, 123, 125, 126, 132, 151, 152, 153, 159, 161
Milia, Marc, 122
Millen, Matt, 96, 98, 99
Miller, Brian, 135
Miller, Desmond, 144
Miller, Eugene "Shorty," 8, 19, 20, 21
Miller, Jim, 126
Mills, Zack, 141, 142, 144
Milne, Brian, 130, 131, 132
Minnesota, University of, 120, 127, 148
Mira, George Jr., 109
Missouri, University of, 19, 80, 81
Mitchell, John G., 9, 11
Mitchell, Lydell, 68, 75, 78, 79, 80, 81, 83, 84, 85, 88, 89, 118
Mitinger, Bob, 47, 52, 57, 59
Mock, James C., 9, 11
Moeller, Gary, 114, 121, 128
Monk, Art, 118
Moore, Lenny, 47, 49–50, 52, 67, 83, 118
Morelli, Anthony, 153, 155
Morris, John, 6, 9, 11
Moscrip, Andy, 16
Municipal Stadium (Philadelphia), 57
Murray, Daniel, 161

N

Nagurski, Bronko, 61
Natale, Dan, 85, 91
Nebraska, University of, 27, 28, 102, 130–131, 132–134
Nessel, John, 85
Nevers, Ernie, 61
Nixon, Richard, 79, 80, 81
Nolan, John, 40
North Carolina State (NC State), 86, 91, 96, 99
Northwestern University, 125, 132, 141
Norton, Negley, 37, 39, 40
Norwood, Jordan, 153, 155
Notre Dame, 80, 81, 108, 121, 169

O

O'Hora, Jim, 51
O'Neal, Brian, 126
O'Neil, Ed, 70, 85, 88
Ohio State (OSU), 20–21, 52–53, 54–55, 72, 91, 98, 120, 122–123, 125, 126, 128, 157, 159, 160–161
Ohio University, 86, 88
Oklahoma, University of, 85, 109, 161
Onkotz, Dennis, 65, 66, 68, 69, 70, 71, 72, 75, 76
Opfar, David, 106
Oregon, University of, 26, 59, 132–134
Oregon State, 157
Osborne, Duke, 27
Osborne, Tom, 133, 134

P

Pae, Dick, 59
Paffenroth, Dave, 103
Page, Paul, 44
Palm, Mike, 27, 33
Parker, Jim, 53
Paterno, David, 151
Paterno, George, 162
Paterno, Jay, 96, 161, 172
Paterno, Joe (Joseph Vincent) "JoePa," 6, 7, 46–47, 48, 52, 61, 62–64, 65, 66–69, 70, 71, 73, 74, 75, 76, 77, 78, 79, 81, 82, 83, 85, 86, 87, 88, 89, 91, 93, 96, 98, 99, 100, 106, 107, 110, 111, 112, 113, 114–115, 116, 118, 119, 120, 121, 122, 123, 124, 125, 126, 129, 131, 132, 135, 136, 137, 141–142, 143, 144, 146, 147, 149, 151, 152, 153, 154, 155, 157, 158, 159, 161, 162–173
Paterno, Sue, 66, 142, 164, 166, 172, 173
Paxson, Scott, 145
Pennsylvania, University of, 13, 37
Peoples, Shonte, 122
Percy Field, 20
Perkins, Dan, 135
Perrimen, Brett, 112
Petchel, Elwood "Woody," 36, 40, 41, 44
Peters, Chuck, 37, 38
Petrella, "Pepper," 38
Petruccio, Tony, 92
Phillips, Anwar, 145
Pittman, Charlie, 64, 65, 67–68, 73, 76, 79, 96, 166
Pittsburgh, University of (Pitt), 16, 18, 26, 37, 39, 41, 42, 48–49, 50, 68, 92, 93, 99, 116, 117
Plum, Milt, 50, 52, 53, 55
Posluszny, Paul, 70, 71, 147, 148, 151, 153
Potsklan, John, 40, 41
Pryor, Terrelle, 157, 160
Purdue University, 141, 158

Q

Quarless, Andrew, 151

R

Radecic, Scott, 104
Rados, Tony, 49
Rafferty, Tom, 91
Rauch, Dick, 27
Ravotti, Eric, 123, 125
Redinger, Pete, 28
Reed, Dan, 14
Reid, Mike, 65, 68, 69, 72, 75, 76
Reitz, Mike, 79
Ressler, Glenn, 59
Rice, Simeon, 131
Rice University, 25
Richards, Jack, 21
Richardson, Wally, 122
Ricker, Dutch, 6, 25
Riggins, John, 72
Rivera, Marco, 130
Robinson, Dave, 59–60, 61, 70
Robinson, John, 127–128, 139
Robinson, Michael, 147, 149, 150, 155
Rockne, Knute, 169
Roepke, Johnny, 34
Rogel, Fran "Punchy," 36, 40
Rose, James Reuben, 9, 11
Ross, Robert, 42
Rowell, Buddy, 49
Royal, Darrell, 79, 83
Royster, Evan, 155, 156, 158
Rozier, Mike, 103
Rubin, Mark, 157, 160
Rutgers University, 96, 98, 164

S

Saban, Lou, 67
Sabol, Joe, 52
Sacca, John, 119, 121, 122, 124
Salaam, Rashaan, 133
Sales, Tyrell, 146, 157
Samford (Howard College), 171
Sandusky, E. J., 96, 139
Sandusky, Jerry, 70, 96, 168
Sandusky, Jon, 96
Sargeant, Lydell, 146, 158
Schembechler, Bo, 119
Schlichter, Art, 98
Schmidt, Herb, 139
Scholl, Leroy, 16
Schwartzwalder, Ben, 78–79
Scirrotto, Anthony, 146, 160–161

Scott, Austin, 149
Scott, Bryan, 142
Seelig, Mark, 111
Sefter, Steve, 104
Shafer, Raymond, 80–81
Shaffer, John, 106, 108, 111
Sherry, Jack, 48, 51
Short, Brandon, 70, 136
Shuler, Mickey, 92, 96
Shuman, Tom, 85, 86, 87, 91
Sidler, Randy, 92, 96
Sieminski, Chuck, 59
Simon, John, 42
Skorupan, John, 70
Smaltz, Bill, 38
Smear, Steve, 69, 72, 75, 76, 78
Smith, Andrew Latham, 13, 16
Smith, Bubba, 119
Smith, Chester L., 44
Smith, Neal, 65, 68, 72, 76
Snell, George, 28
Southern California, University of (USC), 30, 31, 33, 62, 121, 127–128, 154, 160, 161
Southern Methodist University (SMU), 42, 44, 45
Spaeth, Matt, 148
St. Bonaventure, 23
Stagg, Amos Alonzo, 26, 173
Stellatella, Sam, 57, 58
Stewart, Vin, 127
Stoyanovich, Bill, 126
Straub, Bill, 52
Stynchula, Andy, 54
Suhey, Joe, 93
Suhey, Kevin, 93
Suhey, Larry, 93
Suhey, Matt, 93
Suhey, Paul, 93, 96, 98–99
Suhey, Steve, 38, 40, 93
Sullivan, Edward, 28
Sweeney, Jim, 116
Syracuse University, 34, 35, 37, 40, 41, 42, 52, 54, 65, 68, 78, 79, 87, 116, 118, 157

T

Taliaferro, George, 43
Tamburo, Sam, 39, 40, 41
Tarman, Jim, 115
Tate, Mark, 164
Taylor, Phil, 146, 155
Temple University, 41, 91, 98, 116, 151, 157, 173
Tennessee, University of, 83, 120, 126–127
Testaverde, Vinny, 109, 111, 112, 113, 168
Texas, University of, 79, 80, 83, 84, 85, 120, 161

Texas A&M, 153
Texas Christian University (TCU), 53
Texas Tech, 161
Thomas, Blair, 108, 110
Thorpe, Jim, 23
Toretti, Sever, 51
Trevor, George, 15
Triplett, Wally, 39, 40, 41, 42, 43, 44

U

UCLA, 68

V

Valentine, Sam, 52, 55
Vanderbilt University, 55
Vermont, University of, 12
Very, Dexter "Dex," 19, 20
Vorhis, Larry, 16

W

Walker, Doak, 44, 45
Walker, Herschel, 100, 103, 104, 106, 168
Walter, John, 104
Warner, Curt, 101, 103, 104–105, 106
Warner, Glenn "Pop," 26, 27
Washington, University of, 108
Washington State, 39
Way, Charley, 27
Weller, John S., 9, 11
Welsh, George, 75
Welty, Dan, 20
West Virginia (WVU), 41, 42, 45, 50, 68, 88, 116, 117, 118, 171
Western Maryland College, 47, 48
Whatley, Robin, 73
Wheatley, Tyrone, 122
White, Bob, 108, 109
Williams, Bob, 39, 41
Williams, Derrick, 154, 155, 157, 158, 161
Wilson, "Lighthorse" Harry, 20, 24, 25, 26, 28, 30, 31
Wisconsin, University of, 50, 151, 158
Wolosky, John "Shag," 37, 39, 40, 41, 42, 44
Woodruff, George, 169
Woodson, Abe, 49
Wozniak, John, 116

Y

Yale University, 15, 16, 63
Yeckley, Ed, 16

Z

Zapiec, Charlie, 69, 70, 79, 83